Using
Dreamweaver
MX

Other Computer Titles

by

Robert Penfold

Other Titles of Interest

Using Dreamweaver MX

Robert Penfold

Bernard Babani (publishing) Ltd
The Grampians
Shepherds Bush Road
London W6 7NF
England
www.babanibooks.com

Please note

Although every care has been taken with the production of this book to ensure that any projects, designs, modifications, and/or programs, etc., contained herewith, operate in a correct and safe manner and also that any components specified are normally available in Great Britain, the Publisher and Author do not accept responsibility in any way for the failure (including fault in design) of any projects, design, modification, or program to work correctly or to cause damage to any equipment that it may be connected to or used in conjunction with, or in respect of any other damage or injury that may be caused, nor do the Publishers accept responsibility in any way for the failure to obtain specified components.

Notice is also given that if any equipment that is still under warranty is modified in any way or used or connected with home-built equipment then that warranty may be void.

© 2002 BERNARD BABANI (publishing) LTD

First Published - October 2002

British Library Cataloguing in Publication Data

A catalogue record for this book is available from the British Library

ISBN   0 85934 530 0

Cover Design by Gregor Arthur

Printed and bound in Great Britain by Cox and Wyman

Preface

No doubt many potential users of Dreamweaver are reluctant to give the program a chance because it is the standard web design program for professional users. In general, top programs for the professionals have a reputation for being difficult to learn and use. Dreamweaver "breaks the mould" by being straightforward to learn and use while still having the power to produce large and sophisticated web sites. Whether you wish to build a simple text-only web site or a huge site having all the "bells and whistles", Dreamweaver can handle the task and it will not make life unnecessarily difficult. Beginners at web site design can start with a simple site and develop it into something more sophisticated as their expertise increases. Those with some experience of web site design should soon learn to produce impressive results using Dreamweaver.

Although Dreamweaver is an HTML editor, it is not necessary to learn HTML coding in order to use the program effectively. It can be used to design web pages by placing text and images on the WYSIWYG (what you see is what you get) design view, and then letting Dreamweaver write the code. It is possible to expand the capabilities of the program by adding your own code, and ultimately you may well wish to do things this way. Initially though, it is easier to concentrate on designing pages using the WYSIWYG method. Very sophisticated sites can be produced in this way, so it is by no means essential for Dreamweaver users to learn HTML coding.

Dreamweaver is available in a Windows PC version and for Macintosh computers. The PC version was used in the production of this book, but in use there is very little difference between the two. The differences are mainly brought about by the use of different conventions in the way the two types of computer are used, and by differences in the nomenclature used in menus. Provided you are reasonably fluent in the use of a Macintosh computer you should have little difficulty following the methods described in this book. Even if you use the PC version you will still need to know the fundamentals of using the computer, but with either version you do not need to be a computer expert.

No previous experience with Dreamweaver or of web design is required to use this book. It seems reasonable to assume that anyone learning to use Dreamweaver is familiar with using web sites and knows a few Internet basics. This book can be used on its own to learn about Dreamweaver, but it is strongly recommended that it is used in conjunction with the program itself. The only way to learn about any creative software is to try it out, follow a few examples, and then try some ideas of your own. PC and Macintosh demonstration programs can be downloaded from the Macromedia web site (www.macromedia.com), and these are fully operational for 30 days. About an hour or so per day for half that period should be sufficient to become reasonably skilled in using Dreamweaver.

Robert Penfold

Trademarks

Microsoft, Windows, Windows XP, Windows Me, Windows 98 and Windows 95 are either registered trademarks or trademarks of Microsoft Corporation.

Dreamweaver MX, Flash MX, and Fireworks MX are registered trademarks or trademarks of Macromedia Inc.

All other brand and product names used in this book are recognised trademarks, or registered trademarks of their respective companies. There is no intent to use any trademarks generically and readers should investigate ownership of a trademark before using it for any purpose.

Contents

1

User interface 1

2

Background 27

3

The basics 41

4

Adding text 59

5

Paragraphs and lists 81

6

Images 99

7

Local sites 125

8

Links 149

9

Frames 177

10

Tables 201

11

Layers 231

12

Forms and Flash 251

13

Style sheets 273

14

Uploading 307

User interface

Dabbling

Programs for building web sites tend to have reputations for being difficult to learn and use. I suppose it is fair to say that learning to use a program like Dreamweaver MX is a bit more difficult than learning to use a typical word processor. This does not mean that mastering Dreamweaver MX is difficult in absolute terms, but unlike many modern word processors, it is not "child's play". With a word processor it is possible to produce letters and other simple documents just by "playing" with the program to see what things do. In fact it would probably be possible to produce quite long and sophisticated documents in this way, given sufficient time.

With a program like Dreamweaver MX you are unlikely to produce a worthwhile web site using the "suck it and see" method. This approach works well enough with word processors, drawing programs, and many applications programs. However, with these programs you can produce the finished article without any outside assistance. These days virtually all programs have the ability to import files from other pieces of software, but you can still produce a great deal of excellent work without using this facility.

The situation is different with an application like Dreamweaver MX, where the finished article is often largely assembled from components produced using other programs. I will not say that it is impossible to produce a sophisticated web site using Dreamweaver MX alone, because it might just be possible. I will state categorically that this is not the normal way of tackling things. Trying to produce a top quality web site using Dreamweaver MX alone is a bit like trying to make a table and chairs using a full set of carpentry tools but no wood. Dreamweaver MX is best regarded as the tools for the job, but not the raw materials.

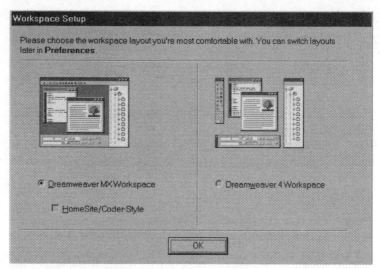

Fig.1.1 There is a choice of a new look or the traditional Dreamweaver screen layout

Ideally you should learn a little background information and have some source files to experiment with prior to trying out Dreamweaver MX for the first time. Being realistic about things, few people will be able to resist the temptation to run the program and start clicking on a few icons at the earliest opportunity. Consequently, we will look at the user interface first, and then consider some background information. However, you may wish to return to this section after reading the next chapter in order to make sure you have a clear understanding of the user interface. Later chapters cover each part of the user interface in detail, explaining how Dreamweaver MX can be used to assemble professional-looking web sites.

This book can be used as a sort of primer so that you have a good idea of how things work when you finally start using Dreamweaver MX. It is not primarily intended for use in this way though, and ideally you should have a computer with Dreamweaver MX installed so that you can actually try out the facilities of the program and experiment with them. There are plenty of examples to follow, but in order to exploit any creative program it is necessary to experiment and "do your own thing". In this way you learn just what the program can and can not achieve, and gain fluency in its use.

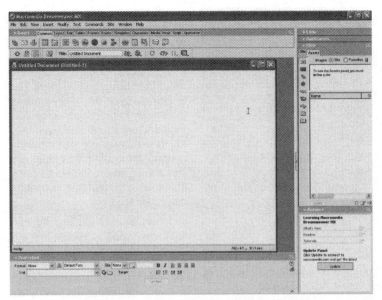

Fig.1.2 The opening screen should look something like this

Note that it is not essential to buy Dreamweaver MX in order to try it out. A demonstration version sometimes appears on the cover discs of computer magazines, and it is also available as a free download from the Macromedia web site at www.macromedia.com. The file for the Dreamweaver MX demonstration is substantial at around 50 megabytes, and it should take about three hours or so to download using a 56k modem. It should only take around 20 minutes using a broadband connection, but either way it is worth the effort. Once installed you have what is actually a fully working version of Dreamweaver MX, but it will only operate for 30 days. This should be more than adequate to go through the examples in this book and do some experimenting of your own. The Save function of the demonstration program is fully operational, so you can save your work ready for use if you should decide to buy "the real thing".

Two versions

When Dreamweaver MX is run you should get something like the screen of Figure 1.1. This offers two versions of the user interface. Those who are familiar with Dreamweaver 4, the predecessor of Dreamweaver MX,

Fig.1.3 The expanded version of the Files window

might prefer to use the alternative layout on offer. Anyone using this book will presumably have little or no experience of Dreamweaver 4, and should therefore accept the default setting. This gives the Dreamweaver MX workspace (screen layout). All the Macromedia programs will use what is essentially the same screen layout, so having learned to use Dreamweaver MX you should find it easy to use any of the other products in the range such as Flash MX.

In order to accept the default settings simply operate the OK button without altering the radio buttons or the checkbox. This launches the main program, and to some extent the appearance depends on the screen resolution used, the sizing of the windows, etc., but there should be a main window, complete with a menu bar (Figure 1.2). The new Macromedia MX screen layout has a Properties window at the bottom of the screen, and a work area above this that initially contains a blank document in a normal resizable window.

There are some windows or panels down the right-hand side of the screen. Each of these windows has a small arrowhead just to the left of the name in the bar at the top. The arrowhead points downwards when the window is expanded or to the right when it is minimised (Figures 1.3 and 1.4 respectively). Simply left-click on the arrowhead in order to toggle one of these windows from one state to the other. This method can also be used with the Properties window incidentally.

One way of closing a window is to left-click on the button at the extreme right-hand end of the name bar. This produces the small pop-up menu of Figure 1.5, and selecting the Close Panel Group option closes the panel. An alternative method is to activate the Window menu (Figure 1.6), which lists the available windows. A tick against the entry for a window indicates that it is open. A window can be toggled on or off by selecting its entry in the Window menu. Thus, if you need to launch a window that is not currently on the screen, it is merely necessary to select its entry in the Window menu. Note that some panels are multipurpose, and that with these the tabs beneath the name bar are used to select the desired function.

Bars

With previous versions of Dreamweaver there is a fairly standard toolbar beneath the menu bar, plus a vertical toolbar down the left-hand side of the screen. This aspect of the interface has been changed somewhat in the MX version, which can have up to three toolbars beneath the menu bar (Figure 1.7) and lacks the vertical

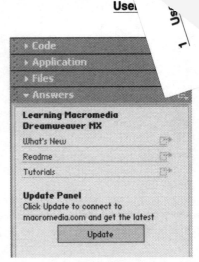

Fig.1.4 Here the Files window is minimised

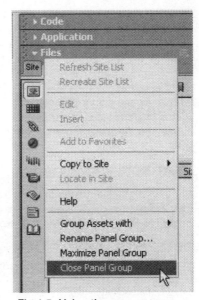

Fig.1.5 Using the pop-up menu to close a group

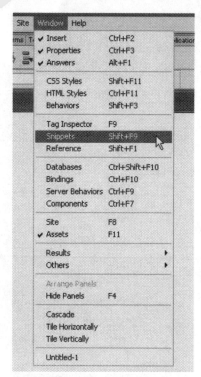

Fig.1.6 *As one would expect, the windows can be controlled via the Window menu*

toolbar. Two of the toolbars are simple types that can be toggled on and off via the Toolbar submenu in the View menu (Figure 1.8). The Standard toolbar has familiar functions such Copy and Paste. The Document toolbar is mainly concerned with the type of view provided in the document window. This is something that will be considered in more detail later.

The third toolbar is the Insert type, and it can be expanded or minimised by way of the usual arrowhead at the left end of the title bar. It has a row of tabs along the very top, within the title bar, and this permits the desired set of tools to be selected. This toolbar replaces the vertical tools palette used in previous versions of Dreamweaver. Like its predecessor, it is likely to be used a great deal in normal use as it gives easy access to a wide range of facilities.

Interfacing

Compared with many programs the Dreamweaver MX user interface can look a little cluttered and messy, but you have to bear in mind that it is being used to perform tasks that are rather more complex than most

Fig.1.7 *Dreamweaver MX can have three toolbars including the Insert palette*

pieces of software. The user interface of Dreamweaver MX is not particularly cluttered by the standards of graphic oriented programs, and it is really quite efficient. Things are kept as straightforward as possible by having windows and palettes that are context sensitive. In other words, the contents of the window or palette changes according to the type of thing you are doing at the time.

This avoids filling the screen with unnecessary elements that are not relevant to the types of task being undertaken. It has to be admitted that context sensitive windows and palettes are not to everyone's liking, and some users prefer a consistent user interface. However, with complex software,

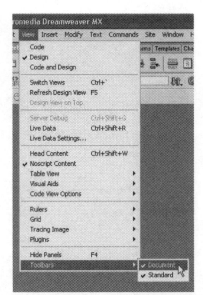

Fig.1.8 The two normal toolbars are controlled via the View menu

even if you are using a high-resolution screen, there is usually no practical alternative to this way of doing things.

Most people find a well designed context sensitive interface easier to learn than one having vast numbers of tools, etc., permanently on the screen. As these things go, Dreamweaver MX does not have one of the more challenging user interfaces. If you would really prefer not to use this type of interface any more than is absolutely necessary, then use the conventional menu system wherever possible and use the palettes, etc., only when there is no alternative.

Insert panel

In its standard form the Insert panel has icons that act as buttons, and it is shown in this form in Figure 1.7. To select an alternative version go to the Edit menu and select the Preferences option. This will bring up a window like the one in Figure 1.9. The range of options available depends on the category selected in the left-hand column. In this case it is the default category (General) that is required. The Insert Panel entry near the bottom of the window provides three options, which are Text Only,

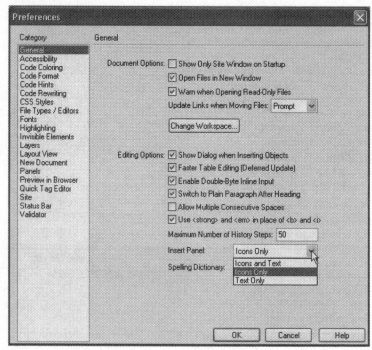

Fig.1.9 The General section of the Preferences window

Icons Only, and Text and Icons. Selecting the text option changes the Insert Panel to one like Figure 1.10.

Since the text takes up more room than the icons, the Insert bar has to expand to the right, and it is quite likely that there will be inadequate screen space to accommodate it. Whether it is too wide to fit depends on the screen resolution in use, but in most cases there will be inadequate space to show all the bar at once. Where appropriate, the rest of the bar

Fig.1.10 The Text version of the Insert panel

Fig.1.11 Revealing the missing section of the Insert panel

can be revealed by left-clicking the downward pointing arrow at the left end of the bar (Figure 1.11). Left-click the upward pointing arrow at the left end of the bar in order to revert to the main section of the bar.

The text version of the bar has the advantage of clearly naming each button, making it unnecessary to remember the function of each one. The drawback is that the palette shows only a relatively limited number of tools at any one time, making it necessary to switch between the two sections. Also, bear in mind that positioning the cursor over an icon in the Icon Only version of the bar brings up a short description of the icon under the pointer. Even so, you might prefer to use this version while learning to use the program. The Text and Icons version (Figure 1.12) has the same problem as the Text version, and it uses the same up and down arrows to switch between the two views. This is perhaps the best option when initially learning to use Dreamweaver MX, because you can clearly see the function of each button, and you will gradually become familiar with the icons. Once fully familiar with the icons, the Icons Only mode can be used.

Whichever version of the bar you decide to use, its function is exactly the same. It largely duplicates the Insert menu, and its numerous submenus. It gives quick access to a range of objects that can be added to a web page. It is not necessary to understand the available objects at this stage, but some are fairly straightforward, such as image, table, and date. The Common palette is the default version of the Insert bar, but several other versions are available via the tabs. These replace the pop-out menu of earlier versions of Dreamweaver and make it easy to quickly select the required version of the bar. Note that all versions are available

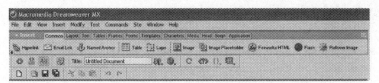

Fig.1.12 The Text and Icons version of the Insert panel

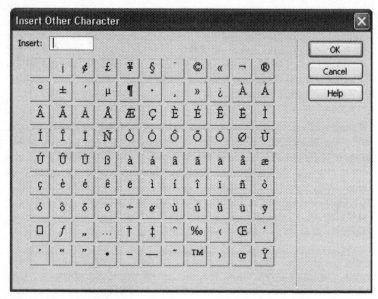

Fig.1.13 This window enables special characters to be added to documents

in Text Only, Text and Icon, and Icon Only guises. Various types of objects are covered in detail later in this book, but here is a brief description of the type of objects found in some of the palettes in the Insert bar.

Common

As its name suggests, this palette contains the objects that are used the most frequently, and hence it is the default palette. It is used for things such as images, the date, layers, and tables.

Characters

This palette gives easy access to text characters that are not included on an ordinary QWERTY keyboard. Typical examples are the © copyright symbol, the ® and ™ trademark symbols, and currency symbols such as the Euro (€). In other words, what are often referred to as symbols in word processor terminology and when dealing with some graphics programs. The button at the right end of this palette is the Other Character type, and operating this produces the window of Figure 1.13. This provides access to a further range of symbols.

Forms

If you have ever filled in an online questionnaire, order form, etc., you will have made use of text boxes, radio buttons, checkboxes, and simple menus. This palette provides the special components of this general type that are needed when producing forms.

Frames

Frames are used in many web sites these days, and the idea of frames is to divide a web page into multiple and effectively independent HTML pages. If you look at anything other than a very basic web page you will notice that it is divided into separate zones, and in most cases each of these is a frame. This palette provides access to framesets that enable the frames to peacefully coexist on the same web page. This facility is available if you are using Dreamweaver MX or versions 3 or 4, but is not included in earlier versions.

Head

This palette is used to place objects into the Head tag of a web page. This could, for example, be a META tag containing a keyword to help Internet search engines find your web site. Objects of this type are not actually visible on finished web pages, but they are still an important part of most web sites. Dreamweaver 4 had a palette called Invisibles that included further invisible objects. For example, named anchors were available via this palette. Many web sites use very long pages rather than large numbers of pages. It can then be useful to have a link to a particular position on the page rather than just a general link to the top of the page. An invisible object called a named anchor can provide a link of this type. This object, like the others previously in the Invisibles palette, has been relocated. Named Anchors are added via the Common palette.

Media

This is roughly comparable to the Special palette in the previous versions of Dreamweaver. It is used to add such things as Java applets, ActiveX controls, and plug-ins. Neither the Media nor the Special palette are included in versions prior to Dreamweaver 4.

Text

This palette gives access to the usual text formatting facilities such as bold and Italic. Note though, that web pages and HTML do not give quite the same freedom with text as word processors and desktop publishing programs, so some of the facilities in this palette might not work in quite the expected manner.

Layout

The Layout palette enables you to change the way that documents are viewed in Dreamweaver MX. By default the program operates with the Standard View, but it can be set to Layout View by operating the appropriate button. The Standard View and Layout View buttons are labelled as such even in the Icons Only mode (Figure 1.14), so they are easily identified. The two buttons to the left of the Standard View button enable tables to be produced quickly and easily in this mode. Tables can be used to display data in tabular form, but they can also be used as means of accurately laying out web pages. The two buttons to the right of the Layout View button enable layout tables to be produced, but only when the Layout View is in use. Layout tables are designed to make life easier when using tables as a means of accurately laying out pages.

Fig.1.14 The Layout palette

Properties Inspector

The window towards the bottom of the screen is the Properties window or Properties Inspector as it is also known. This is very similar to equivalent features in many graphics and desktop publishing programs. If you select some text for example, the Properties Inspector will show various parameters of that text, such as the font, letter size, and alignment. In addition to ordinary desktop publishing and word processor properties there will also be web site related parameters such as link information. The Properties Inspector is context sensitive, so the parameters it displays will change to suit the item or items selected for inspection. Figures 1.15

Fig.1.15 The Properties Inspector with text selected

*Fig.1.16 This version of the Properties Inspector is produced when the
selected object is an image*

and 1.16 respectively show the Properties Inspector with some text and
an image selected.

Of course, although this window is called the Properties Inspector, it can
be used for more than just looking at the properties of the selected objects.
It is really a properties editor rather than an inspector. If some text is
selected, its font, size, etc., can be changed using the Properties
Inspector. In Figure 1.17 the mouse has been left-clicked on the
arrowhead beside the font listing, and this has brought up a list of available
fonts. Left-clicking on one of the fonts in the list changes the text to that
font.

Colour is important in web design, and the Properties Inspector makes
colour changes easy. Operating the menu button to the right of the Size
label and menu brings up a colour palette, as shown in Figure 1.18.
Left- clicking on the one of the squares in the colour chart changes the
selected item or items to the chosen colour. Alternatively, operating the
button with the circular icon at the top of the colour palette brings up the
new window of Figure 1.19. Here you can produce your own custom
colours that can then be applied to objects.

Using buttons, menus, etc., it is possible to alter the size of images, text
styles and alignment, or any property that is shown in the Properties
Inspector. When designing a page you are likely to change your mind

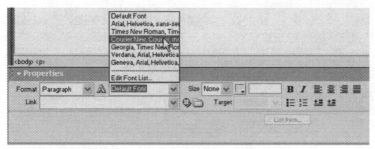

Fig.1.17 The font menu of the Properties Inspector

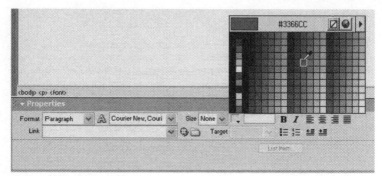

Fig.1.18 The Properties Inspector has a pop-up colour palette

quite frequently about factors governing the appearance of objects, and the Properties Inspector makes it possible to quickly implement these changes. It is important to practise using this feature and to become reasonably expert in its use.

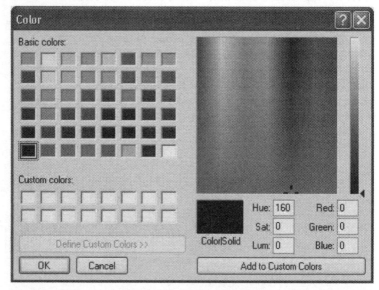

Fig.1.19 With this window it is possible to produce custom colours

Now you see it

A useful feature of Dreamweaver MX is the ability to easily retract or expand the panels down the right-hand side of the window. There is an arrowhead pointing to the right and about half way up the group of panels (Figure 1.20). Left clicking this arrowhead retracts the panels into the right-hand side of the main window, leaving just a left-pointing arrowhead (Figure 1.21). Left clicking this arrowhead causes

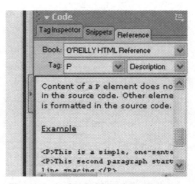

Fig.1.20 Left-clicking the arrow retracts all the panels

the panels to pop out again. This makes it easy to remove the panels when more space is required for the document, and then return them to the screen again afterwards. Note that you can not simply resize the document window to take it on top of the panels, Properties Inspector, etc. It is restricted to otherwise unused areas of the screen.

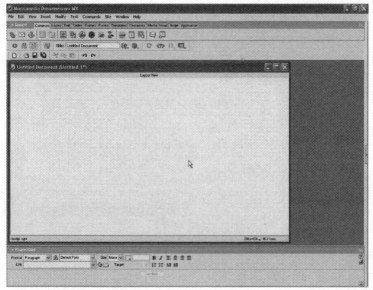

Fig.1.21 The screen with all the panels retracted

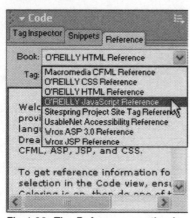

*Fig.1.22 The Reference section is
part of the Help system*

Reference

The menu system, the toolbars, the Properties Inspector, and the document window are where most of the action takes place when using Dreamweaver MX. However, the panels down the right-hand side of the screen provide access to a huge range of features, and they can certainly not be ignored. The Reference window in the Code panel is part of the built-in help system. In Dreamweaver 4 it provides three online reference books dealing with HTML, JavaScript, and CSS.

The range of material on offer has been expanded in Dreamweaver MX, and the Books menu of this window provides a choice of eight publications (Figure 1.22). The two menus beneath the Books menu

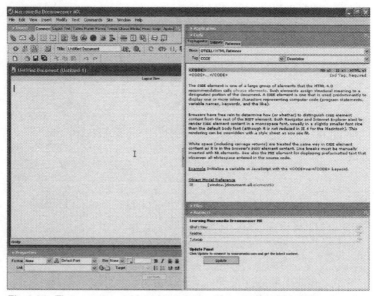

Fig.1.23 The panels can be dragged to a much greater width

enable the required topic to be selected.

This built-in reference library is undoubtedly a useful feature, but it is probably of most use to advanced users rather than beginners. The default width of the panels is quite narrow, making it difficult to use the reference material properly. The right-hand edge of the panels can be

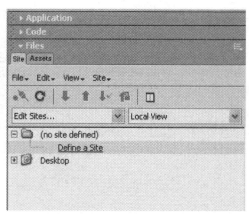

Fig.1.24 The Site window is an important part of Dreamweaver

dragged to increase or decrease their width though, so it is easy to temporarily widen the panels (Figure 1.23). Some of the other panels can be closed in order to expand the Reference window vertically.

Files panel

The files panel is designed to give centralised control over the assets (image files, etc.) used in your web sites. By default there are two tabs in the Files panel. The one on the left is the Site tab, which produces a panel like the one shown in Figure 1.24. This is used to define sites and give various views that enable you to see the make-up of each site. Initially it is largely inoperative because there are no sites defined. The second tab brings up the Assets panel (Figure 1.25), and this enables you to see the image files,

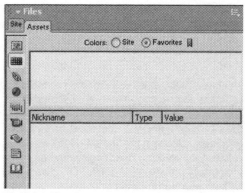

Fig.1.25 The Assets section of the Files group

colours, etc., used in the site. The buttons down the left-hand side of the panel allow other types of asset to be selected, such as colours and URLs. Again, with no sites defined there is nothing initially for the panel to show. Operating the Favorites radio button at the top of the panel results in only the selected assets being shown rather than all assets of the relevant type in the site.

History

The History palette (Figure 1.26) shows the last actions performed on the current frame. Try bringing up this palette on the screen by selecting Others from the Window menu and selecting History from the submenu that appears. Then type some text onto the main document window.

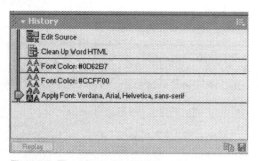

Left-clicking on this window will produce a standard text cursor towards the top left-hand corner, and some text can then be typed onto the screen. If you use the Properties Inspector to change the text style, font, and colour you will find that each change is listed in the History palette. Like the History palette in some graphics programs, it does not merely show each change, but can be used to undo and redo actions. Move the slider at the left of the screen upward to undo actions, and move it down again to reinstate them.

Fig.1.26 The History palette provides a very useful Undo/Redo facility

Note that this feature is in addition to the standard facility to undo and redo the last action, which is available from the Edit menu. In fact Dreamweaver MX has a multistage undo and redo facility available from the File menu, and the same feature is available from the usual Undo and Redo buttons in the Standard toolbar. The menu and button methods are useful if you only need to go a few steps backwards or forwards and the History palette is not active. Of course, the History palette responds to changes made via either of these methods. The History palette can also be used to generate and replay a sequence of commands, giving a form of macro facility.

Code View

With Dreamweaver MX it is possible to produce web pages by using a largely or even totally visual approach. In other words, you add text by typing it onto the screen, change its size or colour by selecting the text and setting the required parameters using the Properties Inspector, and so on. Changes made can be seen on the screen, but the screen of Dreamweaver MX is one thing and the screen of a browser is another. Dreamweaver MX has to convert the web pages you generate into code that standard browsers can interpret correctly. The code used by browsers is HTML, and the Code Window shows the code that is generated by Dreamweaver MX. This is actually a simple editor, and it can be used to add your own code or modify the existing code.

Document window

This is the main window that has the menu bar, etc., at the top, and it is the one that shows the WYSIWYG representation of web pages. The left-hand section of the status bar at the bottom of this window shows the relevant HTML tags for the current selection. Further along the status bar there is a box that shows the size of the document window in terms of pixel width and height. If you drag the window to resize it, the status display will show the window's new size. There are some popular preset sizes available if you left-click on the size box to bring up a menu (Figure 1.27).

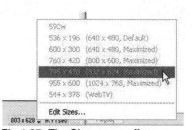

Fig.1.27 The Size menu offers several preset sizes

The Preferences window for the Status bar appears (Figure 1.28) if you select the Edit Sizes option, and it is then possible to edit the existing sizes or add new ones.

The box to the right of the size indicator is the statistics indicator, and it shows the size of the web page in terms of kilobytes, together with the download time using a 28.8k modem. Incidentally, other standard modem speeds are available via the Preferences window for the status bar (Figure 1.29). We would all like to produce dynamic and exciting web pages, but it is as well to keep the download times reasonably short. Users will not appreciate your artistry if they get fed up waiting for the page to

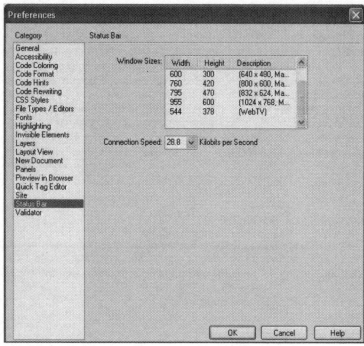

Fig.1.28 The Preferences window for the Status bar

download and move on to another site! Bear in mind that the indicated download time assumes a perfect connection. Real world loading delays are likely to be somewhat longer than the figure indicated.

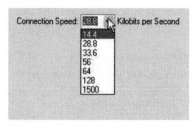

Fig.1.29 The default modem speed can be changed

Customising

A degree of customisation is possible with the document window via the View menu. The first three options enable this window to show the HTML code, the normal design view, or both using a split screen (Figure 1.30). Even with the Design window blank, there will still be some code

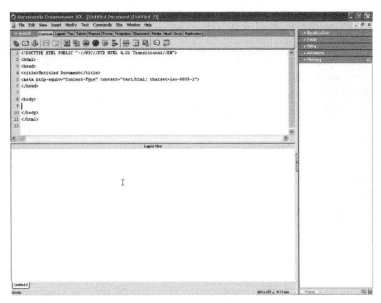

Fig.1.30 Code and Design views can be shown simultaneously

in the Code window that defines the page itself. Amongst the other options there is the ability to show a grid on the screen, and the Grid Settings option in the submenu brings up the window of Figure 1.31. This enables the size and colour of the grid to be adjusted, and either dots or lines are available. The Snap to Grid option in the submenu enables the grid to operate as a snap grid as well as a visual type.

Another option in the View menu enables rulers to be displayed along the left and top edges of the document area, and the rulers can be calibrated in inches, centimetres, or pixels. These can also be very useful when you need to position objects with good precision. Select Rulers and then the Show option to turn the rulers on or off. Select Rulers and then Pixels, Inches, or Centimetres to set the units of measurement. Figure 1.32 shows the document window with both rulers and a line grid

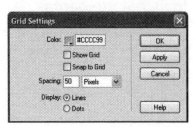

Fig.1.31 The Grid Settings window

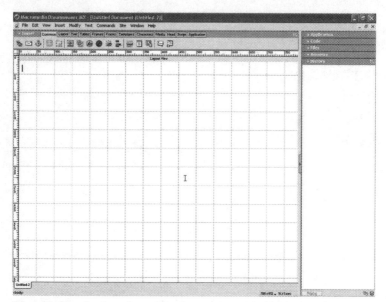

Fig.1.32 The Design view with rulers and a grid of lines switched on

added, but in normal use you would probably settle for one or the other and not both. Placing the pointer at the point where the two rulers join and then dragging the origin to the desired point on the screen relocates the origin for the rulers. Cross hairs appear on the screen (Figure 1.33) while this is being done. Go to the View menu and select Rulers and Reset Origin to reset the 0-0 origin to the top left-hand corner of the screen.

Invisible elements

The main document window gives a WYSIWYG view of the web pages you produce, and the pages therefore appear the same within Dreamweaver MX as they will when viewed using a browser. Obviously this is normally what is required, and it avoids having to load web pages into a browser in order to see what they will look like in use. On the other hand, web pages often include things that are hidden away in the background and are not supposed to be seen by users. An example of this is comments added into the code by the programmer to remind him or her what each section of code is for. These invisible elements can be

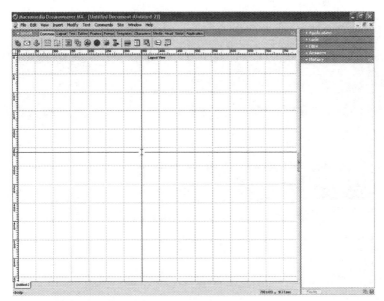

Fig.1.33 A crosshairs cursor can be used

made visible or hidden from view by going to the View menu and selecting Visual Aids and then Invisible Elements. This operates in standard toggle fashion, and there is a tick against the menu entry when this feature is enabled. You can select the elements that are shown on the screen via the appropriate preferences window. Go to the Edit menu, select Preferences, and then left-click on Invisible Elements in the list on the left.

Editing text

Text can be typed into the main document window, which is in many ways like a text editor or word processor. The usual Cut, Paste, and Copy options are available from the Edit menu. To select text either double-click on a word to select that word, or hold down the left mouse button and drag the cursor over the text you wish to select. If the window is used in split mode to show the code and design views simultaneously, text selected in one section of the window will also be selected in the other section (Figure 1.34). Anything selected in the Design window will also be highlighted in the Code Inspector palette if this is already active

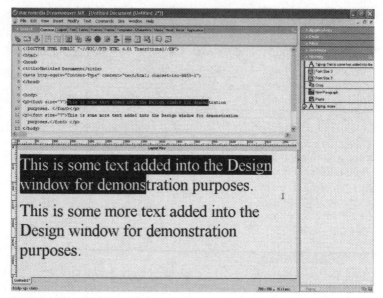

Fig.1.34 Text selected in one view is also selected in the other view

or if it is launched after a selection has been made. Left-clicking on a paragraph tag (<p>) in the code view or the Code Inspector will select the appropriate paragraph in the design view.

Entering and editing text into the document view of Dreamweaver MX is not quite as free and easygoing as entering text into a modern word processor, but a lot of word processor style features are present. Chapter 4 explains the finer points of typing or loading text into Dreamweaver MX.

Fig.1.35 It is no longer possible to drag a window from one group to another

Finally

It is perhaps worth pointing out that where panels are grouped together, such as the Application and Code palettes, they can not be dragged from one palette to another. This facility was present in Dreamweaver 4, but it has apparently been removed from

Dreamweaver MX for legal reasons. The error message of Figure 1.35 will appear if you try to drag one of the tabs from its palette. It is still possible to move a panel to another palette group, and this is achieved by right-clicking on the appropriate tab. Next the Group With option is selected from the pop-up menu, and then the appropriate group is selected from the submenu (Figure 1.36). Dreamweaver retains

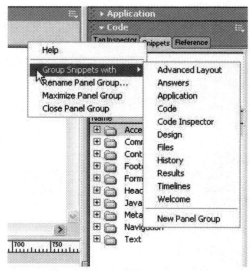

Fig.1.36 It is still possible to move a palette from one group to another

a good range of customisation features that enable the user interface to be moulded to suit individual users.

1 User interface

Background

Beneath the surface

Web pages are written using what could be regarded as a form of programming language, known as HTML (hypertext mark-up language). As its name suggests, it is actually more like a mark-up language used in a desktop publishing program than a true programming language. Those of us that can remember desktop publishing in the days before that term had been invented can also remember the relatively crude way in which pages were produced. There were no true WYSIWYG (what you see is what you get) desktop publishing programs for the early PCs and other computers of that era.

Instead, embedded codes were used to indicate that pieces of text should be in a certain font, style, and size. What appeared on the monitor was the text plus the embedded codes in the standard font of the text card. This was usually a pretty crude monospaced font. In order to see what a page looked like you had to print it out. If there were any problems or you simply did not like some aspect of the page design, the embedded codes had to be changed and then the page was printed out again. This sounds like slow and tough going, and it was.

Modern desktop publishing programs do not work on this basis, and the monitor does provide something close to a true WYSIWYG display. The resolution of even a good monitor is usually well below the final printed resolution, requiring some compromises to be made in the version displayed on the monitor, but you get a very good idea of what the final printed version will look like before it is proof printed.

This is not to say that the embedded codes have disappeared, and they are still used by some programs. There is often a mode that enables the user to see the raw text plus these codes, and even make changes to the text and the embedded codes. However, with a modern WYSIWYG desktop publishing program there is no need to use or know anything about the method of coding. You can simply format pages using the palettes, pop-down menus, etc. The program displays a good facsimile of the final printed version, generates the embedded codes, and eventually converts the text and code into the finished product.

Originally it was necessary to understand HTML before you could produce web pages, because there was no WYSIWYG program that would do the job for you. The situation has changed over the years of course, and there are now plenty of programs that enable web pages to be produced by those having no understanding of HTML. In some cases the program may totally shield the user from the underlying HTML code, but even though you can not see it the code is still there. HTML is the language understood by web browsers, and it is what all web site and web page creation programs have to generate.

Roundtrip HTML

Dreamweaver is a WYSIWYG program that generates web sites in HTML. Producing web pages using Dreamweaver is in many ways like using a WYSIWYG desktop publishing program, and changes made to the font size or colour of some text will be immediately represented on the display. The HTML code will also be changed, and the user can look at the code that the program generates. Dreamweaver's main claim to fame is that you are not restricted to simply looking at the HTML code, and you can make manual changes to it. This is what is called "roundtrip" HTML in Dreamweaver terminology.

With most HTML editors that have a WYSIWYG mode you can not manually change the code that is generated. All changes have to be made via the program's tools and menus rather than by direct changes to the HTML. This may seem a rather strange way to do things, but these programs can only handle HTML code written in a specific fashion. Any code produced manually may not conform to the program's way of doing things and can not be interpreted properly. In some cases Dreamweaver may not be able to understand the code you have written, but it will still leave it intact rather than trying to change or delete it. Provided you have written the code correctly, it will be carried through to the web site and will work properly.

On the face of it, roundtrip HTML is not of any importance. You can produce web pages using the tools, menus, etc., without the need for any manual editing of the code. Indeed, you do not need to see the code let alone make changes to it. To some extent this is true, and beginners will prefer to use the WYSIWYG approach rather than trying to write any HTML code themselves. One reason it is of importance to more advanced users is because HTML has not reached the stage where it is properly standardised. It is still being developed to meet the increasing demands that are placed upon it. With Dreamweaver you can add up-to-date HTML code that Dreamweaver can not understand, and it will be used in the web site. Whether all browsers will be able to interpret it correctly is another matter. You should always endeavour to develop sites that will still be usable by people who do not have the very latest versions of the popular browser programs. Another reason for adding your own code is that little enhancements that are not otherwise possible using Dreamweaver can be incorporated into web pages.

Although Dreamweaver enables you to write your own HTML code, it has to be emphasised that you do not need to know anything about HTML in order to use the program effectively. It is tempting to say that you can get by with Dreamweaver if you know nothing about HTML code, but you can actually do much more than get by with it. Very sophisticated sites can be produced using Dreamweaver in its WYSIWYG mode, and no "home made" HTML code. On the other hand, as with many things in computing, the greater your knowledge of how things work, the better the results you are likely to produce. Also, with a deep understanding of how things work you are in a much better position to sort out problems when things do not go according to plan.

If you only wish to produce some relatively straightforward web sites there is probably no need to bother too much about learning HTML code, now or ever. If you wish to produce web sites that push the technology to its limits you will certainly have to learn about HTML, and probably a few other things as well. Even if you decide not to learn HTML coding, I would certainly recommend learning a few basics of this subject, and you will certainly need to understand some of the terminology.

Mark-up

HTML is derived from SGML (standard general mark-up language), which is a standard for the representation of text in digital form. Like Adobe's popular PDF (portable document format) it was designed not to be specific to one type of computer or operating system. This cross-platform capability is retained in HTML, and web pages can therefore be viewed correctly on a Mac, a PC using any practically any version of Windows, Linux, or whatever, or on any system that has a suitable browser program. Another reason for the success of HTML is its hyperlink feature, or just plain "links" as they are often called. If you use the Internet you can hardly fail to have seen these. Practically every web page has links to other pages in the same site, to pages in other sites, or in some cases to other places on the same over-length web page. Most browsing is done by clicking on links rather than typing web addresses into the browser.

HTML basics

You can get an instant example of basic HTML by running Dreamweaver and launching the Code Inspector. Although the default web page will be empty initially, it still has a basic HTML description, and this will be visible in the Code inspector (Figure 2.1). Each HTML page must have certain tags, and these are the HTML, head, title and body tags. A tag indicates what the code is describing, and in the case of the HTML tag it is the page itself. Many (but not all) tags use opening and closing containers. If you look at the code for the default page you will notice that it starts with "<html>" and finishes with "</html>". These are respectively the opening and closing containers, and because the HTML tag is for the entire page, they appear at the beginning and end of the code.

Most elements of HTML code are comprised of three sections, which are the tag itself, the attribute, and the value. For example, there is typically a section like this:

<body bgcolor="#FFFFFF" text="#000000">

</body>

Here body is clearly the tag, and the attribute is "bgcolor", which is the background colour. The attribute is in double quotation marks, and is a numeric value that determines the background colour. Although #FFFFFF may not look like a number, that it is because it is in hexadecimal and not ordinary decimal numbering. Hexadecimal, or just "hex" as it is often called, operates in base 16 and uses numbers from 0 to 9 plus letters from A to F. The hash (#) sign indicates that the number is in hexadecimal and not in decimal. A value of #FFFFFF is the maximum value that can be used and gives a white background. The relevant hexadecimal number is shown in the colour swatch when a colour is selected. Try adding some text in the Design window, selecting it, and then changing its colour using the Properties window. This should result in some code appearing in the Code window, complete with a six-digit value for the colour. This value will be the same as the one that appeared in the swatch window when the colour was selected.

Try changing the value to #AAAAAA in the Code window and then left-click on the main document window. This should change the background

```
<!DOCTYPE HTML PUBLIC "-//W3C//DTD HTML 4.01 Transitional//EN">
<html>
<head>
<title>Untitled Document</title>
<meta http-equiv="Content-Type" content="text/html; charset=iso-8859-1">
</head>

<body>

</body>
</html>
```

Fig.2.1   Some HTML code displayed in the Code Inspector

to a mid-grey colour. Repeat the process using values of #00FFFF, #FF00FF, and #FFFF00. These should produce background colours of cyan, magenta, and yellow respectively, which are the three primary colours. Each primary colour has its own two-digit strength value, and by using the appropriate value for each one it is possible to produce any colour within the video system's repertoire. In the case of colour it is not usually worthwhile doing things manually, because the program provides a colour mixing tool to make the job much easier. However, this simple example does serve to show the basic way in which the coding operates.

Tags

When just about anything is added to an HTML page, at the code level it is a tag plus an attribute and a value. In Figure 2.2 a bitmap image has been added to the page. The image is selected in the design view, so its code is shown highlighted in the Code Inspector to the right of the image. The tag is "<img", and the attribute that follows this is "src", or the source of the image in other words. The value is the path and filename for the image file. It will be apparent from this that the value in HTML code does not have to be a numeric value. It can be whatever data is needed to permit the object to be displayed correctly. Note that the tag selector in the bottom left-hand corner of the Design/Code window shows the relevant tag or tags for whatever is selected in this window.

You can learn quite a lot about HTML code simply by adding objects into the design view of and then examining the code that Dreamweaver generates. Unlike some WYSIWYG web programs, Dreamweaver

*Fig.2.2 The highlighted text in the Code Inspector window is the
HTML code for the image of an anchor*

produces what is usually efficient and straightforward HTML code, so it
is relatively easy to see what is going on. You should find it quite easy to
edit things like text and the names of objects using the code view or the
Code Inspector. Once you have grasped a few basic concepts, learning
HTML code should not be too difficult.

Why use HTML

Using HTML may seem to be doing things the hard way, but there are
good reasons for using a mark-up language for web pages. It is possible
that we will all have high-speed Internet access before too long, but until
then the average Internet connection can only handle data at a rate of a
few kilobytes per second. The screen image on an average computer is
a bitmap that contains around one to eight megabytes of data. A simple
web page sent as a bitmap would require the transfer of a similar amount
of data, and a large scrollable page would require a much larger transfer.
Data compression techniques could reduce the amounts of data involved,
but it could still require something like 100 to 500 kilobytes per page.
This represents a download time of around 20 seconds to one minute

per page with a 56k modem and a pretty good telephone connection. With a poor connection these times would have to be doubled or trebled.

Using a mark-up language such as HTML it is possible to reduce simple web pages to just a few kilobytes of data. Complex pages can still require the transfer of substantial amounts of data, especially where large colour photographs are involved. However, HTML helps to keep amounts of data to low levels where this is possible, and keeps download times relatively short. A few compromises may be involved in using a mark-up language, but at present the advantages far outweigh the drawbacks. Where some degree of interactivity is required, simply downloading pages as bitmaps will not give the desired result anyway. With an increasingly interactive Internet there is no real alternative to HTML, JavaScript, etc.

File types

As pointed out in the previous chapter, Dreamweaver is mostly used in conjunction with files generated using other programs. These programs mostly work in their own file formats, but can also generate files in certain standard formats so that they can export work to programs like Dreamweaver. Although Dreamweaver can not handle a huge range of file types, it can handle the most important ones for web use, and most programs of relevant types can therefore export files to Dreamweaver. These are the most important of the standard file types:

Jpeg or Jpg

Whether called Jpeg or Jpg, it is pronounced jay-peg. This is now the most common format used for bit maps. A bitmap is an image that is made up of dots, or pixels as they are termed. A computer monitor produces images in this fashion, and any type of graphic can be represented as a bitmap. However, it produces large files and often gives relatively poor results when applied to line drawings. This file format is mainly used with photographic images, or pseudo photographic images, where it enables good results to be obtained without resorting to large file sizes. The modest file size is achieved using compression, and with some programs you can use varying degrees of compression and up to three different types.

Note that the small file sizes obtained when using high degrees of compression are obtained at the expense of reduced picture quality. In Internet applications it is clearly helpful to have small files in order to keep download times to a minimum. On the other hand, there is no

Fig.2.3 This Jpeg image has been subjected to minimal compression and has a file size of about 900k

point in having an image that downloads quickly if no one can see what it is meant to be! The borderline between acceptable and unacceptable quality is a subjective matter, and can only be determined using the "suck it and see" approach. Figure 2.3 shows a photograph that has been saved in Jpeg format using minimal compression, and Figure 2.4 shows the same photograph with maximum compression. These produce file sizes of about 900k and 100k respectively, and there is surprisingly little difference between them. However, with a colour image any artefacts added by the compression tend to be more noticeable, so this monochrome image is perhaps overstating the case for using large amounts of compression.

*Fig.2.4 This version of the image has been compressed to about
100k of data*

GIF

The full name for this format is CompuServe GIF, and programs that use
it have to be licensed by CompuServe. This format is generally preferred
for line art such as graphs and most diagrams, or practically any non-
photographic images. In fact the GIF image format is sometimes used
for monochrome photographs, but these days Jpeg is the more popular
choice for images of this type. With suitable images it combines small
file sizes and high quality. Up to 256 colours is supported, and these
can be any colours rather than those from a predetermined set. No
compression is used with this format, but the file sizes are kept small by
the inherently compact method of storing images. With a line art format
the image is stored on the basis of (say) a line of a certain width going
from one co-ordinate to another, rather than as a set of pixels to depict

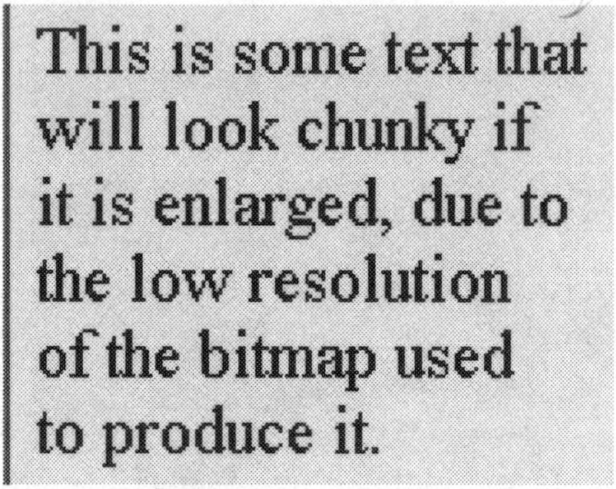

This is some text that will look chunky if it is enlarged, due to the low resolution of the bitmap used to produce it.

Fig.2.5 Bitmaps tend to give poor results when enlarged

the line.   An advantage of this system is that images are produced in high quality on high-resolution printers, etc. The higher the resolution of the output device, the higher the quality of reproduction with line art images. Bitmap images, unless very large numbers of pixels are used, produce   rather chunky looking results when printed large. Figure 2.5 shows an example of this effect. GIF files can be used for simple animations incidentally.

Png

This is a relatively new file format for images, and it is apparently pronounced pong, as in nasty smell or Ping-Pong. It is designed to be a sort of universal licence-free image format that will eventually replace the GIF format. Although relatively new, any reasonably modern browser should be able to handle Png images (Internet Explorer 4 or later for example). These days many graphics programs can export images in this format.

Txt

This is a simple text file, and any word processor or text editor should be able to produce a file in this format. It is important to realise that this type of file can only handle basic text, and that all or virtually all formatting information is lost when a file is saved in this format. Hard carriage returns should be retained, but text size, font, and colour information are lost. Tabulation tends to go astray when text is swapped using this format. You can use a word processor to generate blocks of text and then format them in Dreamweaver, but it might be better to export the text in HTML format. In practice this method will not always give perfect results every time, but no more than a small amount of editing should be needed to restore any lost formatting. Most modern word processors such as Microsoft's Word can save documents in HTML format.

Swf

Files in Macromedia Flash format. These are used to provide animations including rollovers, etc.

Aif or Aiff

A sound file format.

File types are usually indicated by a three or four letter extension to the filename. For instance, a file called myphoto1.jpg would be a bitmap image in Jpeg format. Three-letter extensions were used in the days of MS/DOS, but this limit is not present in modern operating systems. However, some people still use three-letter extensions, and it is for this reason that some extensions exist in three and four-letter versions. Thus, a Jpeg image file can have jpg or jpeg as its extension.

Conversion

Such is the importance of the web these days that practically any graphics program can produce files in GIF or Jpeg format. In many cases both formats will be available, while in others only one or the other will be available, depending on the types of image the program is designed to handle. Being relatively new the Png format is less well supported, but as pointed out previously, it is nevertheless supported by many modern graphics packages. It is included as an output format in the later versions of Adobe PhotoShop for example. If your graphics program does not support at least one of the popular web graphics formats you are certainly using the wrong program for this type of work.

If you are not prepared to switch to a different program there is the option of using a conversion program. A file saved in a standard graphics format can be converted to a GIF, Jpeg, or Png file using one of these programs. Commercial software of this type seems to be a bit "thin on the ground" these days, but it can usually be found from one of the larger shareware suppliers. Graphics programs such as PhotoShop and Paintshop can inport and export images in a wide range of file formats and can therefore be used as conversion programs, although this is rather under-utilising their abilities.

Other formats

There are other file formats in use on the Internet, but most of these are not used in quite the same way as (say) a Jpeg image that forms part of a web page when it is viewed using a browser. It is more usual for these other file formats to be downloaded and then viewed and (or) heard via a suitable program such as a media player. Some of the more common of these file types are listed here:

AVI

A movie format that can also handle sound.

Mpeg or Mpg

Another movie format that can handle sound as well.

Mov

Apple QuickTime movie/animation files.

PDF

This is the Adobe portable document format. It is actually a general-purpose file format that can handle text and any type of image. This book was sent to the printers in the form of a PDF file for example. A high degree of compression is used, but results of excellent quality are produced. Adobe Acrobat reader is needed to view PDF files, but the reader program is free from the Adobe web site and is available for several types of computer and various operating systems. The popular web browsers link to the reader program so that they can effectively be used to display PDF documents. This format is a popular choice for complex and (or) large documents.

MP3

An audio format that uses a large amount of compression but still manages to produce some impressive results.

MIDI

MIDI was originally designed for use with synthesisers and other electronic musical instruments. A MIDI file can be played by having a synthesiser connected to the MIDI port of a computer, but these days most sound cards can play MIDI files, albeit with a fair amount of help from the sound-card's driver software.

Note that the standard web graphics file types can be used where large or complex images need to be downloaded, and they are not restricted to use within web pages.

DHTML

DHTML is an extension of HTML that uses a variety of technologies to permit clever things to be achieved. For example, graphics or other objects can change when the pointer is placed over them, or other things can change when the pointer is at a certain point on the page. These are languages that DHTML uses in addition to standard HTML, with a brief explanation of each one.

JavaScript

This should not be confused with the Java programming language, which is completely different. The Java name was licensed by Netscape from Sun Microsystems, but only the name was used, not Java technology. JavaScript is now very popular and is used to add all manner of clever tricks to web sites. It is often used to provide better interactivity with the user. For instance, many financial web sites can produce graphs showing price data for shares and this type of thing. Without JavaScript a chart has no interactive capability. If you wish to zoom in on part of the chart, either it is not possible at all, or fresh parameters have to be set and then the chart is redrawn "from scratch". With JavaScript charts you can use the mouse to indicate the part of the chart that is of interest, and then you get a zoomed view of that section.

Using JavaScript it is rather like using a charting application on your computer rather than just downloading web pages, and I suppose that when using JavaScript you are downloading and using a program on your computer. JavaScript is used in other ways, such as for rollovers and testing browser compatibility. Note that you do not have to learn JavaScript in order to use it with Dreamweaver. If you should decide to learn JavaScript it is more difficult to master than HTML, but should not be difficult for anyone having some previous programming experience.

CSS

CSS stands for Cascading Style Sheets. This is a relatively new page layout system but it is supported by any reasonably up-to-date browser. It is designed to give better and more precise control over page layouts than HTML.

DOM

DOM is the acronym for document object module, and it provides a link to external scripting and programming protocols such as ActiveX. It also enables so-called plug-ins to be used, such as Flash or Shockwave.

XML

XML (Extensible Mark-up Language), like HTML, is based on SGML. Extensible simply means that it can be extended, and it is extended by designers creating their own tags. XML is a subject that goes beyond the scope of this book.

WMA

WMV

These are Windows media files, and are respectively for audio and video files. Of course, the video version can include sound as well. They have been somewhat overshadowed by the MP3, AVI, and MPG file formats, but are nevertheless in widespread use.

The basics

Basic pages

Armed with the background knowledge of the previous chapter and the knowledge of the Dreamweaver user interface gained in chapter 1, the best way forward is to produce some simple web pages. If you have experience with a word processor, or better still a desktop publishing program, producing simple web pages using Dreamweaver should be relatively straightforward. Even if you have only limited computing experience it should not be that difficult, but it is assumed here that the reader has a basic knowledge of how to use his or her computer. It is also assumed that the reader has used the Internet and knows what web pages look like and how they are used.

Open

As with most programs, Dreamweaver can load existing files so that they can be updated, or new files can be created "from scratch". At this point there will obviously be no existing HTML files of your own to open, but some sample files are loaded onto the hard disc during the installation process. If you wish to load and look at these go to the File menu, choose the Open option, and then use the file browser to select one of the example files. These will be in the samples folder in the Dreamweaver MX folder. For a Windows installation the normal route to the Dreamweaver MX folder is:

C:\ProgramFiles\Macromedia\DreamweaverMX

The program may default to the appropriate folder if you have not experimented with the Open function previously. There will probably be several subfolders and a number of files to choose from. Left-click on the Open button and the selected file will be displayed in the main document screen.

By default the file browser will show any type of file that Dreamweaver can open. However, left-clicking on the downward pointing arrowhead at the right end of the "File of type" text box produces a list of file types (Figure 3.1). You can then select a specific file type, which makes it easier to find the one you require in a folder that has a large number of files of various types. As is now standard practice,

Fig.3.1 Using the file type filter

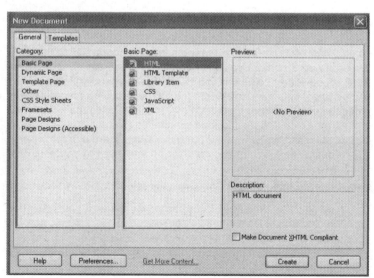

Fig.3.2 You will usually select HTML when creating a new document

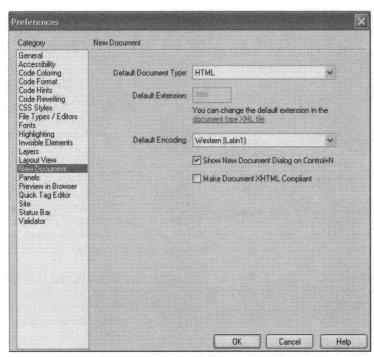

Fig.3.3 A different type of default document can be selected

Dreamweaver MX has a list of recently opened files listed near the bottom of the file menu. In order to load one of these simply left-click on its entry in the list.

New and Save

To create a new document go to the File menu and select New. This brings up the window of Figure 3.2, where you select the type of document to be created. Initially you will only need to create basic HTML pages, and this is the default option. In due course you may wish to use a different type of default document, and this setting can be changed by choosing Preferences from the Edit menu. Select New Document in the menu down the right-hand side of the Preferences window, and it should then change to look like Figure 3.3. The menu at the top enables the default document type to be altered. When initially trying out the New

Fig.3.4   The Save As window appears when saving a document for the first time

command just settle for the existing default and operate the Create button to produce the new but empty document.

Having created web pages you will need to save them to disc for later use. To save the current page select Save from the File menu, which will bring up the usual file browser window (Figure 3.4). By default documents are called Untitled1, Untitled2, etc., but you can edit the name in the text box to something more suitable and then operate the Save button to save the document to disc under this name. Of course, once a document has been saved, it is immediately saved to disc the next time the Save option is selected. Its existing name will be used, and the original copy will be overwritten. Dreamweaver does not make backup copies of old versions when new versions of files are saved. Use the Save As option to save the document under a different name.

Extensions

By default, files are saved with an htm extension in the case of PCs, or an html extension if you use a Mac. Dreamweaver MX enables the default extension to be altered by going to the Edit menu and selecting the Preferences option. The General section enables the default extension to be altered or the extension to be left out altogether. There is no easy way of making either of these changes using Dreamweaver MX, but in practice it is unlikely that you will need to change the default extension.

One use of the Save As feature is to save copies of a document to disc so that they can be opened and modified later. This provides a quick means of generating several web pages that are basically similar, although it is necessary to take great care to remove anything from the original that is not needed in the new version. There is also a template feature, and it is well worthwhile investigating this when you have become more fluent at using Dreamweaver.

You may sometimes make unsatisfactory modifications to a page and wish to revert to the original version. The History palette is one option here, but provided the document has not been saved since you started altering it there is an easier option. Simply close the document

Fig.3.5 Operate the No button to exit without saving

without saving it. Select Close from the Edit menu and then operate the No button when you are asked if you wish to save changes to the document (Figure 3.5). With Dreamweaver MX, unlike previous versions, you are not asked if you wish to Exit Dreamweaver. Dreamweaver MX remains open, and the original version of the document can then be opened in the normal way. In order to close a document but save any changes that have been made, use the same process but left-click on the Yes button when asked if you wish to save changes to the document. Alternatively, save the document and it will then be closed as soon as the Close function is used.

Page Properties		
Title: Untitled Document		OK
Background Image:	Browse...	Apply
Background:		Cancel
Text:	Visited Links:	
Links:	Active Links:	
Left Margin:	Margin Width:	
Top Margin:	Margin Height:	
Document Encoding: Western (Latin1)	Reload	
Tracing Image:	Browse...	
Image Transparency:	100%	
Transparent	Opaque	
Document Folder:		
Site Folder: C:\Documents and Settings\Robert\My Documents\		Help

Fig.3.6 The Page Properties dialogue box

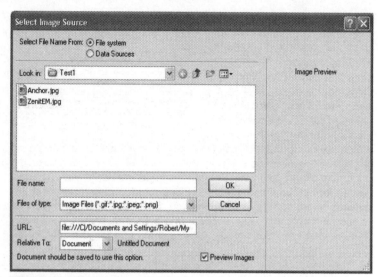

Fig.3.7 The file browser is the easier and more reliable method of locating the required image file

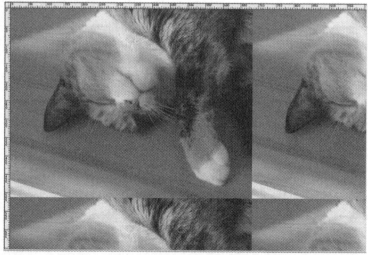

Fig.3.8 A background image that uses the tiling method. This works best with an image that is small relative to the page size, rather than an image that almost fits the page, as here

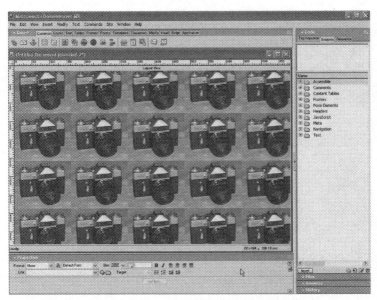

Fig.3.9 Here the tiles are small enough to give a good effect

Page properties

The Properties Inspector provides control of the characteristics of individual objects on a page, but it is also possible to set default characteristics for an entire page. In order to bring up the Page Properties window (Figure 3.6) select Page Properties from the Modify menu. Note that there must be a document open or Page Properties option will not be active. Most of the options available from this dialogue box are fairly straightforward. The Title option sets the text that will appear in the title bar of the web page. There are colour charts that enable background, text, and link colours to be selected, or you can type in the colour values. A background image can be chosen, and the filename (with full path) can be typed into the appropriate text box. There is file browser available though (Figure 3.7), and this is the easier and more reliable way of selecting the required file.

If the background image is larger than the web page it will not be resized to fit the page, but will instead be clipped. In other words, the left-hand and (or) bottom of the picture will be cut off. Similarly, if the image is too small to fill the web page it will be made to fit the page using the tiling

Fig.3.10 A tracing image added to the page. This will not be visible when the page is viewed using a browser

method (Figure 3.8). Ideally, where necessary the image should be resized using a graphics program so that it is the correct size for the web page. If you wish to use the tiling method, it works best if the picture is small in relation to the page size so that a large number of tiles are used (Figure 3.9). If the image is nearly as large as the page, the viewer tends to get the impression that something has gone awry when the page loaded. An advantage of the tiling method is that it enables a small image file to be used, which helps to keep download times short.

Tracing image

The Tracing Image option enables an image to be placed on the page, and its transparency can be set so that it can be reduced to a weak background image if required (Figure 3.10). This image will be visible in Dreamweaver, but it will not be carried through to the final web page. Its purpose is to aid the production of a page that is being copied from a paper mock-up produced using a graphics program. When viewed within Dreamweaver the tracing image will hide any ordinary image that it overlaps, but any hidden images will appear properly when the web page

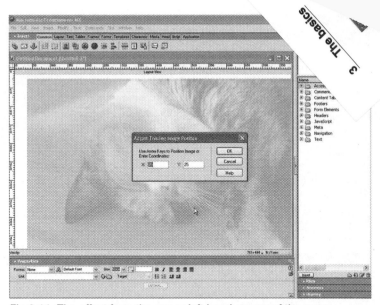

*Fig.3.11 The offset from the upper left-hand corner of the page
is adjustable*

is viewed using a browser. To hide the tracing image go to the View
menu, then select Tracing Image and Show. This option toggles the
image on and off.

There are further options in the Tracing Image submenu that enable the
position of the image to be altered, including the Adjust Position setting.
This brings up a simple dialogue box (Figure 3.11) that enables the offset
from the top right-hand corner of the screen to be altered. In the example
of Figure 3.11 it has been set to 30 pixels across (X) and 25 pixels down
(Y). Choosing Reset Position results in the image being returned to its
previous position. Align With Selection aligns the top right-hand corner
of the image with the corresponding corner of whatever object is selected
at the time. In the example of Figure 3.12 the image has been aligned
with a short text string. Of course, this option will not do anything unless
something is selected when the command is issued.

Web pages often have a pale image used as the background, but the
tracing image facility is obviously not usable in this fashion because the
image is not visible on the final web page. Instead, the background
image must be added using the background image facility. The image

Fig.3.12 Here the image has been aligned with the top of the text string

can be faded using the brightness and contrast controls of a graphics program prior to it being imported into Dreamweaver.

It is useful to bear in mind that you do not have to operate the OK button and exit the Page Properties dialogue box in order to see what any changes look like. Operating the Apply button will immediately implement any change. Obviously the Page Properties window will often partially obscure the image underneath, but you can usually see the page well enough to gauge whether or not the desired effect has been achieved. The Page Properties window can always be moved slightly if necessary.

Colour conscious

The subject of colour selection has been mentioned previously in this book, and it is worthwhile looking at the subject in a little more detail here. As we have already seen, the colour of objects is set using a six-digit hexadecimal number, but in Dreamweaver, as with most programs, there are colour palettes that make it easy to select the desired colour without bothering with hexadecimal values. You simply select the colour you require from a chart, or mix the colour if nothing in the preset selection is suitable. Dreamweaver then adds the appropriate hexadecimal value into the HTML code.

If you have used any graphics software you should be familiar with colour palettes, and should not have any difficulty in using the colour selection facilities of Dreamweaver. Even with no experience of this type of software, the basic colour chart selection method requires no further comment. Just left-click the "eyedropper" on the required colour to select it. Although various parts of Dreamweaver permit colour selection, things have been kept as simple as possible by having the same colour picker in each case.

The "eyedropper" tool can actually be used to select a colour from anywhere within a Dreamweaver window, but not outside the areas of the screen used by Dreamweaver. Actually, the "eyedropper" changes to a conventional pointer outside the main Dreamweaver window, but it still seems to operate as a colour picker. However, this tool is probably of most use for selecting colours from within the main Dreamweaver window. If an image is displayed within the document window for example, any colour used in that image can be selected using the "eyedropper" tool. Also, a menu of alternative colour sets can be produced by left-clicking on the arrowhead in the top

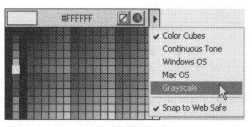

Fig.3.13 The colour sets menu

right-hand corner of the colour picker window (Figure 3.13). As pointed out previously, a colour-mixing palette can be produced by operating the button with the circular icon just to the left of the arrowhead. This makes it easy to produce any desired colour.

Suppose that a strong but dark blue is required, similar to navy blue. The main part of the window on the right gives the colours of the rainbow at the top, and the same colours diluted with an increasing amount of mid-grey towards the bottom of the panel. In other words, there are saturated colours at the top and increasing unsaturated versions of these colours towards the bottom. Nothing on this panel meets our requirements, but a strong blue colour can be selected by left-clicking on a mid-blue colour towards the top of the panel. The cross hairs sight

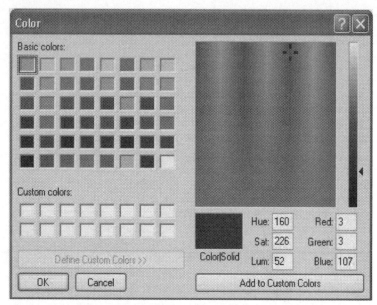

Fig.3.14 Using this colour palette it is possible to mix any desired colour that the 24-bit system can handle

moves to show the new colour selection. The slider to the right of the panel shows the selected colour in the middle, with increasing amounts of white towards the top, and black towards the bottom. In this example we require black added to the blue to darken it, and the slider is set towards the bottom of its range. If you try to approximate the settings shown in Figure 3.14 you should end up with a suitably dark blue colour.

The colour chart in the left-hand section of the window can be used as an alternative method of providing a basic colour that can then be adjusted using the slider control. The range of colours available here is relatively limited, but it will often provide a suitable basis for the required colour. Simply left-click on the required colour to select it and then adjust the slider control. In order to add a newly mixed colour to the custom colours beneath the main colour chart, first left-click on the rectangle you wish to contain the new colour. Then left-click on the Add to Custom Colours button to assign the new colour to the selected rectangle.

Web friendly

The problem in selecting web page colours on one computer is that they may be somewhat different when displayed on another computer. One reason for this is simply that different monitors produce different colours from the same colour values. In actual fact, the same monitor will produce different colours depending on how it is set up. A second problem is that not all computers have the same colour capabilities. Apart from differences between Macintosh computers and PCs, there can be differences between computers of the same general type. Some PCs have simple graphics cards offering relatively few colours, while others have graphics systems that can handle millions of different colours. A further complication is that the operating system and applications software might impose limits on the colours that can be used.

There is a set of so-called "browser safe" or "web safe" colours that can be reproduced by the popular Microsoft and Netscape browsers in both their Windows and Macintosh versions. Using these 200 or so colours does not guarantee that precisely the specified colour will be produced on every computer, but it does at least keep the inevitable divergences to a minimum. The "browser safe" colours are those that have 00, 33, 66, 99, CC, or FF as the hexadecimal values for each of the primary colours, but note that a few of the possible combinations are not guaranteed to always be spot on. In the menu of Figure 3.13 you will notice that there is a Web Safe option. When this is selected the "eyedropper" tool will only produce "web safe" colours and where necessary the chosen colours will be adjusted to the "web safe" colour that produces the nearest match.

Of course, the system colours produced using the colour mixing palette can be any colours within the repertoire of 16.7 million or so that this method supports, and in most cases will not be of the "web safe" variety. This does not mean that system colours will not work in practice. It simply means that the precise colours you choose will not necessarily be exactly matched when they are displayed on real-world monitors using popular browsers. As pointed out previously, even using "web safe" colours there will be variations from one computer to another. On the other hand, using the safe versions minimises any differences, and as the range of 216 safe colours is adequate for most purposes, it makes sense to use them unless there is a good reason to opt for a system colour instead.

It has to be pointed out here that the Macintosh version of Dreamweaver has somewhat enhanced colour selection facilities compared to the

Fig.3.15 The browser preview facility used with Internet Explorer

Windows version. These can be useful if you are experienced at using one of these alternative methods, but it is otherwise best to use the more straightforward methods of colour selection.

Colour choice

There is a temptation to choose bright contrasting colours that make your web pages as lively as possible. However, when choosing colour schemes you first need to consider whether ultra-bright colours are appropriate to the type of site you are designing. Colours that are suitable for a site devoted to holidays in the Caribbean might not be well suited to a site covering more sombre matters such as bereavement or legal advice. Whether bright or subdued colours are used, the main concern should always be readability. Pairs of colours that are normally considered good combinations do not always work well when used as background and text colours. Readability is generally best if there is good contrast between the text and the background, and I mean contrast in the light and dark sense rather than in terms of colour contrast.

Try setting the background to a well saturated yellow colour and adding some equally well saturated green lettering to the document. With small

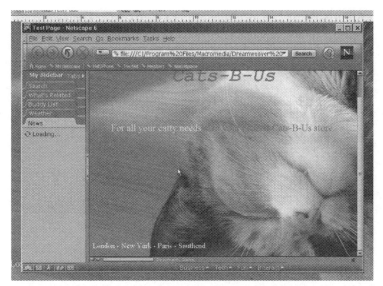

Fig.3.16 The browser preview facility used with Netscape 6

lettering it will probably be difficult to read the words at all. With large letters the text will be much more easily read, but it will not exactly leap out from the page. If the text is altered to a slightly darker green it will stand out much more clearly from the background, and the small text should be perfectly readable. Change the background to a paler yellow and things should improve still further. The page should also be less hard on the viewer's eyes as well. If the text is now changed to a pale green it will blend back into the page again.

There is no excuse for using colours that provide poor readability, because Dreamweaver makes it easy to change colours, and it does not take long to experiment with various colour combinations. Obviously each page in a site can have its own colour scheme, and in some cases this might be the best way of doing things. However, the generally accepted wisdom is that a site works best if a fixed colour scheme is used.

Proof of the pudding

Dreamweaver displays a WYSIWYG view of web pages in the main document window, but as different browsers treat web pages in slightly different ways you can not totally rely on the document window to show

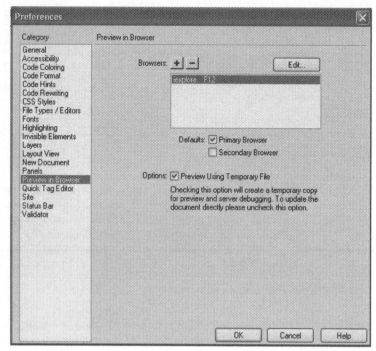

Fig.3.17 The Preview in Browser section of the Preferences window

you a true representation of how pages will look in a "real world" browser. The only way to discover exactly how web pages will look "in the flesh" is to load them into web browsers. As most Internet users have either Netscape or Microsoft browsers, the best way to test your new web pages is to use recent web browsers from both companies to view the pages. Netscape and Microsoft browsers are available as free downloads and are often to be found on the "free" cover-mounted discs of computer magazines.

In order to view a page using a browser, open the page in Dreamweaver, go to the File menu, select Preview in Browser, and then select the appropriate browser from the list. If the browser program is not already running it will be launched automatically and the web page will be loaded into it. Figure 3.15 shows a simple web page being previewed using Microsoft's Internet Explorer 5, and Figure 3.16 shows the equivalent when using Netscape 6. Note that changes made in Dreamweaver will

not be carried
through to the page in
the browser. In order
to view changes first
close the browser and
then select the
browser preview
option again.

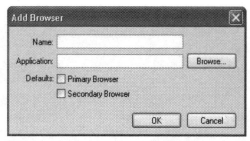

Fig.3.18 Adding a browser to the list

A browser normally
has the ability to load
files from disc as well
as web pages from
the Internet, so it is possible to save a page to disc and then load it into
a browser. Bear in mind though, that operating systems do not normally
allow two programs to access the same file simultaneously. Before using
a browser to open a file created using Dreamweaver, make sure the file
is closed in Dreamweaver.

Adding a browser

When Dreamweaver is installed it will detect the default browser and this
should be included in the list of browsers when the preview facility is
selected. Other browsers may not be detected and included in the list,
and any browser installed after Dreamweaver was installed will not be
included. To add a browser to the list, first go to the File menu and then
select Preview in Browser and Edit Browser List. This will bring up the
Preferences window of Figure 3.17. Next operate the + button to bring
up the Add Browser dialogue box (Figure 3.18), and then either type the
path to the browser program file and its name or use the Browse option.
Operating the Browse button produces the usual file browser. The Name
field in the Add Browser window is used to identify the browser in the list
that appears when the preview facility is selected. Add a suitable name
here such as Netscape or Explorer. Tick the appropriate check box if
you wish the newly added browser to be used by Dreamweaver as the
primary browser. Finally, left-click the OK button and the browser will be
added to the list. To remove a browser program from the list, left-click
on its entry to highlight it and then operate the – button.

If you are producing straightforward web pages it is unlikely that there
will be any discernible difference between the Dreamweaver WYSIWYG
display and what you see using a browser. Significant differences are
only likely to occur if a web page uses some up-to-the-minute feature, or
possibly if the browser is an old and out-of-date version.

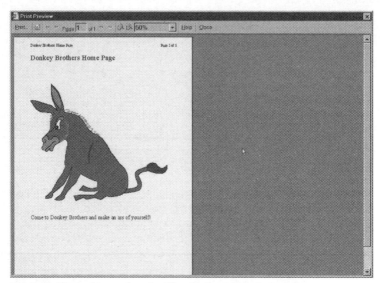

Fig.3.19 The print preview facility of Internet Explorer 5.5

Printing

Surprisingly perhaps, Dreamweaver does not have the usual Print option under the File menu, or anywhere else come to that. There is a Print Code option, but this only gives a printout of the HTML code, not compiled pages. As the output of the program is only intended to be viewed on a monitor this is not necessarily an important omission, but it can sometimes be handy to have hard copy of your web design work. There is no major difficulty in printing out pages, and it is just a matter of loading them into a suitable browser and printing them from there. Modern Microsoft and Netscape browsers all have facilities to print documents, but for the best printing features it is probably best to use the most recent version you can find. Figure 3.19 shows the print preview facility of Internet Explorer 5.5.

Adding text

Input

A lot of background information of one type or another has been provided in the previous chapters, but there are still some topics that need to be covered. However, having digested the first three chapters you are in a position to start making some web pages using the text manipulation facilities of Dreamweaver. There are two basic methods of getting text into Dreamweaver, and the more obvious one is to simply type it into the document window. Dreamweaver incorporates many of the standard facilities for entering, formatting, and checking text, including a word processor. Therefore, if you are building a web site "from scratch", there is probably no point in entering text other than direct into Dreamweaver's document window.

However, if preferred you can import text from a word processor, text editor, or practically any program that can produce text. One reason for doing things this way is that you may prefer to work using a word processor that you are familiar with rather than using Dreamweaver's word processing features. Another possible reason is that you already have text that has been prepared for other purposes, and you now wish to use it in web pages. As will be explained in more detail later in this chapter, any formatting of the text may or may not be carried into Dreamweaver, depending on the method of importation used. Of course, plain text can be formatted once it has been imported into Dreamweaver, but there is no point in formatting it in a word processor and then doing the job again in Dreamweaver. If the text is ready formatted you should try to take that formatting forward into Dreamweaver. Provided you are using modern mainstream programs this should not be difficult to achieve.

Text cursor

Entering text straight into Dreamweaver and formatting it is not very difficult, and anyone having some experience of modern word processing should be able to work out the basic processes by using a little trial and

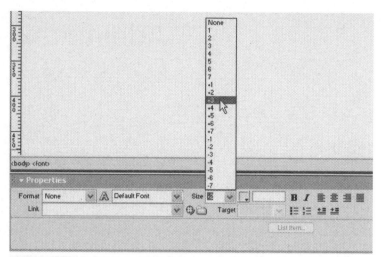

Fig.4.1 The text size can be changed using the Properties Inspector

error. The basics of word processing using Dreamweaver will be covered here for the benefit of those who lack experience with word processors, but it will only be covered fairly briefly. The document window should be set to design view, so select Design from the View menu if it is currently in the code view mode. If the text cursor is not already present, left-clicking on the document window will produce it. The text cursor is blinking vertical line, and initially it will be towards the top left-hand corner of the screen. The text cursor is separate from the mouse pointer, and the pointer will still be present when the text cursor is on the screen.

Anything typed at the keyboard will now appear in the document window in standard word processor fashion. Dreamweaver has a word-wrap facility, so there is no need to add carriage returns at the end of each line. These are added automatically by the program, which will not put any line breaks within words. The text size, font (letter style), and colour will all adhere to whatever default settings have been set.

Text size

There is more than one way to set text size in HTML, and using style sheets it is possible to set a point size in standard word processor or desktop publishing fashion. Without style sheets the relative method

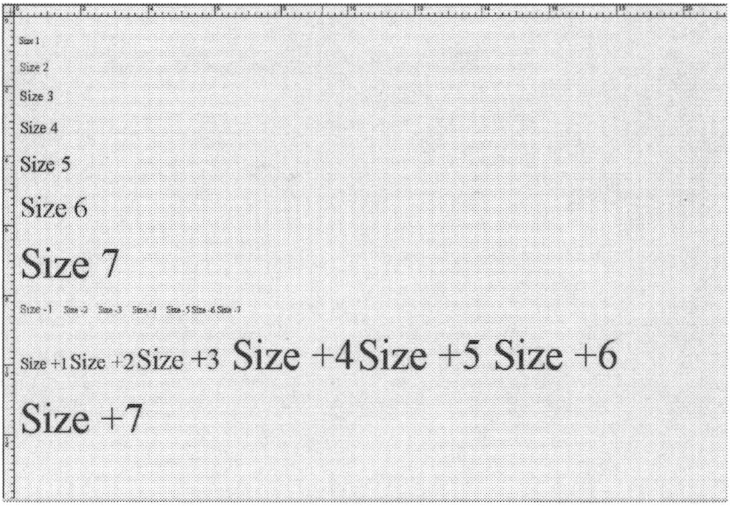

Size 1
Size 2
Size 3
Size 4
Size 5
Size 6
Size 7
Size -1   Size -2   Size -3   Size -4   Size -5 Size -6 Size -7
Size +1 Size +2 Size +3 Size +4 Size +5 Size +6
Size +7

Fig.4.2 A useful range of text sizes are available

has to be used, where the font size is relative to the base size. The basic font size will vary somewhat from one browser to another, but is usually around 10 to 14 points. If you select some text in the document window and then look at the available sizes in the Properties Inspector (Figure 4.1) you will find that there is a choice of two different ways of setting the text size. There are absolute sizes from 1 to 7, and relative sizes from −1 to +7. The absolute sizes are still relative in that the size actually obtained depends on the base size, which is whatever size is set for text size 3. Make this larger or smaller, and the other sizes shift accordingly.

On the face of it there are more text sizes available using the relative values, but as can be seen from Figure 4.2, some of these values simply duplicate other sizes, and there are still only seven sizes available. The point size used as the base size for various types of text can be set by going to the Edit menu, selecting Preferences, and then selecting Fonts as the category in the Preferences window (Figure 4.3). However, there is usually no point in doing so, and (say) boosting the text size in Dreamweaver will not result in the text being increased in size when the page is viewed in a browser. It is up to users to set the base text size of their browser to something sensible for the screen resolution they are using. This prevents (say) minute text being produced when a high screen resolution is in use.

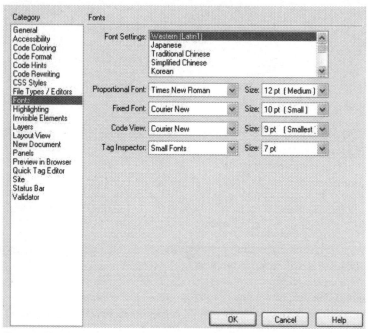

Fig.4.3 The base font size can be changed using the Preferences window, but there is normally no point in doing so

Try making some text larger using this method and then use the browser preview facility to view the page. The text will not be larger in the browser's version of the page, since the base size used by the browser will not have changed. You can get a better match by altering the text size in the browser. With Internet Explorer for example, the text size can be altered by selecting Text Size from the View menu. The default size plus two larger and two smaller sizes are available. It is definitely not advisable to design web pages that only display correctly if the browser is adjusted to produced abnormally large or small text, because no one will bother to make the adjustment. They will just exit the site and go elsewhere!

Fonts

Dreamweaver enables a wide range of fonts (lettering styles) to be used, and it is easy to change selected text from the default font to another style. Click on the arrowhead to the right of the current font description

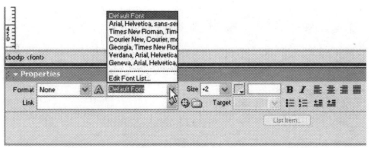

*Fig.4.4 Fonts can be changed using the pop-up menu of the
        Properties Inspector*

in the Properties Inspector and a list of fonts will appear (Figure 4.4).
Simply left-click on the desired font and the selected text will change
accordingly. Note that you do not have to specify a font. Dreamweaver
uses the Default Font setting if no font is selected, and the font used will
then depend on the default setting of the browser used to display the
page. This will usually be something fairly conservative such as Times
Roman, but will obviously vary somewhat from one browser to another
and one user to another.

There is a major problem when specifying a font, which is simply that a
font can only be displayed by a browser if that font is actually installed
on the computer concerned. The problem is made worse by having
different names for the same font. Swiss and Helvetica for example, is
the same font under different guises, and these are not the only names
in use for this font. There is little point in using an exotic font if it is not
installed on most computers and the majority of browsers will forced to
revert to some sort of default font.

HTML eases the problem of different names for much the same font by
allowing lists of fonts to be used. Browsers then go through the lists,
one by one, entry by entry, until an installed font of the same name is
detected. It is still possible that no suitable font will be found, and that
some browsers will have to use the default font. However, this method
does maximise the chances of a suitable font being found if there is one
installed on the computer. It is not a major disaster if the default font is
used, because the web page should still be perfectly readable and usable.

You can edit existing font lists or make your own by going to the Text
menu and selecting Font and then Edit Font List. Selecting Edit Font List
from the list of fonts in the Properties Inspector has the same effect, and
also brings up the window of Figure 4.5. In order to edit one of the lists,

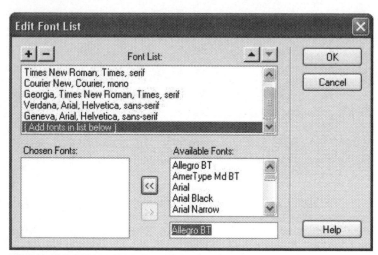

Fig.4.5 The dialogue box for editing font lists

left-click on its entry in the upper part of the window and the list of fonts will then appear in the text box in the bottom left-hand corner of the window. The fonts installed on your computer appear in the text box to the right of this one. To add one of the installed fonts to the list, first left-click on its entry to highlight it and then operate the << button to add it to the list. To remove a font from the list, left-click on its entry and then operate the >> button. To add the name of a font that is not installed on your PC, type its name into the text box beneath the list of installed fonts and then operate the << button.

The make a new list, first left-click on the (Add fonts in list below) entry in the font list. Then add and remove fonts from the new list in the usual fashion. To add more than one list, left-click the + button to add extra blank entries in the font list. Fonts are then added or removed from the additional lists in the usual way. Operate the OK button when you have finished, and the new list or lists will then be available via the Properties Inspector and the Text menu. Initially you will probably prefer to use the default font lists rather than making your own, but it is worth experimenting a little and making your own dummy list so that you get to understand the process of creating and editing lists. You should then have no difficulty in making the "real thing" when the need arises. To remove a list, you can either delete all its entries using the >> button to remove them one at a time, or select its entry and then operate the – button. To move a list

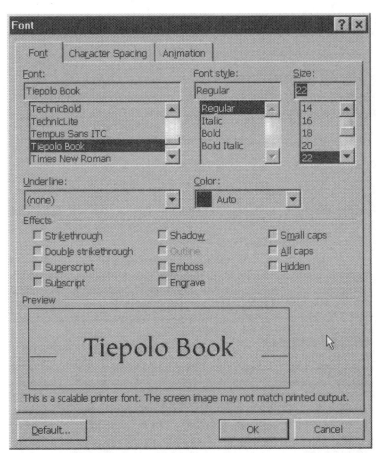

Fig.4.6 The font preview facility of Word 97

up or down one position in the font list, select it and then operate the up
or down button.

Dreamweaver does not have a font preview facility, and you can only
view a new font within Dreamweaver by adding it to the available fonts
and then using it in the document window. When choosing new fonts it
is quicker and easier to view them in a program that does have some
form of font preview facility, such as Microsoft Word. Figure 4.6 shows
the font preview facility of Word 97, and this is obtained by selecting the
Font option from the Format menu. The required font, size, etc., are

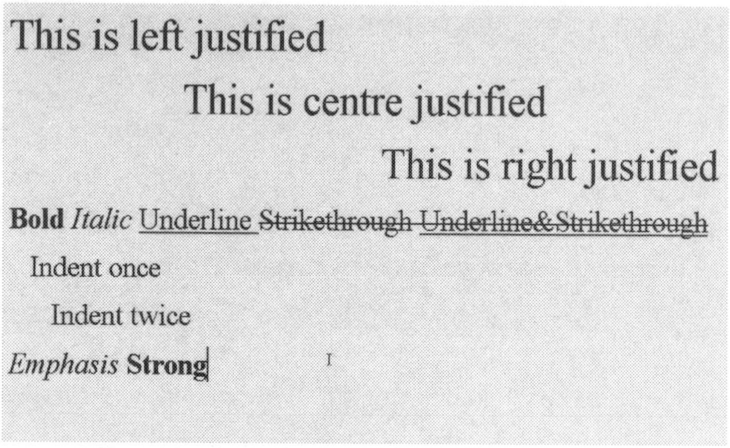

This is left justified

This is centre justified

This is right justified

Bold *Italic* Underline ~~Strikethrough~~ ~~Underline&Strikethrough~~

Indent once

Indent twice

Emphasis **Strong**

Fig.4.7 Various text styles and justifications

selected using the controls in the upper part of the window, and the corresponding font is previewed in the lower section of the window. Similar facilities are to be found in many other programs.

Styles/effects

Various text effects, or styles as they are also known, can be applied to text by first selecting it and then selecting the required effect using the Properties Inspector or the Text menu. Several of the available styles are shown in Figure 4.7. The B and I buttons in the Properties Inspector provide the usual bold and italic text. The three buttons next to these provide left, centre, and right justification. The centre option is very useful for headings. Dreamweaver 4 has no full justification option, but the fourth justification button in Dreamweaver MX provides this facility. Figure 4.8 shows a block of dummy text that has full justification.

The two buttons at the right-hand end of the lower row provide indenting and what in Dreamweaver terminology is called "outdenting". The indent button can be operated two or more times to provide deeper indenting. The "outdent" button reverses an indent operation and places the text back one tabulation position to the left.

Further effects are available from the Text menu if the Style option is selected. These include underlining, strikethrough, and emphasis effects. Note that it is possible to combine two or more effects, and you can have

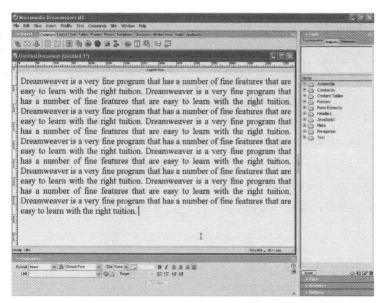

Fig.4.8 Dreamweaver MX can produce fully justified text

something like a bold and underlined heading that is centre justified. However, it is best not to get carried away and start adding effects just because they are there. Effects should be used in a manner that will enhance your web pages and not just for the sake of it.

Getting physical

With HTML there are two style categories called physical and logical styles. The physical variety are the familiar ones such as bold, italic, and underline, which are used in most computer programs that can handle text. If an effect of this type is selected, the text displayed in browsers will include that effect. The logical effects such as emphasis and strong work in a slightly different fashion. In most browsers these two effects will be displayed the same way as italic and bold text, but they can also be interpreted in other ways in order to make something clever happen. For example, the intonation of the voice could be altered in a browser that provides text to speech conversion. In most cases you will only require the physical effects, and it is best to stick to these initially.

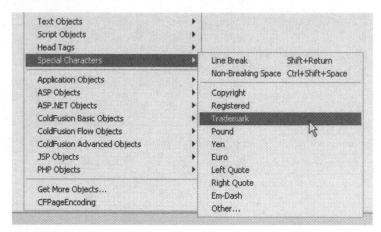

Fig.4.9 Dreamweaver has numerous submenus. This one gives access to special characters

Special characters

Special characters such as copyright and trademark symbols are easily added using Dreamweaver. To add a special character using the main menu system, select Special Characters from the Insert menu, and then left-click on the required character to select it from the list that appears (Figure 4.9). Alternatively, a small but useful range of special characters is available from the Characters section of the Insert toolbar. Selecting the Other option in the Special Characters submenu launches the Insert Other Character window (Figure 4.10), and it can also be launched using the right-most icon in the Characters section of the Insert toolbar. Simply select the required character by left-clicking on its icon in the palette and then operate the OK button. The character will be placed at the current position of the text cursor, so make sure that the cursor is in the correct place before issuing this command.

Spelling check

Dreamweaver incorporates a spelling checker that operates in much the same way as the equivalent facility in a word processor program. What it actually does is compare each word in the document with the words listed in its reference dictionary. If no match for a word in the document can be found, the spelling checker points out the offending word. Of

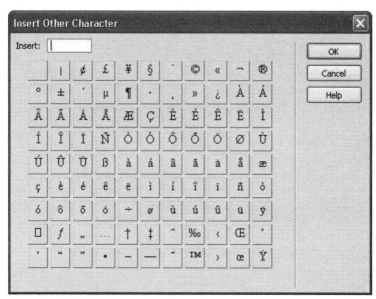

Fig.4.10 This window provides an easy way of selecting special characters

course, the word in question might be perfectly all right, but not in the reference dictionary for some reason. Names, technical terms, new words, slang words or anything out of the ordinary is likely to be pointed out by the spelling checker. Some words of these types are included in the reference dictionary, but it would be unrealistic to expect everything to be included.

Once a suspect word has been pointed out it is up to you to decide whether or not to correct the word or leave it unaltered. The spelling checker will suggest some alternative words to use. All it is doing here is to look through its dictionary for words that are similar to the suspect word. Provided the first one or two letters in the word are correct, this method will often produce the correct word.

In order to start the spelling checker go to the Text menu of the main document window and then select the Check Spelling option. The checker will start immediately and will point out the first error if it finds one (Figure 4.11). The offending word will also be highlighted in the main document window. In this example the "k" character was omitted from the word "checker". Using the scrollbar to scroll down through the

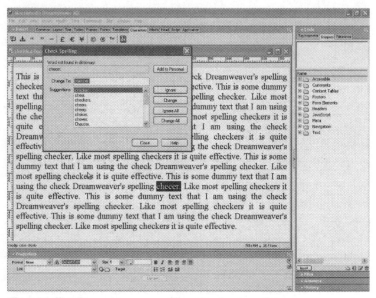

Fig.4.11 The Dreamweaver spelling checker in action

list of suggested alternatives will usually unearth the correct word, and in this case the first suggestion was the right one. To change the incorrect word to one of the suggested alternatives simply left-click on the correct word in the list and then operate the Change button. Alternatively, double-click on the correct word.

Using the Change All button has the same effect, but it will also result in any further instances of the misspelled word being automatically corrected. If the right word is not listed, manually correct the text in the Change To text box and then operate the Change or Change All button. If the word is actually all right, operate the Ignore button to leave it unchanged and continue checking the document. Using the Ignore All button instead has the same effect, but any other instances of the word will also be ignored.

If a correct word is pointed out by the checker it is possible to add it to the reference dictionary so that it will not be pointed out again if it crops up in future documents. Just operate the Add to Personal button in order to add the word to the dictionary. Note though, that only the word in your text will be added to the dictionary. Where appropriate, plurals and other possible variations on the word must be added separately.

Once the spelling checker has completed its task it will provide an onscreen message to that effect. Operate the OK button to exit the checker and return to the

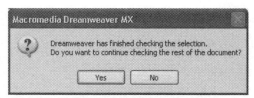

Fig.4.12 Operate the Yes button to check the rest of the document

document. Operate the Close button at any time to exit the spelling checker immediately and return to the document. Incidentally, the spelling checker can be used to check a single word or a section of text by selecting the word or text and then starting the spelling checker. Once the word or words in question have been checked, Dreamweaver will ask if you wish to check the rest of the document (Figure 4.12). Operate the No button to exit to the document window or Yes to check the rest of the document.

Find and Replace

This is another standard word processing feature that is incorporated in the Dreamweaver document editor. It is an option in the Edit menu. The Find and Replace facility simply finds the next occurrence of a specified text string starting from the current cursor position. Once found the string can optionally be replaced with another text string. This is useful if you realise that (say) a name has been repeatedly misspelled. For example, if you find that you have repeatedly used "Windows ME" instead of "Windows Me", the Find and Replace facility makes it easy to replace all the instances of "ME" with "Me".

On its own, the Find facility provides an easy way to jump to a particular point in a long document if you know a certain word appears at or near that point. For example, you might wish to go to the part of a document that mentions free beer, and by using "free beer" as the search string the Find facility should home straight in on the appropriate part of the document. Clearly the Find and Replace facility will work best using search words that are unusual, and there is little point in using common words that crop up throughout a document.

To search the current document for a string of characters, load the document into the document window if you have not already done so. Then select Find and Replace from the Edit menu, which will bring up a window like the one in Figure 4.13. The text you wish to search for is

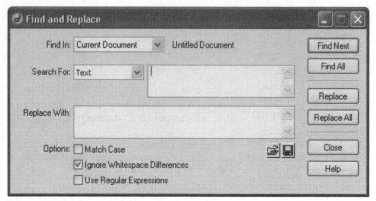

Fig.4.13 The Find and Replace dialogue box

typed into the larger Search For text box. The smaller text box enables you to search for something other than simple text, but we will settle for the default text option. If you wish to find some text but do not wish the automatically change it, do not put anything in the Replace With text box.

Having entered a suitable search string, operate the Find Next button to find the first occurrence of the text in the document. Assuming that a suitable text string is present in the document, it will be highlighted in the document window, but the Find and Replace window will still be present on the screen (Figure 4.14). You can edit the document and return to the Find and Replace window when you have finished. Operate the Find Next button to find the next occurrence of the string in the document, or operate the Close button if you have finished. An alternative way of exiting this facility is to close the Find and Replace window once the first occurrence of the string has been found. To find further occurrences select the Find Next option from the Edit menu. Note that any occurrences of the specified string will be found, even if the string is found within a word. For example, using "put" as the search string would find "put" in the word "putty".

If you wish to use the Replace facility, operate the Replace or Replace All button instead of the Find Next button. The Replace option is the safer of the two, as it will highlight the first occurrence of the string that it finds. You can then operate the Replace button to replace the text with the new string, or operate the Find Next button to move on to the next occurrence. The Replace All option instantly replaces all the matches with the new text string, but it can be reversed using the Undo facility if a mistake is

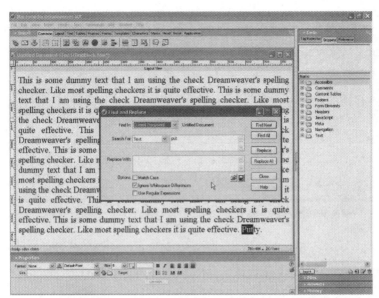

Fig.4.14 The search string has been found and it is shown highlighted in the document window

made and the document becomes seriously scrambled. Note that leaving the Replace With textbox empty will result in matches being replaced with nothing, which is an easy way to delete all occurrences of a string.

The search facility of Dreamweaver is quite comprehensive, and there are several variations available on the basic search function. Operating the Find All button instead of the Find Next button causes the appropriate section of the Results window to be opened, and a list of the occurrences of the text string is provided (Figure 4.15). The list shows where the text string was found, which will be the current document in every case if that is all that was searched. However, there are other options available in the Find In menu towards the top of the Find and Replace window (Figure 4.16). A folder on a disc can be searched, as can an entire site or selected

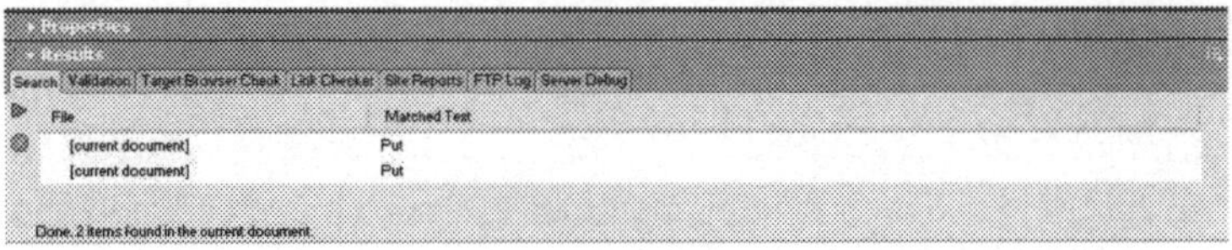

Fig.4.15 The Find All option produces a list of all matches

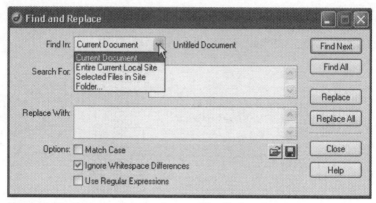

Fig.4.16 Various sources can be used for find and replace operations

files in a site. Double-clicking on an entry in the list of occurrences will open the source of that entry, if it is not already open. The selected string will be shown highlighted.

Normally the search is not case sensitive. If you specify (say) "help" as the search string, the Find Next function will also locate strings such as "Help" and "HELP". Tick the Match Case checkbox to make the search case sensitive. A match will then occur only if the search string exactly matches every character in a text string in the document.

Replace caution

I think it is worth re-emphasising that a certain amount of care has to be exercised when using the Replace function. If no text is used in the Replace With text box, the matched text strings will be replaced with nothing. As already pointed out, this could be useful if you genuinely wish to erase text strings rather than replace them with something. It can cause a lot of accidental damage if you simply forget to add some text into the Replace with text box. Remember that this facility will replace any occurrence of a string, even if it occurs within a word. For example, replacing "put" with "take" would result in "putty" being changed to "takety". The Replace option is much safer than using Replace All type, since the Replace option requires each change to be confirmed. This gives you an opportunity to abort any inappropriate changes. Remember that the Undo option of the Edit menu will reverse a search and replace operation that goes wrong.

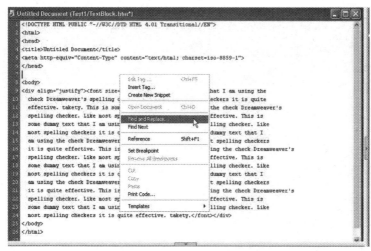

Fig.4.17 Find and Replace is also available for the Code window

The Find and Replace function is available in both the Code and Document views incidentally. In the Code view it can be used via the normal route, or right-clicking anywhere in the actual code part of the window (but not on the title bar, menu bar, etc.) will bring up a small menu that gives access to this function (Figure 4.17). It is worthwhile putting some text into the document window and then experimenting a little with the find and replace functions. The basics of these functions are easily mastered with a little experimentation.

Importing

As already pointed out, the facilities of Dreamweaver are such that it is not essential to import text from other programs. In fact there is not normally any point in doing so when producing simple web sites that do not have large amounts of text. However, if the need should arise, it is not usually too difficult to import text into Dreamweaver. The obvious route is to use the standard Cut, Copy, and Paste facilities. Normally this method preserves any formatting of the original text, including fonts, text sizes and colours, left and right justification, etc.

Unfortunately, text imported into Dreamweaver using the Paste function does not retain any formatting information, and it is converted into plain text. This might seem to be rather weak compared to most programs,

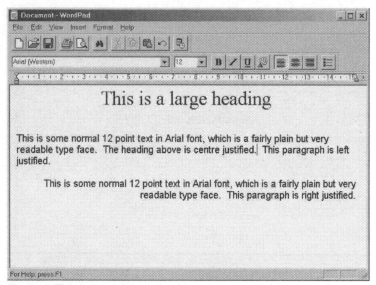

*Fig.4.18   This is a small sample of text that has been formatted in the
Windows Wordpad text processor*

but bear in mind that Dreamweaver operates in HTML, and it would have
to convert the pasted text into HTML code in order to retain the formatting.
It is unrealistic to expect this sort of thing from a simple paste facility.
Figure 4.18 shows some formatted text in the Windows ME Wordpad

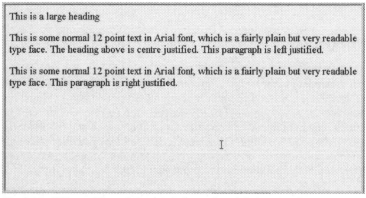

*Fig.4.19   All formatting of the text is lost when it is imported
into Dreamweaver*

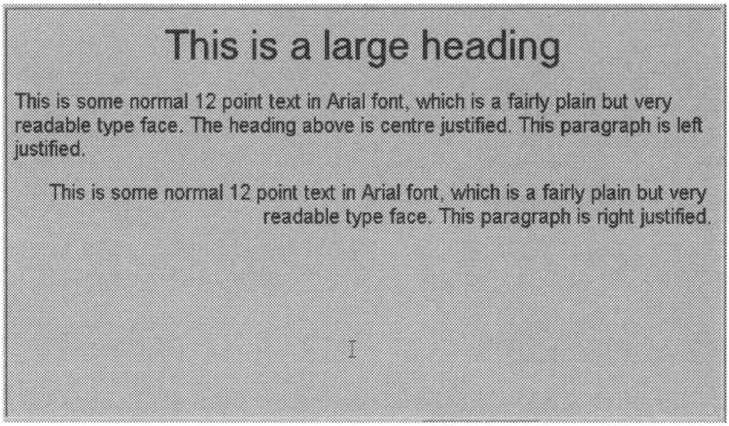

Fig.4.20 Importing this text into Dreamweaver as an HTML file has largely retained the original formatting

program. Figure 4.19 shows the same text when pasted into Dreamweaver, and a number of changes are apparent. In Dreamweaver the text is all in the default font at the basic text size, and it is all left justified.

Most programs that can handle text can save files as simple ASCII files, which have a "txt" extension. These can be loaded into Dreamweaver using the Open command, but this method also results in the loss of formatting information. In this case the formatting disappears because it is not included in the file, and not because of any shortcoming in Dreamweaver. Of course, having loaded the text into Dreamweaver, any formatting that has been lost can be reapplied using the program's formatting commands.

Where possible it makes sense to retain any formatting of the original text, and there is usually a way around the problem if you use an up-market word processor that has good export facilities. Such is the importance of the Internet that many word processors now have the ability to save documents in HTML format. These files can then be opened in Dreamweaver in the usual way, and the formatting should be retained. Being realistic about matters, it is likely that there will be some changes in the formatting, but these will mostly be relatively minor. A small amount of editing should be sufficient to take care of any problems that do occur. Figure 4.20 shows the same text as Figures 4.18 and 4.19, but this time it has been exported from a word processor as an HTML file and then opened in Dreamweaver. This time the text is about the right size and

has the correct justifications. The grey background colour is the one that was used in Word, and it has been correctly carried through to

Fig.4.21 This error message appears if the Word version can not be determined

Dreamweaver. The only slight problem is that the font used for the heading has changed, but this is easily corrected in Dreamweaver.

Word cleanup

If you produce text on a word processor and then load it into Dreamweaver it is quite likely that the word processor in question will be Microsoft Word. This has the ability to save documents in HTML format, so transferring your documents into Dreamweaver, complete with formatting, should be perfectly straightforward. Unfortunately, in practice the HTML documents produced using Word might be a bit approximate when

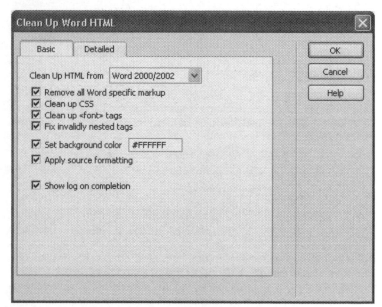

Fig.4.22 Various types of correction can be applied

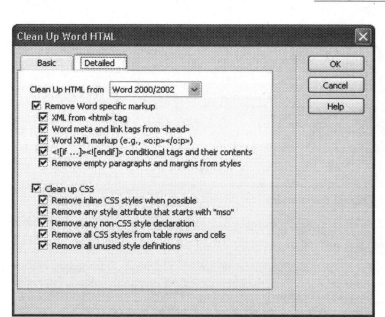

Fig.4.23 Further options are available from this dialogue box

transferred to another program. There will not be problems in every case, but they can and do occur. Fortunately, Dreamweaver has a facility to clean up HTML code produced using Word, and this could be very useful if you have problems using documents originated in Word.

To use the Word cleanup feature start by loading the HTML file into Dreamweaver in the usual way. The go to the Commands menu and select the Cleanup Word HTML option. If the document you loaded was not originated in Word, or was produced using an old version, the error message of Figure 4.21 will appear. You may continue by manually selecting the version of Word, but it is probably not worthwhile continuing unless the document was produced in a suitable version of Word. There is a command for cleaning up HTML from any source, and it would be sensible to try this instead.

Assuming that Dreamweaver detects the version of Word in use, the window of Figure 4.22 will appear. The menu near the top of the window enables Word 97/98 or Word 2000/2002 to be selected, but the correct version should be chosen by default. In both cases there are checkboxes

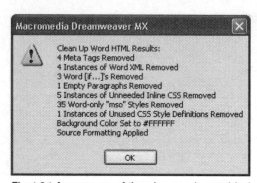

that are used to select the types of correction that will be made. Operating the Detailed tab brings up further options, and these are again different for Word 97/98 and Word 2000. Figure 4.23 shows the Word 2000/2002 version. If you know the source of the problem or problems

Fig.4.24 A summary of the changes is provided

you can be selective, or you can simply let Dreamweaver sort out any errors that it thinks it finds.

Even if you let Dreamweaver "do its own thing", you might prefer to deselect the option to change the background colour. Whatever background colour was in use when the document was saved will be used as the background colour of the HTML version. If you deliberately set the required colour before saving the document, you will not require Dreamweaver to change the colour. It is set to white by default, but you can set the hexadecimal code for another colour.

Once everything has been set as required, operate the OK button. A message like the one in Figure 4.24 will then give details of the changes that have been made. Operate the OK button to return to the document, which should reflect the changes made by Dreamweaver.

Paragraphs and lists

Paragraphs

When dealing with HTML paragraphs you have to forget the basic rules of grammar. In HTML a paragraph is whatever text appears between the paragraph tags, and this could be as little as a single character. Paragraphs are easy to understand if you are used to a desktop publishing program such as Adobe PageMaker. Programs such as this use a similar system whereby anything between two carriage returns, or the top and bottom of the document and a carriage return, is considered to be a paragraph.

A number of predefined paragraph styles are available, with each one having its own font and size settings, and effects (bold, italic, etc.). In fact there is also very precise control over things like line and character spacing, justification, and so on. To set a paragraph to the required style it is just a matter of placing the text cursor somewhere in the paragraph and then left-clicking on the appropriate entry in the paragraph palette.

Dreamweaver handles things in a similar fashion when formatting text in the main document window, but in a greatly simplified fashion. If you go to the Text menu of the main window and select Paragraph Format, a menu of available paragraph types is produced (Figure 5.1). The same options are available from the Format menu of the Properties Inspector incidentally.

Most of the paragraph formats are heading styles, and as one would expect for headings, the text sizes are mostly quite large and the text is in a bold font. There are six heading sizes, with 1 as the largest and 6 as the smallest (Figure 5.2). Size 5 is actually about the size of normal text, and size 6 is somewhat smaller, and it is the four largest sizes that are of most use for headings and subheadings.

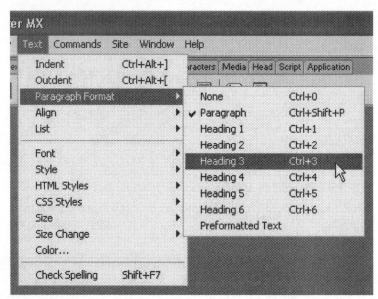

Fig.5.1 Several paragraph formats are available from the Text menu

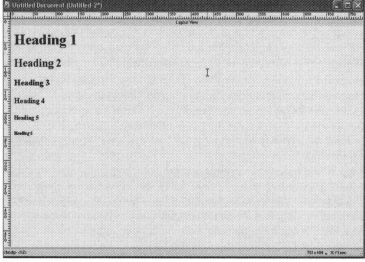

Fig.5.2 The six heading paragraph styles

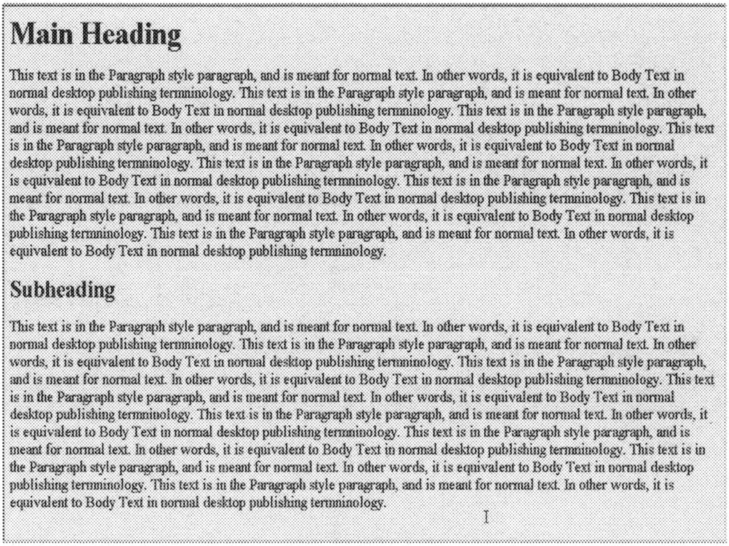

Main Heading

This text is in the Paragraph style paragraph, and is meant for normal text. In other words, it is equivalent to Body Text in normal desktop publishing terminology. This text is in the Paragraph style paragraph, and is meant for normal text. In other words, it is equivalent to Body Text in normal desktop publishing terminology. This text is in the Paragraph style paragraph, and is meant for normal text. In other words, it is equivalent to Body Text in normal desktop publishing terminology. This text is in the Paragraph style paragraph, and is meant for normal text. In other words, it is equivalent to Body Text in normal desktop publishing terminology. This text is in the Paragraph style paragraph, and is meant for normal text. In other words, it is equivalent to Body Text in normal desktop publishing terminology. This text is in the Paragraph style paragraph, and is meant for normal text. In other words, it is equivalent to Body Text in normal desktop publishing terminology. This text is in the Paragraph style paragraph, and is meant for normal text. In other words, it is equivalent to Body Text in normal desktop publishing terminology. This text is in the Paragraph style paragraph, and is meant for normal text. In other words, it is equivalent to Body Text in normal desktop publishing terminology.

Subheading

This text is in the Paragraph style paragraph, and is meant for normal text. In other words, it is equivalent to Body Text in normal desktop publishing terminology. This text is in the Paragraph style paragraph, and is meant for normal text. In other words, it is equivalent to Body Text in normal desktop publishing terminology. This text is in the Paragraph style paragraph, and is meant for normal text. In other words, it is equivalent to Body Text in normal desktop publishing terminology. This text is in the Paragraph style paragraph, and is meant for normal text. In other words, it is equivalent to Body Text in normal desktop publishing terminology. This text is in the Paragraph style paragraph, and is meant for normal text. In other words, it is equivalent to Body Text in normal desktop publishing terminology. This text is in the Paragraph style paragraph, and is meant for normal text. In other words, it is equivalent to Body Text in normal desktop publishing terminology. This text is in the Paragraph style paragraph, and is meant for normal text. In other words, it is equivalent to Body Text in normal desktop publishing terminology. This text is in the Paragraph style paragraph, and is meant for normal text. In other words, it is equivalent to Body Text in normal desktop publishing terminology.

Fig.5.3 This page uses three paragraph styles

The Paragraph paragraph style is intended for normal text, and it is the equivalent of body text in desktop publishing terminology. Figure 5.3 shows a page containing four paragraphs, one of which is a heading in the Heading 1 format. Two of the other paragraphs are in the Paragraph format and the remaining one is a subheading in Heading 2 format. The paragraph styles provide an easy way of applying some basic formatting to text, but you have to resort to the Properties Inspector and (or) the menu system in order to do more sophisticated formatting.

Try typing some headings and a couple of blocks of text into the document window, and then experiment with the paragraph styles. To set a paragraph to the Heading 1 style for example, left-click somewhere within the paragraph so that the text cursor (the flashing vertical line and not the mouse pointer) is positioned within the paragraph. Then select Paragraph Format and Heading 1 from the text menu. Note that using a paragraph style does not prevent further formatting using Properties Inspector or the menu system, or by editing the HTML code come to that.

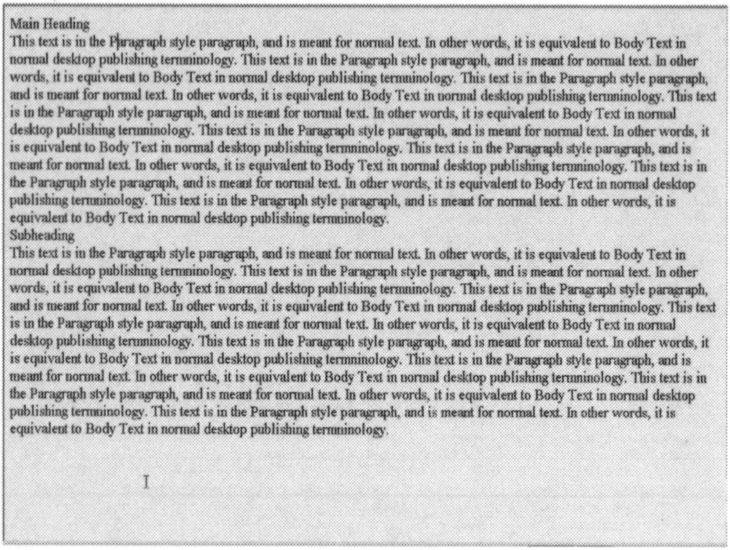

Main Heading
This text is in the Paragraph style paragraph, and is meant for normal text. In other words, it is equivalent to Body Text in normal desktop publishing terminology. This text is in the Paragraph style paragraph, and is meant for normal text. In other words, it is equivalent to Body Text in normal desktop publishing terminology. This text is in the Paragraph style paragraph, and is meant for normal text. In other words, it is equivalent to Body Text in normal desktop publishing terminology. This text is in the Paragraph style paragraph, and is meant for normal text. In other words, it is equivalent to Body Text in normal desktop publishing terminology. This text is in the Paragraph style paragraph, and is meant for normal text. In other words, it is equivalent to Body Text in normal desktop publishing terminology. This text is in the Paragraph style paragraph, and is meant for normal text. In other words, it is equivalent to Body Text in normal desktop publishing terminology. This text is in the Paragraph style paragraph, and is meant for normal text. In other words, it is equivalent to Body Text in normal desktop publishing terminology. This text is in the Paragraph style paragraph, and is meant for normal text. In other words, it is equivalent to Body Text in normal desktop publishing terminology.
Subheading
This text is in the Paragraph style paragraph, and is meant for normal text. In other words, it is equivalent to Body Text in normal desktop publishing terminology. This text is in the Paragraph style paragraph, and is meant for normal text. In other words, it is equivalent to Body Text in normal desktop publishing terminology. This text is in the Paragraph style paragraph, and is meant for normal text. In other words, it is equivalent to Body Text in normal desktop publishing terminology. This text is in the Paragraph style paragraph, and is meant for normal text. In other words, it is equivalent to Body Text in normal desktop publishing terminology. This text is in the Paragraph style paragraph, and is meant for normal text. In other words, it is equivalent to Body Text in normal desktop publishing terminology. This text is in the Paragraph style paragraph, and is meant for normal text. In other words, it is equivalent to Body Text in normal desktop publishing terminology. This text is in the Paragraph style paragraph, and is meant for normal text. In other words, it is equivalent to Body Text in normal desktop publishing terminology. This text is in the Paragraph style paragraph, and is meant for normal text. In other words, it is equivalent to Body Text in normal desktop publishing terminology.

Fig.5.4 This version of the page uses line breaks instead of carriage returns

Line breaks

You will probably have noticed that adding a carriage return does not take the text cursor to the beginning of the next line, but moves it two lines further down the screen. A blank line is inserted between one paragraph and the next, but this is a sort of "no go" area for the text cursor, which can not be positioned within this part of the document. This is the standard HTML way of handling things, but you might not always wish to have this blank line between blocks of text. The blank line can be avoided by using a line break rather than a carriage return. To insert a line break, or soft return, as it is also known, hold down the Shift key and then press Enter. Incidentally, a soft return is the character that is automatically inserted at the end of a line when the word wrap facility wraps text around onto the next line.

Figure 5.4 shows the same page of text that was used in Figure 5.3, but with line breaks rather than carriage returns. The lack of blank lines between paragraphs is readily apparent, as is the fact that the same paragraph style is used for all four paragraphs. The problem here is that the lack of carriage returns means that the text becomes one long paragraph, and as such it has just the one paragraph style. However,

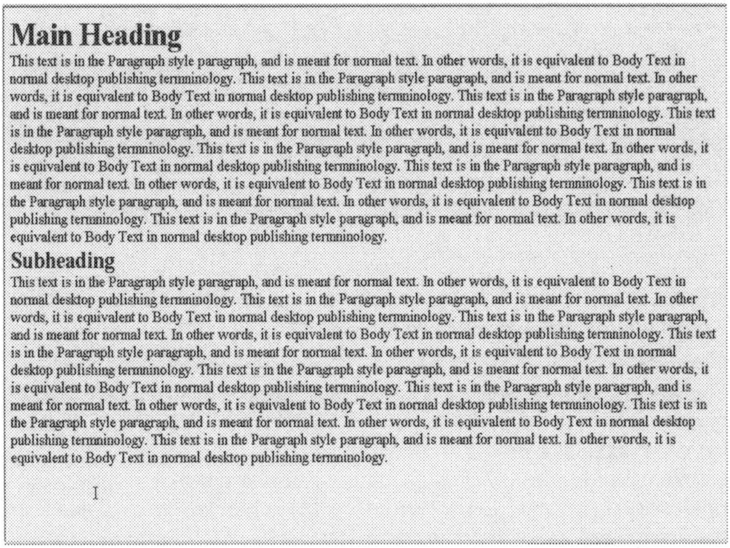

Main Heading

This text is in the Paragraph style paragraph, and is meant for normal text. In other words, it is equivalent to Body Text in normal desktop publishing terminology. This text is in the Paragraph style paragraph, and is meant for normal text. In other words, it is equivalent to Body Text in normal desktop publishing terminology. This text is in the Paragraph style paragraph, and is meant for normal text. In other words, it is equivalent to Body Text in normal desktop publishing terminology. This text is in the Paragraph style paragraph, and is meant for normal text. In other words, it is equivalent to Body Text in normal desktop publishing terminology. This text is in the Paragraph style paragraph, and is meant for normal text. In other words, it is equivalent to Body Text in normal desktop publishing terminology. This text is in the Paragraph style paragraph, and is meant for normal text. In other words, it is equivalent to Body Text in normal desktop publishing terminology. This text is in the Paragraph style paragraph, and is meant for normal text. In other words, it is equivalent to Body Text in normal desktop publishing terminology. This text is in the Paragraph style paragraph, and is meant for normal text. In other words, it is equivalent to Body Text in normal desktop publishing terminology.

Subheading

This text is in the Paragraph style paragraph, and is meant for normal text. In other words, it is equivalent to Body Text in normal desktop publishing terminology. This text is in the Paragraph style paragraph, and is meant for normal text. In other words, it is equivalent to Body Text in normal desktop publishing terminology. This text is in the Paragraph style paragraph, and is meant for normal text. In other words, it is equivalent to Body Text in normal desktop publishing terminology. This text is in the Paragraph style paragraph, and is meant for normal text. In other words, it is equivalent to Body Text in normal desktop publishing terminology. This text is in the Paragraph style paragraph, and is meant for normal text. In other words, it is equivalent to Body Text in normal desktop publishing terminology. This text is in the Paragraph style paragraph, and is meant for normal text. In other words, it is equivalent to Body Text in normal desktop publishing terminology. This text is in the Paragraph style paragraph, and is meant for normal text. In other words, it is equivalent to Body Text in normal desktop publishing terminology. This text is in the Paragraph style paragraph, and is meant for normal text. In other words, it is equivalent to Body Text in normal desktop publishing terminology.

Fig.5.5 Variations in text size, etc., can be accommodated within a paragraph

you can use the Properties Inspector or the Text menu to put the headings in bold print and a larger text size, as in Figure 5.5, and the closed-up style will be retained.

Remember that a number of special characters are available from the Characters section of the Insert toolbar, which is useful if you forget the keyboard codes. The line-break icon is the one at the left end of the bar (Figure 5.6). Just position the text cursor where you require the line break and then left-click on the line break icon. Alternatively, drag the icon to the position in the document where the line break is required. The pointer becomes a vertical line like the text cursor, making it easy to insert the line break at the appropriate point in the text.

Spaced out

When typing text into the document window you may have noticed that hitting the spacebar once has the usual effect, but two or more operations do not insert any more spaces. You can press the spacebar all day, but only one space character will be produced. The Tab key does not operate in the usual fashion either. Operating the Tab key once produces a single

Macromedia Dreamweaver MX - [Untitled Document (Untitled-1*)]
File Edit View Insert Modify Text Commands Site Window Help
Insert
Common Layout Text Tables Frames Forms Templates Characters Media Head Script Application
Layout View

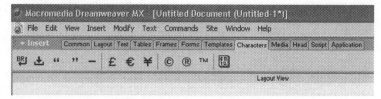

Fig.5.6 The button at the left end of the row inserts line breaks

space character, and further operations have no further effect. In other words, it has the same effect as the spacebar.

There is a way around this in the form of the non-breaking space character. This can be added using the Characters section of the Insert toolbar, and its icon is the second one along from the left end of the bar. In other words, it is the one on the immediate right of the line break button. The simple list of Figure 5.7 was produced with the aid of line breaks and non-breaking spaces. Do not forget that the indent facility available from the Properties Inspector or the Text menu can be used to shift paragraphs to the right, as in the version of the list shown in Figure 5.8.

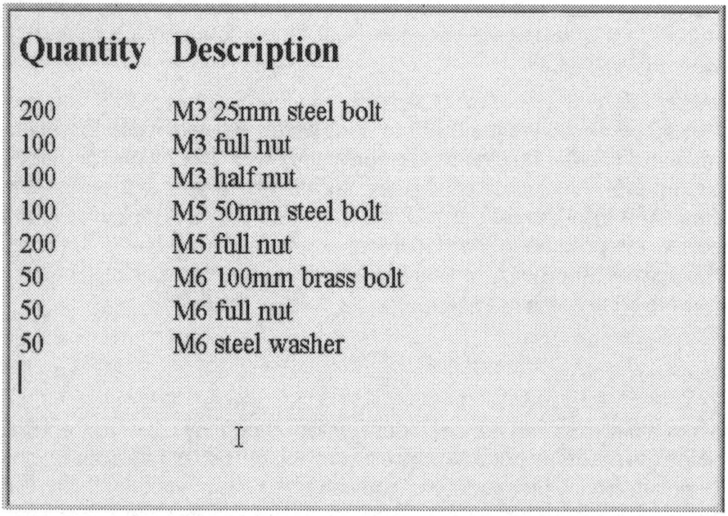

Quantity Description
200 M3 25mm steel bolt
100 M3 full nut
100 M3 half nut
100 M5 50mm steel bolt
200 M5 full nut
50 M6 100mm brass bolt
50 M6 full nut
50 M6 steel washer

Fig.5.7 A simple list produced with the aid of line breaks

Quantity	Description
200	M3 25mm steel bolt
100	M3 full nut
100	M3 half nut
100	M5 50mm steel bolt
200	M5 full nut
50	M6 100mm brass bolt
50	M6 full nut
50	M6 steel washer

Fig.5.8 In this version the list has been moved to the right using the indent facility of the Properties Inspector

Preformatted

There is a Preformatted option in the list of paragraph styles, and this is intended to retain the formatting of simple text that is pasted into the document window, or loaded as a text ("txt") file. The type of formatting in question here is just the positioning of characters, and not anything remotely clever such as fonts, text sizes, colours, etc. Spacing information tends to be lost when simple text is loaded into Dreamweaver, because tabs and several spaces in succession are reduced to single spaces. The table of values shown in Figure 5.9 was loaded into Dreamweaver without selecting the Preformatted option first, and the columns of the original text have been lost completely.

Figure 5.10 shows the same table of values, but this time loaded after selecting the Preformatted option. Unfortunately, although it is closer to the original than the version of Figure 5.9, it is still not perfect. The columns are not aligned properly, and this is a common problem when transferring simple text files from one program to another. The problem usually stems from discrepancies in the amount of space used to represent the tab character. In order to maximise the chances of success it is better to use multiple space characters rather than tabs. This takes longer, but should ensure that the basic formatting remains intact if the text is exported to

```
R1 1 off 27k 5% 0.25W
R2,4,7 3 off 10k 5% 0.25W
R3,5 2 off 100k 1% 0.5W
R6 1 off 1k 5% 0.25W
R7,8,9 3 off 47k 5% 0.25W
R10 1 off 2M2 5% 0.25W
R11,15 2 off 4k7 5% 0.5W
R12,13,14 3 off 220k 5% 0.25W
R16 1 off 380R 5% 0.25W
R17 1 off 22k 5% 0.25W
R18,19,20 3 off 68k 1% 0.5W
```

Fig.5.9 The text characters are all intact, but the formatting of this text has been lost completely

```
R1      1 off   27k 5%  0.25W
R2,4,7     3 off   10k 5%  0.25W
R3,5       2 off   100k   1%  0.5W
R6      1 off   1k  5%  0.25W
R7,8,9     3 off   47k 5%  0.25W
R10     1 off   2M2 5%  0.25W
R11,15     2 off   4k7 5%  0.5W
R12,13,14  3 off   220k    5%  0.25W
R16     1 off   380R    5%  0.25W
R17     1 off   22k 5%  0.25W
R18,19,20  3 off   68k 1%  0.5W
```

Fig.5.10 Preformatting has retained some of the formatting, but things are still far from right

```
R1          1 off   27k    5%    0.25w
R2,4,7      3 off   10k    5%    0.25w
R3,5        2 off   100k   1%    0.5w
R6          1 off   1k     5%    0.25w
R7,8,9      3 off   47k    5%    0.25w
R10         1 off   2M2    5%    0.25w
R11,15      2 off   4k7    5%    0.5w
R12,13,14   3 off   220k   5%    0.25w
R16         1 off   380R   5%    0.25w
R17         1 off   22k    5%    0.25w
R18,19,20   3 off   68k    1%    0.5w
```

*Fig.5.11 Some non-breaking spaces have been added to fix the
formatting of the text*

another program. Where things do go wrong, some added non-breaking
spaces should soon sort things out again (Figure 5.11).

Preformatted text is in a simple monospaced font, like the text produced
by simple text editors. If the text is pasted into Dreamweaver there should
be no difficulty in changing the font, text size, etc., but doing so might
alter the basic formatting of the text. In order to retain accurate formatting
the text should all be the same size and in a monospaced font.

Lists

Dreamweaver has some useful facilities for producing lists. The easiest
way to understand these is to make a simple list and then try formatting
it in various ways. Make a list of something like the months in the year or
the days of the week (Figure 5.12). Dreamweaver supports two normal
types of list called ordered or numbered lists, and bulleted or unordered
lists. We will start with the ordered variety. To convert the basic list to an
ordered list, first select all the text in the list. Then select List and Ordered
List from the Text menu. Alternatively, if the Properties Inspector is active
operate the Ordered List button. This is the button beneath the italic "I"

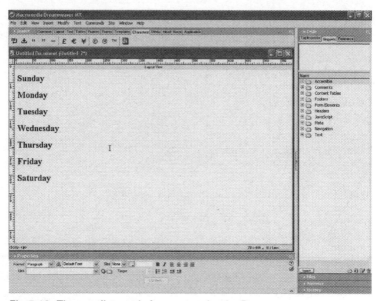

Fig.5.12 The raw list ready for processing by Dreamweaver

Fig.5.13 The ordered list

button. This should produce something like Figure 5.13, where things have not entirely gone to plan.

The seven entries have been numbered properly, but an empty eighth entry has been added. This is due to a carriage return at the end of the list being selected, and Dreamweaver has correctly numbered this additional line. The unwanted "8." can be deleted manually, just like any other text. To a large extent it is possible to edit the list like normal text, but note that any lines that are added will produce automatic renumbering of the list. This can be clearly seen in the version of Figure 5.14, which has had the spurious "8." removed and two more lines added. The list has been automatically adjusted so that the entries are now numbered from 1 to 9.

Try adding items to your list. Place the text cursor at the end of the line immediately before the position where the new line is required. Press the Return key to add the new line and move the cursor onto that line. The list will be renumbered, and a number will be added for the new line. Finally, type in the text for the new entry. To remove an item from the list, first select the text for the item and press the Delete key to erase the text. Then press the

Fig.5.14 The edited list

Backspace key to delete the number for that entry. The number and its full stop can not be selected like normal text, but it can be deleted using the Backspace key. The list will then close up to remove the blank line and the entries will be automatically renumbered.

Unordered list

An unordered list is produced in much the same way as an ordered type, with the text for the list first being selected. However, List and then Unordered List are selected from the Text menu, or the Unordered Text button is operated on the Properties Inspector. This is the button immediately on the left of the Ordered Text button. Try this on your ordered list, and it will change to a bulleted list like the one in Figure 5.15. This demonstrates the point that a list can be ordered or bulleted, but it can not have bullets and numbers. To change a list back to normal text, first select the text in the list and then operate the appropriate List button of the Properties Inspector. Alternatively, select the text, go to the Text menu and select List and then the appropriate type of list from the submenu. A third alternative is to select the text, go to the Text menu, select List, and then None from the submenu.

Fig.5.15 The bulleted list

If you accidentally end up with text in a list that should not be included, the same basic method can be used to remove that text from the list. Note that a list is ended by inserting two carriage returns. This avoids the situation whereby everything you add after a list is merged into the list by Dreamweaver.

List properties

It is possible to alter some of the settings that govern the appearance of lists. First, there must be at least one line of a list in the document window, and the cursor must be placed within that line. Next the Properties option is selected from the List submenu

of the Text menu. Alternatively, operate the List Item button in the Properties Inspector. Either way, a window like the one of Figure 5.16 will appear on the screen. The menu at the top permits the type of list to be set. If the list is a bulleted type, the menu beneath permits normal

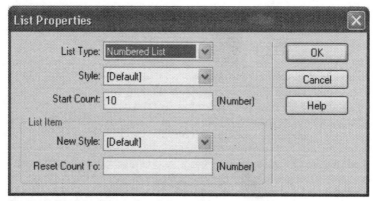

Fig.5.16 The List Properties dialogue box

(circular) or square bullets to be selected. The third menu is only applicable to ordered lists, and it permits the start number to be changed. In the list of Figure 5.17 for example, the starting number has been set at 10.

The two menus in the lower section of the window apply to the entry in the list that contains the text cursor, whereas the upper section pertains to the list as a whole. With a bulleted list, the New Style menu permits each entry to be set individually to the round or square bullet style. In the case of an ordered list it gives the options of using a Roman numeral or a letter (a, b, c, etc.) instead of a number. For ordered lists the Style menu in the upper section provides the same options, but for the entire list rather than an individual entry. The bottom menu enables the count to be reset to the specified value at the entry that contains the cursor. The count progresses normally from this new starting value. In the list of Figure 5.18 for instance, the count has been set to start at 10, and it has been reset to one at the Thursday entry.

Definition list

A third form of list is available in Dreamweaver, and this is the definition list. This operates using pairs of lines, with the first line of each pair containing a term and

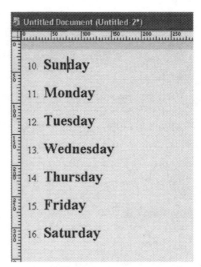

Fig.5.17 The start number for this list has been set at 10

Fig.5.18 The count can be reset at any point in the list

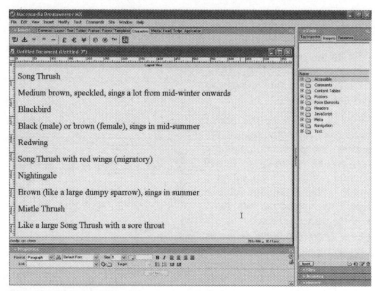

Fig.5.19 The definition list prior to formatting

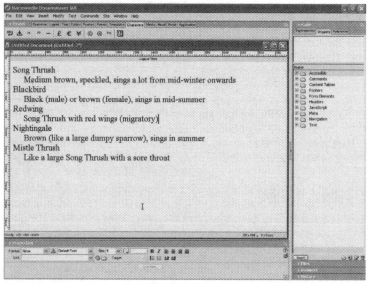

Fig.5.20 The formatted definition list

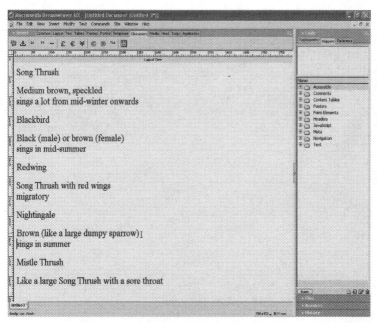

Fig.5.21 Entries can occupy more than one line

the second containing a definition for the term. The term can actually be anything that you need to define, such as a name. To try out a definition list, type some pairs of lines containing terms and definitions into the document window, as in Figure 5.19. To turn the completed text into a definition list it must first be selected. Then select List from the Text menu, and Definition from the submenu that appears. The list should then be formatted like the one in Figure 5.20, with odd-numbered lines left unaltered and the even-numbered lines indented. There is no button for definition lists on the Properties Inspector incidentally.

Both terms and definitions can occupy more than one line if they are word wrapped onto additional lines, or you split them across two or more lines using soft carriage returns. For example, the original text of Figure 5.21 is formatted as in Figure 5.22 when it is turned into a definition list. The completed list can be edited much like ordinary text. In Figure 5.23 for example, the terms are in bold print and the definitions are in Italics.

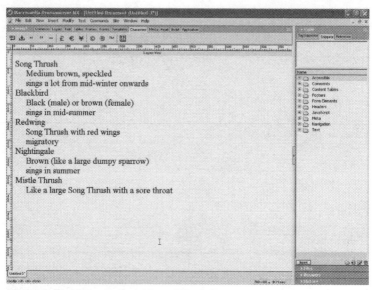

Fig.5.22 The formatted version of Fig.5.21

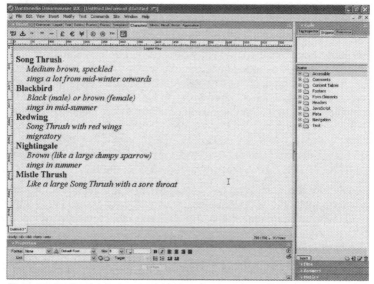

Fig.5.23 Definition lists can be edited much like ordinary text

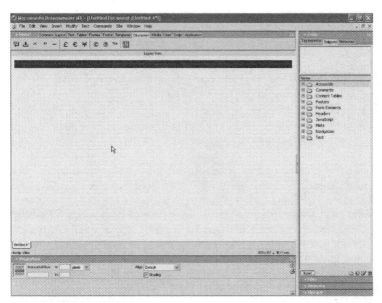

Fig.5.24 Rules with default settings added to a page

Rules

Dreamweaver has a facility to place horizontal rules on the page, and these pairs of lines can be used to break up a page into definite sections. Obviously the same effect can be obtained by adding extra line spacing between parts of a page, but some designers prefer to use rules. To experiment with rules first make sure that the text cursor is on a blank line. Then select Horizontal Rules from the Insert menu, which will insert a pair of default rules on the line currently occupied by the text cursor. The new rules will be selected, and will therefore be shown highlighted on the screen. If it is not already running, launch the Properties Inspector, which will show the characteristics of the rules (Figure 5.24). Note that horizontal rules are also available from the Common page of the Insert palette (Figure 5.25).

By default the rules occupy the full width of the page, excluding the narrow margins outside the text area of course. The width and height of the rules can be specified in the W and H textboxes. The little pop-down menu to the right of the width text box enables the width dimension to be

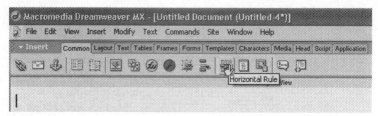

*Fig.5.25 Rules can be added using the Common page of the
          Insert palette*

specified in screen pixels or as a percentage of the default value. The
height setting is always in pixels. The Alignment menu provides the
usual left, right, and centre alignment, although this is only of relevance
if the rules are set at something less than the full page width. Operation
of the Shading text box is perhaps the opposite of what one might expect.
There is nothing between the two lines when this box ticked, but shading
is added when the box is not ticked. With a little experimentation you
should soon master the use of rules. Figure 5.26 shows some example
rules together with the settings used for each one.

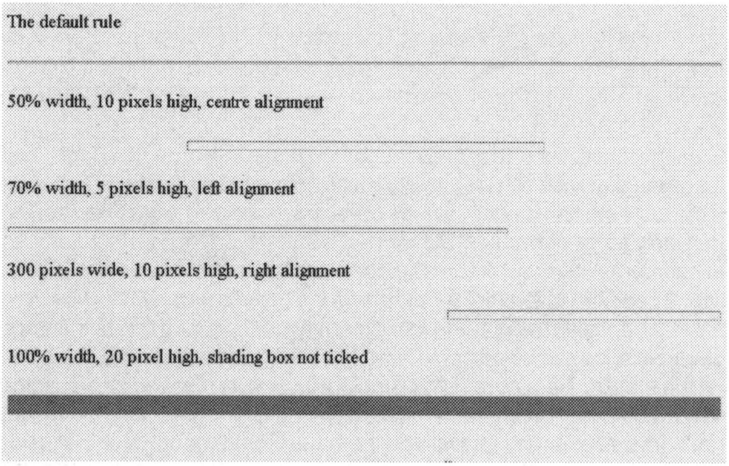

The default rule

50% width, 10 pixels high, centre alignment

70% width, 5 pixels high, left alignment

300 pixels wide, 10 pixels high, right alignment

100% width, 20 pixel high, shading box not ticked

Fig.5.26 Various examples of rules added to a page

Images

Getting the picture

Images are not an essential part of a web site, and it is possible to produce attractive and functional sites without them. In the early days of the Internet images were in fact something of a rarity, and they had to be downloaded and displayed using a suitable program. Being realistic about it though, images will significantly improve the look of most web sites, and in some cases can improve functionality as well. These days small to medium size images can be downloaded quite quickly, and they can be included as a normal part of a page that will be displayed in browsers correctly.

Loading an image into Dreamweaver is fairly straightforward provided it is in one of the standard formats for web use. The image is inserted at the current cursor position. To load an image via the menu system go to the Insert menu and select the Image option. Alternatively, left-click on the Insert Image button in the Common section of the Insert palette (Figure

Fig.6.1 The Image button of the Insert palette

6.1). Either way, this brings up a slightly enhanced version of the usual file browser (Figure 6.2). It has the usual controls to let you locate and select the required file, which can be on your computer or on the Internet. Obviously your PC must have an Internet connection if a URL is used instead of the path and filename of an image file on disc.

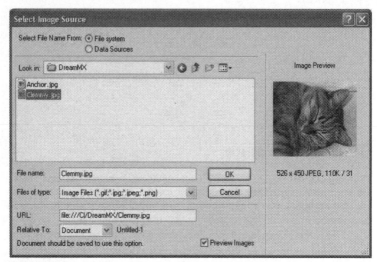

Fig.6.2 The browser used when loading an image

Fig.6.3 The image loaded into the document

To make a document-relative path, your document should be saved first.

A 'file://' path will be used until you save your document.

☐ Don't show me this message again.

[OK]

Fig.6.4 This warning message appears if the file is not stored on the local site

The file browser has a couple of extra features in the right-hand section of the window. If you left-click on the entry for an image file, a small preview image is shown in this section of the window. Beneath the image its file size is given, together with the approximate download time using the default modem speed. For bitmaps, the dimensions of the image in pixels are also provided. It pays to keep an eye on the file sizes and download times, especially when dealing with colour photographs. There is usually no point in using images that will take minutes to download and have resolutions that are too high for most monitors to display properly anyway. Small images will usually do the job just as well and will download much more quickly.

Having found the required image file, select it, operate the Select button, and it will be loaded into the document (Figure 6.3). There might be a warning message displayed on the screen first, such as the one of Figure 6.4. This is pointing out that the image being loaded is not stored on the root folder of the site, and it is asking if the file should be copied there. Root folders and local sites are covered in the next chapter, but in general all files for a site must be stored within the local site so that they are available when the site is published. Therefore, you should answer Yes and have the file copied to your local site. Another warning message is produced if you have not saved the document prior to loading an image. In this case just click on the OK button to continue.

With the image loaded into the document, left-clicking anywhere on the image will select it. If the Properties Inspector is active it will then change

Fig.6.5 The version of the Properties Inspector for editing images

to show the characteristics of the image (Figure 6.5). It will also show a thumbnail version of the image in the panel at the left-hand end of the window. Also, three handles (the small rectangles) will appear on the image itself. These are on the right and bottom edges of the image, and the bottom right-hand corner. If you are familiar with image-editing software you should have no difficulty in using the handles, which operate in the standard way. If not, load an image into a blank page and experiment with the handles. Their purpose is to enable the image to be resized by dragging the handles.

The handle at the bottom enables the image to be stretched or compressed vertically, and the handle on the right provides the same function horizontally. The handle at the corner of the image enables it to be resized in both planes. When resizing an image you need to be aware that changes in the aspect ratio of the image are likely to occur, and these can give some very funny looking results. It is tempting to alter the shape of an image so that it is a perfect fit for the available space, but this will often produce odd looking results. It is generally better to fit text around an image rather than trying to fit the image into a likely looking gap in the text.

Note that you can resize an image without producing a change in its aspect ratio. Hold down the Shift key and then resize the image using the handle at the corner. Instead of the horizontal and vertical sizes being independently adjustable, they will then change together, retaining the original aspect ratio of the image. The size of a bitmap image can be altered by editing the pixel W (width) and H (height) text boxes in the Properties Inspector. This provides an easy way of setting a precise size in pixels, but you again have to be careful to avoid significant changes in the aspect ratio of the image. The thumbnail picture of the image operates as the Apply button, so left-click on this to apply any changes that are made using the Properties Inspector. Left-clicking on the W or H label returns the image to its original width and height respectively.

Size matters

If you resize an image you will notice that the file size given in the Properties Inspector does not change. This is because Dreamweaver is using the image file as the basis of the onscreen image, and it manipulates that file to produce an image of the correct size and shape on the screen. It does not alter the file when changes are made to the image in Dreamweaver's design view. Instead, it alters the way the file is processed to produce the onscreen image. The same is true when a browser downloads the web page. The raw image file is downloaded, and then the HTML code tells the browser how to get the image to display properly.

Clearly it is not a good idea to use a large bitmap image file for what will be only a tiny image on the web page. This gives a long download time for a small image. It is better to reduce the image size using an image editor so that it is imported into Dreamweaver at something reasonably close to the correct size. On the face of it, a small image file can be used to produce a large picture on the screen, giving a short download time. This will work, but stretching a small image in this fashion will inevitably compromise the quality of the displayed image. Note that with any stretching or compressing of a bitmap image, there is the possibility that the image may not look as good when displayed using a browser as it did when viewed using Dreamweaver. Each program has its own method of resizing images, and some work better than others do. The only way to ensure that a bitmap image is reproduced correctly is to leave it at its original size.

The same considerations do not apply to line art such as a GIF image. The file size is determined by the complexity of the image rather than any size considerations. A file of this type will be displayed at a certain size when it is brought into Dreamweaver, and it can be manipulated in the same basic fashion as a bitmap. However, it does not have a natural size in pixels like a bitmap. A line art image is always displayed in the highest quality available from the screen, printer, or whatever. Consequently, a line art image can be made as large as you like, and it should be free from the rough edges that can occur when bitmaps are scaled up.

Multiple selection

To select an image you left-click somewhere within an image, and to deselect it you left-click somewhere outside the image. It is possible to select two or more images by selecting the first one in the usual way,

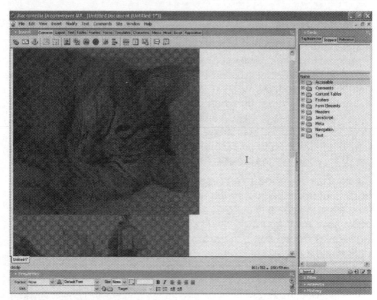

*Fig.6.6 More than one image at a time can be selected. Here
the lower image is only partially visible, but it has clearly
been highlighted*

and then holding down the Shift key while left-clicking on an additional
image or images. The selected images will be shown highlighted, or
perhaps low-lighted would be a better term as they will be quite dark
(Figure 6.6). As the two images will usually have different characteristics,
the Properties Inspector can not meaningfully show the parameters for
two or more images. Consequently, the normal version will be obtained
if the Properties Inspector is active, and it will not be usable with the
images. However, the Cut, Copy, Paste, and Clear (delete) functions
available from the Edit menu will work when multiple images are selected.

Naming

It can be useful to select multiple images, but in order to do most image
manipulation the images must be selected one at a time and controlled
via the Properties Inspector. An image can be named using the text box
just to the right of the thumbnail image. There is not necessarily any
need to do this, but it makes life easier if you will be directly editing the

HTML code and it is essential when using images with JavaScript. If you do add a name, it is best to use only lower-case letters and avoid other characters including spaces.

Image alignment

The Properties Inspector has various alignment options available from the Align menu towards the top right-hand corner of the window. Alignment with images is more complicated than text alignment. There are some 10 alignment options to choose from (Figure 6.7). The Browser Default simply duplicates one of the other nine options, and this is normally Baseline alignment. However, the alignment this provides depends on the default setting of each browser used to view the page. In order to change the image alignment, first

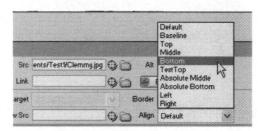

Fig.6.7 Ten image alignment options are available

select the image, and then select the required option from the Align menu of the Properties Inspector. If you place an image in a blank document and then try various alignment options you will probably be surprised by the results, or rather the lack of them. The image is aligned relative to other objects, so you can only see the effect of each alignment option if there is something else on the screen for the image to be aligned with. These brief explanations plus the accompanying illustrations should help to clarify matters.

Middle

This aligns the middle of the image with the baseline of the text (Figure 6.8 top).

Absolute Middle

Similar to the Middle option, but the middle of the image is aligned with the middle of the text (Figure 6.8 middle).

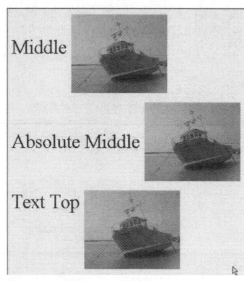

Fig.6.8 Three types of alignment

Text Top

The top of the image is aligned with the top of the text (Figure 6.8 bottom). To be more precise, the top of the image is aligned with the top of the highest text character.

Top

This differs from Text Top in that the top of the image is aligned with the top of the tallest object in the line, not the tallest text character. In the example of Figure 6.9 the picture of the boat is therefore aligned with the top of the picture of the cat, and not with the top of the text. Figure 6.10 shows the effect of changing the alignment of the boat to Text Top.

Fig.6.9 An example of top alignment

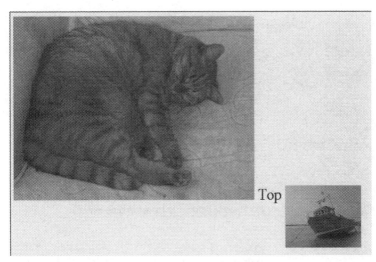

Fig.6.10 The effect of switching to text top alignment

Absolute Bottom

This aligns the bottom of the image to the lowest point on the line. The example of Figure 6.11 uses the same line that was used for Figures 6.9 and 6.10, but with alignment of the boat image set to Absolute Bottom.

Fig.6.11 An example of absolute bottom alignment

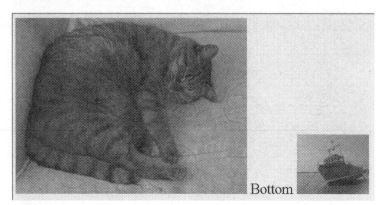

Fig.6.12 The bottom alignment option is used in this version

The important point to note here is that the bottom of the boat picture is aligned with the lowest point in the letter "p", and not with the bottom of the cat picture.

Bottom

With this option the bottom of the image is aligned with the bottom of other elements in the line, but unlike Absolute Bottom alignment, the image is not taken below the text baseline (Figure 6.12).

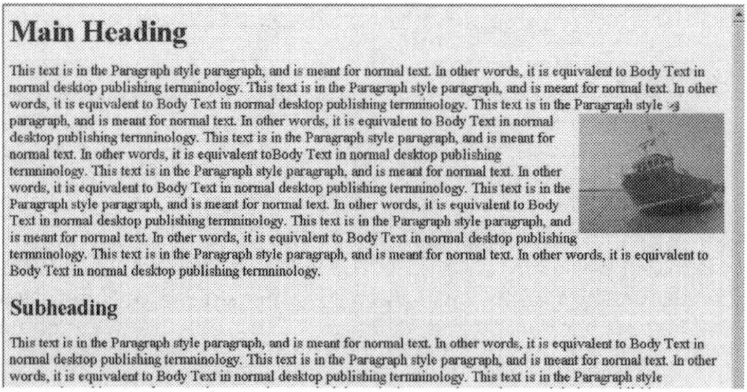

Main Heading

This text is in the Paragraph style paragraph, and is meant for normal text. In other words, it is equivalent to Body Text in normal desktop publishing termninology. This text is in the Paragraph style paragraph, and is meant for normal text. In other words, it is equivalent to Body Text in normal desktop publishing termninology. This text is in the Paragraph style paragraph, and is meant for normal text. In other words, it is equivalent to Body Text in normal desktop publishing termninology. This text is in the Paragraph style paragraph, and is meant for normal text. In other words, it is equivalent toBody Text in normal desktop publishing termninology. This text is in the Paragraph style paragraph, and is meant for normal text. In other words, it is equivalent to Body Text in normal desktop publishing termninology. This text is in the Paragraph style paragraph, and is meant for normal text. In other words, it is equivalent to Body Text in normal desktop publishing termninology. This text is in the Paragraph style paragraph, and is meant for normal text. In other words, it is equivalent to Body Text in normal desktop publishing termninology. This text is in the Paragraph style paragraph, and is meant for normal text. In other words, it is equivalent to Body Text in normal desktop publishing termninology.

Subheading

This text is in the Paragraph style paragraph, and is meant for normal text. In other words, it is equivalent to Body Text in normal desktop publishing termninology. This text is in the Paragraph style paragraph, and is meant for normal text. In other words, it is equivalent to Body Text in normal desktop publishing termninology. This text is in the Paragraph style

Fig.6.13 The text has wrapped properly around this right-aligned image

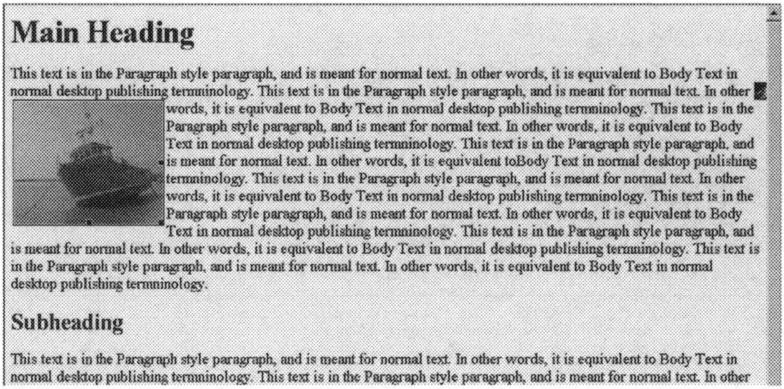

Fig.6.14 An image that uses left alignment

Baseline

Has the same effect as the Bottom option.

Right

This option places the image on the right-hand margin. Assuming left-justified text is used, it will wrap around the image quite well, as in Figure 6.13.

Left

The image is placed on the left-hand margin when this option is selected. With luck, text will wrap around the image, as in Figure 6.14.

Wrapping

Unfortunately, when an image is applied to existing text that is left justified, the text can be forced away from the space to the right of the image, as in Figure 6.15. The same thing can happen when using right alignment with right justified text, although this is a less likely combination. Fortunately, in practice the text will usually wrap around the side of the image, but this is not guaranteed. If text fails to flow around an image correctly, make sure that the correct type alignment has been set. Note that text will not flow around an image if you place the image on the page first, and then use the Paste function to add a block of text above the image. Instead, the image will be moved down the page to make room for the text.

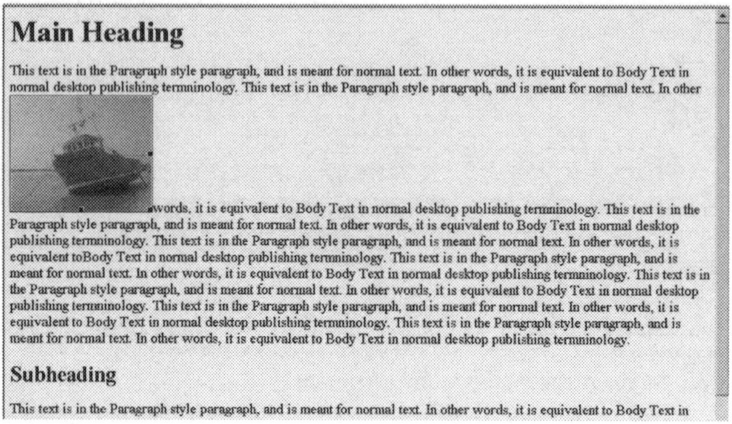

Fig.6.15 The text wrapping does not always give the desired effect

Images tend to be treated as if they were outsize text characters, and it is usually best to think of them in that way. In some ways the facilities offered by Dreamweaver seem crude compared to desktop publishing and up-market word processor programs, but bear in mind that Dreamweaver, unlike desktop publishing and word processor programs, deals in roundtrip HTML. This places some definite restrictions on what can be done.

H and W Space

When dealing with images the Properties Inspector offers additional features that can be accessed via the drop-down panel. If this extra panel is not already displayed, left-click on the downward pointing arrowhead in the bottom right-hand corner of the Properties Inspector to make it appear (Figure 6.16). In order to remove the panel, left-click on the (now) upward pointing arrowhead.

The V (vertical) Space and H (horizontal) Space text boxes can be used to place an exclusion zone around the image, as in Figure 6.17. Here respective horizontal and vertical values of 30 and 20 have been used. This places the image 30 pixels out from the left margin and also keeps the text from encroaching within 30 pixels of the right-hand edge of the image. The text is also prevented from coming within 20 pixels of the top or bottom edges of the picture.

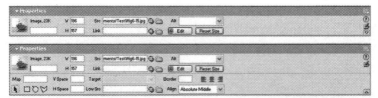

Fig.6.16   The Properties Inspector has a drop-down panel that gives access to more settings, as in the lower version here

Note that if two images are positioned side by side, and they each have a horizontal space setting of 20, the two images will be place 40 pixels apart (Figure 6.18). In fact there are four images in Figure 6.18, with the horizontal and vertical spacing both set at 20 for each image. However, the vertical spacing is clearly larger than the horizontal spacing. This is due to a blank line being added between the upper and lower pairs of images, giving greater vertical spacing than the 40 pixels. This will not necessarily matter, but using a soft return (Shift and Return) after the top right-hand image in place of an ordinary hard carriage return will correct the problem (Figure 6.19).

Fig.6.17   A blank area can be placed around images

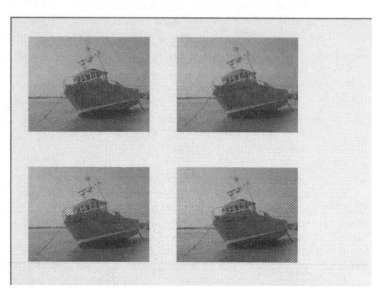

*Fig.6.18 The spacing of these images does not look right due to the
blank line placed between the upper and lower pairs*

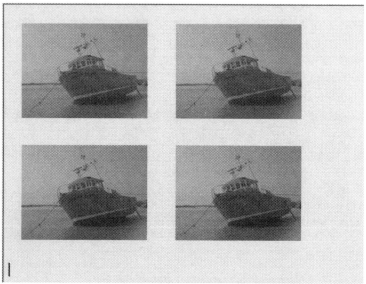

Fig.6.19 A soft return cures the problem of unequal spacing

Border

By default, no border is used around images. Obviously an image-editing program can be used to add a border to an image before it is brought into Dreamweaver. If anything fancy is required, this is the method that must be

Fig.6.20 The Properties Inspector enables a border to be placed around an image

Fig.6.21 A 10 pixel wide border has been added to this image

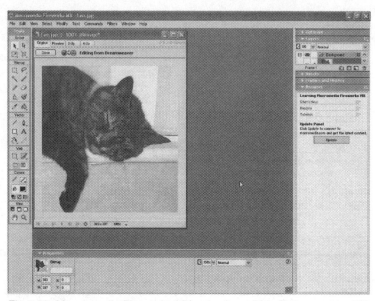

Fig.6.22 Macromedia Fireworks MX operating within Dreamweaver MX

used. A simple border can be added by typing a suitable figure into the Border textbox in the Properties Inspector. This box is in the right-hand section of the window (Figure 6.20). The width of the border (in screen pixels) is equal to the value entered in the textbox. Figure 6.21 shows a photograph that has a border 10 pixels wide. The default border colour is black, but for a linked image the border will assume the link colour. With a non-linked image it is possible to select the image and some text, and then set a colour for them all. However, the text can then be selected in isolation and set to any colour, including the original one. Therefore, it is effectively possible to set any desired colour for the border of a non-linked image.

Also in this part of Properties Inspector you will find the usual three alignment buttons, which operate like the alignment buttons for text. There is also a Reset Size button, which sets the image back to its original size if it has been resized in Dreamweaver.

Image editing

Dreamweaver does not have any built-in image editing capability, but it is possible to edit an image from within Dreamweaver using an external

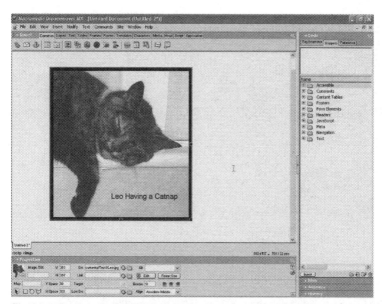

Fig.6.23 Back in Dreamweaver, the text added using Fireworks can be seen on the image

image-editing program. To do this, operate the Edit button, and the appropriate program will then be launched. Figure 6.22 shows an image being edited in Macromedia's Fireworks MX program, but you are not restricted to using Macromedia's image editing software. Other manufacturer's programs such as Corel Photo-Paint can be used from within Dreamweaver, and any graphics program that can handle the appropriate image format should work perfectly well. The image should be opened and loaded into the graphics program automatically, but if anything goes wrong it should be possible to open it manually. When the image editor is running, it might seem as though Dreamweaver has been closed, but it is still there underneath the image-editing window. This point is easily demonstrated by reducing the size of the image editing program's window to reveal Dreamweaver underneath.

Having made your changes, exit the program and elect to save the changes when asked if you wish to do so. Figure 6.23 shows some text added to an image using Fireworks MX, without exiting Dreamweaver. If the changes fail to appear on returning to Dreamweaver, left-clicking on the apply button (the thumbnail image in the Properties Inspector) should update the page to show the changes.

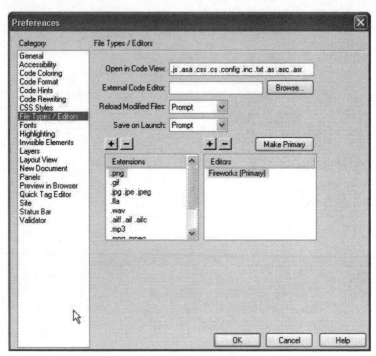

Fig.6.24 Using the Preferences window to control file associations

By default, the image editor used will be the one that the operating system associates with the file type concerned. In order to select a different image editing program go to the Edit menu and choose the Preferences option. Then left-click File Types/Editors in the Category column that occupies the left-hand section of the window. This will produce something like the window of Figure 6.24. In the lower part of the window there is a list of file types on the left-hand side. Left clicking on one of these shows the program associated with that file type on the lower right-hand side of the window. To add a new program to the list of available editors, operate the + button on the right-hand side of the window. Do not use the one on the left side, which is used to add new file types. A standard file browser will appear, and this is used to locate the appropriate program file. Operate the Open button to add the selected program file to the list.

The original program will remain in the list, and will still be the primary editor. In other words, it is the one that will be used by default. To make

It is easy to spot young seagulls due to there brown spotted appearance, plus the cans of lager and the MP3 players.

Young gull photo

Juvenile lesser black backed gull

Fig.6.25   The Alt tag is displayed when the pointer is placed over an image

the new addition the default editor, select it and then operate the – button. To make the new addition the primary editor and leave the original editor in the list, select the newly added entry and then operate the Make Primary button.

Image free

These days most Internet users have browsers that can handle images. However, there are probably still some users with text-only browsers, and others turn off image loading in order to speed things up. It is likely that there will be increasing numbers of portable Internet devices to contend with. At present these mostly have small screens that do not support proper graphics. The lack of images will not necessarily be of importance, but in some cases it could leave users of the site rather

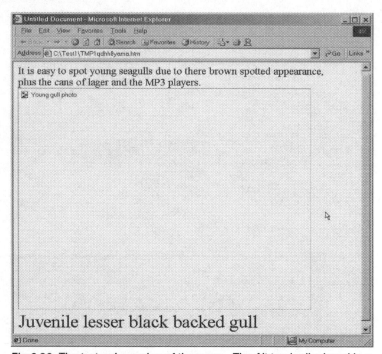

*Fig.6.26 The text only version of the page. The Alt tag is displayed in a
frame where the image would normally appear*

puzzled. There is a way around this problem in the form of an Alt tag.
This is a piece of text that will be used in place of an image if the page is
used with a text only browser. Where the browser supports images, this
text will also be displayed beneath the pointer if it is placed over the
image.

Adding an Alt tag is very simple. Select the image and then type the text
into Alt textbox in the main section of the Properties Inspector. If you try
out this feature, the Alt tag should be displayed if the pointer is placed
over the image, as in Figure 6.25. The same page is shown in Figure
6.26, but image downloading has been switched off in the browser. The
photograph has been replaced with a frame that is empty apart from the
Alt tag, which is displayed in the top left-hand corner. Clearly this type of
thing ruins the impact of web pages, but it does at least give text-only
users a clear indication of what would happen if they were using graphics
enabled browsers.

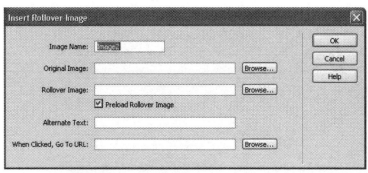

Fig.6.27 The image rollover dialogue box

Low source

A low source image is a low-resolution image that is downloaded quickly and then displayed while the main picture is downloaded. The point of this is that it can provide a complete if rather crude version of a web page almost immediately, even though the final version of the page will take some time to download. For this to work properly the low source image must have a small file size, otherwise it will not appear quickly enough to be worthwhile, and it would significantly extend the download time for the full page. Ideally the file should only be about 1k or so. This usually means using something like a highly compressed greyscale version of a colour photograph, a greatly simplified version of a piece of line art, or something of this nature. It should not be too difficult to produce something suitable using your graphics software.

To use a low source image first select the main image. Then either type the location of the image into the Low Src. textbox in the Properties Inspector, or operate the Browse to File button to the right of the textbox. This brings up the usual file browser, which is used to locate and select the required file. Having pointed the browser to the required file, operate the Select button. Note that only the main image will be displayed in Dreamweaver's design view. You can try loading the page into a browser to test this feature, but the page will probably load so quickly from the hard disc that the low source image will not be seen. Copying the page to a floppy disc and loading it from there might slow things down enough for the low source image to be briefly visible, particularly if the main image has a large file size.

Fig.6.28 This is the "before" image of the rollover

Image rollovers

An image rollover is where there is an image on the page, but a different image is produced when the pointer is placed on that area of the screen. This is achieved using JavaScript, but you do not have to be a JavaScript programmer in order to use rollovers with Dreamweaver. Dreamweaver will generate the program for you. In order to obtain good results the two images should be the same size. To add an image rollover, go to the Insert menu and select Interactive Images and then choose Rollover Image from the submenu. This produces a window like the one in Figure

Fig.6.29 This is the "after" image of the rollover. The previous image is restored when the pointer is moved away from the rollover

6.27. A name for the rollover image can be typed into the upper textbox, or you can just settle for the default. The code is easier to deal with if everything has a meaningful name, but it is not otherwise important.

The Original Image textbox is used to enter the name of the image you wish to use as the one that is normally displayed on the screen. Alternatively, left-click the Browse button to the left of the textbox and use the file browser to locate and select the image. The Rollover Image textbox and Browse button are used in the same way to select the image that will appear when the pointer is positioned over the rollover. By default

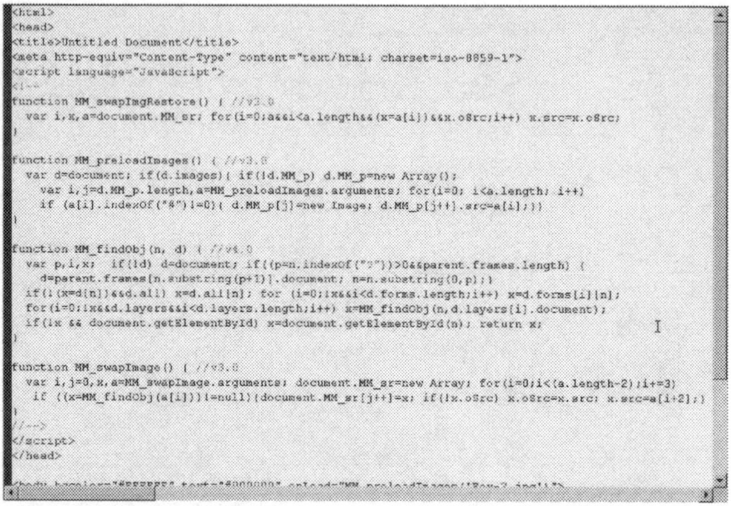

Fig.6.30 *If you examine the code for a rollover you will find that it is written in JaveScript*

the Preload Rollover Image checkbox is ticked, and the rollover image will therefore be loaded at the same time as the rest of the page.

The point of this is that the rollover image will appear immediately when the pointer is placed over the image. If the rollover image is only loaded when it is first needed, the changeover may be too slow and the effect could be lost. Therefore, even if the file size of the rollover is quite small, leave this box ticked. If the image must be linked to another web page, its URL is entered in the textbox at the bottom of the window. Note that the rollover action will occur when the pointer is positioned over the image, but the link will not. The image must be left-clicked, as normal in order to activate the link.

When all the necessary information has been added, left-click the OK button to add the rollover to the page. The original image will be visible in Dreamweaver's design view, but the rollover image will not replace it when the pointer is placed over the image. In order to test this feature you must add a rollover to a page, save the page to disc, close the page in Dreamweaver, and then load it into a browser that can handle JavaScript. Any two images of about the same size will do to try out a rollover. Their main use is in buttons that alter when the pointer is placed over them, with some sort of inverse video effect being used. They can

*Fig.6.31   Precise positioning of the text and graphics in this sort of
layout requires the techniques described later in this book*

also be used for simple visual jokes. The alert fox of Figure 6.28 changes
to the yawning fox of Figure 6.29 if someone is enticed into placing the
pointer over the rollover.

If you experiment with a rollover, try switching Dreamweaver from design
view to code view (go to the View menu and select Code). Much of the
code will look nothing like normal HTML (Figure 6.30), and that is because
it is not HTML but JavaScript. The section between "<script
language="JavaScript">" and "</script>" is the JavaScript program
that Dreamweaver has written for you.

Complex layouts

If you only wish to use simple page layouts having a mixture of text and
graphics, simply adding the images into the text will probably give
satisfactory results. However, for complex results it is better to use tables
and the other methods described in later chapters of this book. These
methods provide more precise control over the positioning of both the
text and the images, making layouts like the mock-up of Figure 6.31
reasonably easy. This type of thing is not possible by simply dropping
text and images direct onto a page.

Local sites

What is it?

Armed with the knowledge in the previous six chapters you should be well on the way to building web sites using Dreamweaver. Making some web pages using text or a mixture of text and graphics should now be reasonably easy, but making some basic web pages and building a web site are not quite the same thing. Anything more than the most simple of single-page web sites will need links. These have been touched upon in previous chapters, but they are sufficiently important to warrant their own chapter. The subject of links is covered separately in chapter 8. In order to build a web site the various files that are used in the site must be organised properly. Before you publish a site on the Internet it must be assembled on the hard disc of your computer. A local site only differs from an ordinary site in that it is on your computer rather than on a server somewhere on the Internet.

If you have experience at producing paper documents using a computer, you may wonder why file management of a web site is difficult. If you are used to producing large documents such as books and catalogues, a web site might seem to be easy by comparison. I suppose one important difference is that paper publications are normally reduced to a single file for the printers. It could take hundreds of files to generate the document, but these are eventually combined into one large file. For example, initially this book will probably consist of around 300 or so files on my computer, but it will be sent to the printer as a single Adobe PDF file. The source files are not needed once the PDF file has been produced, because the PDF file contains all the information needed to produce the printed version of the book.

The situation is very different with a web site, which is not reduced to a single file. It remains a set of files, with matters complicated by the numerous links needed to enable users to navigate around the site. These links must lead the browser to the right file, and must continue to do so once the site is published. If a file is moved, the link must be updated accordingly. Another complication is that the HTML code for a web page does not necessarily represent the complete page. Any graphics for instance, are kept as separate files and are not incorporated into the HTML file. The page will only display properly if the browser can find the image file pointed to by the HTML code.

Absolutely relative

When building a web site it is important to understand the difference between absolute and relative URLs. URL stands for Uniform Resource Location, but it is what most Internet users would simply term a web address. On the face of it, there is no problem in using absolute links at all times. With a link of this type the full name and path to the file is provided. This works fine when providing a link from your web site to another site. You simply provide the full URL such as:

www.babanibooks.com/dreamweaver/contents.html

Any browser can then use that web address to find the correct page, provided it exists. The example web addresses in this book are purely fictitious incidentally, so do not bother trying to find them on the Internet.

The situation is different when dealing with addresses within your newly constructed web site. Your site is assembled on your hard disc drive, and the location of a file would be something along these lines:

C:\mywebsite\images\foxphoto.jpg

Here "C:\" is the root directory of the hard disc on which the local site is stored, and "mywebsite" is the folder used to hold the files for that site. Some of the files are stored in subfolders of the "mywebsite" directory, and the image files are stored in a subfolder called appropriately enough, "images". The file in question here is one called "foxphoto.jpg" that is stored in the "images" subfolder. Using an absolute address for this file is fine while the site is on your computer, but it will not work once the site has been placed on the Internet. The browser of anyone accessing the site will look for the file on drive C: of the hard disc on which the browser is running, and it will obviously draw a blank. Once the site has been published on the Internet, all the addresses change. The absolute address of our example image file would change to something more like:

www.babanibooks/images/foxphoto.jpg

In order to avoid this problem it is essential to use relative addresses for all files within your web sites. With relative addressing, this would be the address of the example image file.

\images\foxphoto.jpg

In order to use relative addressing, there must be a root folder for the site, and all addresses are then relative to this folder. In this example the root site is the "mywebsite" folder, since all the files are stored in this folder and its subfolders. The root folder is whichever one you tell Dreamweaver to use as the root folder, but in practice you do not have any choice over which one to use. For this system to work properly and remain manageable, all the files for a site must be in the root folder itself or a subfolder of the root folder. There must be no files in folders higher up the folder structure, or in a totally different part of this structure.

The reason that relative addressing works, is that the browser knows where it has found the root folder, and it can easily locate any files in that folder or in its subfolders. If a file is called "home.html", there is no path given, just the filename. The browser therefore knows that the file is in the root folder. It does not matter whether the root folder is at "www.babanibooks.com\dreamweaver" or C:\dreamweaver", or anything else. The user will have directed the browser to the correct location, and it will find the file there, wherever that location happens to be. Similarly, if a file is in a subfolder of the root folder, the browser knows where the root folder is located, and it can find files in subfolders by moving down the directory structure from the root folder. If you move your site from one disc to another, or from a disc to an Internet server, once user's browsers have been directed to the root folder they can find everything in the site from there.

Making roots

It is possible to have a system that permitted the browser to be directed to relative addresses up and across the folder structure, but this would be doing things the hard way. In practice it is easier to make and designate a root folder and then have everything in or below that folder. If you will only be producing one web site, the root directory can be a folder of the root directory of the hard disc. In other words, something like:

C:\booksite

Where it is likely that more than one site will eventually be produced it might be better to produce a folder off the root directory of the hard disc,

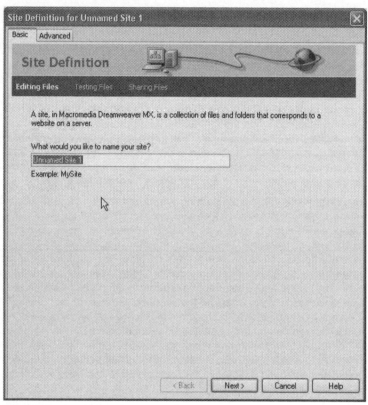

Fig.7.1 A wizard is available to aid site definition

and then have separate subfolders beneath this to act as the root folders for your sites. An example root folder would then be something like this:

C:\websites\booksite

The point of this second method is that it helps to avoid having huge numbers of folders branching directly from the hard disc's root folder, which would tend to complicate file management.

The first step in setting up a new site is to use the operating system or Dreamweaver to generate the folder that will be used as the root directory for the new site. In this case it does not really matter too much which method is used, but in general it is better to handle file management from within Dreamweaver wherever possible. This enables Dreamweaver

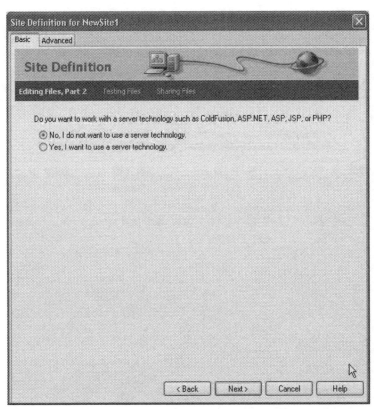

Fig.7.2 Technology such as PHP can be used if desired

to keep track of the files in a site, avoiding error messages and blank areas on pages. Here we will assume that the new folder is to be generated using Dreamweaver and that it will also be designated as the site's root directory at the same time.

New site

There is a wizard that makes it easy to define a new site. To launch this wizard select New Site from the Site menu, which will bring up a window like the one in Figure 7.1. Here a name for the new site is entered into the textbox, or if preferred you can settle for the default name. It is probably best to give the site a meaningful name. Operating the Next

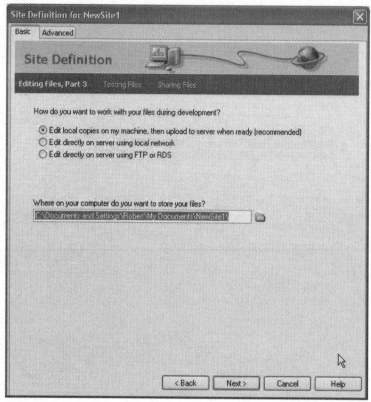

Fig.7.3 Various options for storage of the site are available

button then moves things on to the window of Figure 7.2. Here you can opt to use or not use a server technology such as PHP. Initially you will presumably be designing simple sites that do not require PHP, ASP, etc., so operate the No radio button followed by the Next button.

The next window (Figure 7.3) has three radio buttons that determine where the files for the site will be stored and accessed. One option has the files on the server and accessed via a network, and another has the files on the server and accessed using FTP or RDS. Here we will assume that the files are stored on the hard disc of your PC and then uploaded to the server once the site has been completed. This option is selected using the top radio button, which will probably be the default option. The root directory for the site is selected by typing the path to the

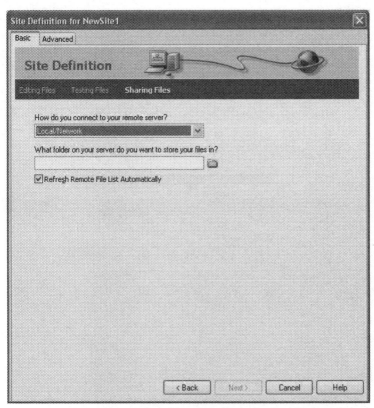

Fig.7.4 The FTP option is normally selected from this window

appropriate folder into the textbox. Alternatively, operate the button just
to the right of the textbox and then select the correct folder using the file
browser that appears. If the folder does not yet exist, the Make New
Folder button of the file browser can be used to add the folder.

Operating the Next button moves things on to the window of Figure 7.4.
The menu is used to select the method used to connect you computer
to the remote server. This will probably be FTP, but another option can
be selected where appropriate. Select the None option if you are simply
experimenting and will not be uploading anything at this stage. The
textbox or file browser is used to select the location on the server where
the files will be stored. With FTP selected using the menu, the window
changes and there are four textboxes (Figure 7.5). Here you enter the

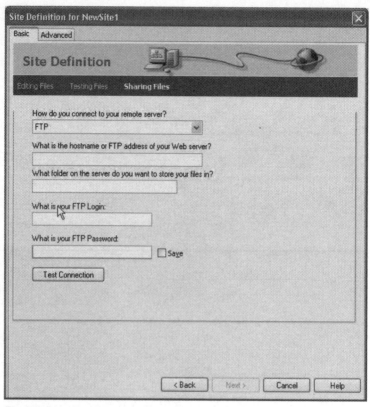

Fig.7.5 Selecting FTP from the menu produces four textboxes

FTP address, the folder on the server that will be used for your site, the FTP login, and your password. Your service provider will supply you with the FTP address, password, etc., and this information must be accurately copied into the relevant textboxes. The Save button is operated if you wish to save the password on your PC so that it does not have to be re-entered each time you login via Dreamweaver. This is more convenient, but means that anyone with access to your PC also has access to your sites and can alter them. The large button enables the connection to the site to be tested.

The next window (Figure 7.6) is only applicable where there are two or more people working on the same web site. Operate the Yes radio button

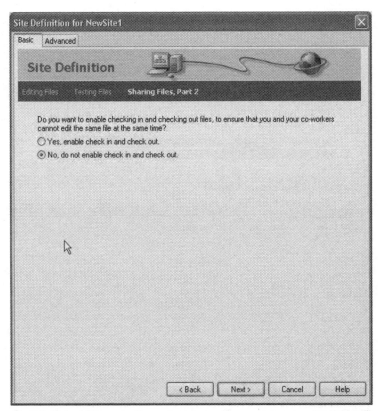

Fig.7.6 Select the no option unless more than one person at a time will work on the site

if you wish to use signing in and signing out to ensure that two people do not work on the same file at the same time. Simply leave the default No setting if you do not wish to use signing in and signing out.

Finally, operating the Next button takes things on to the next window (Figure 7.7) where there is a summary of the settings that have been entered via the previous windows. If you notice a mistake here it is possible to go back and correct the mistake using the Back button. Alternatively, operating the Advanced tab changes the window to look like Figure 7.8. Here you can select a category using the menu on the left, and then make any necessary changes in the main window on the right. It is best not to start playing with these settings unless you are

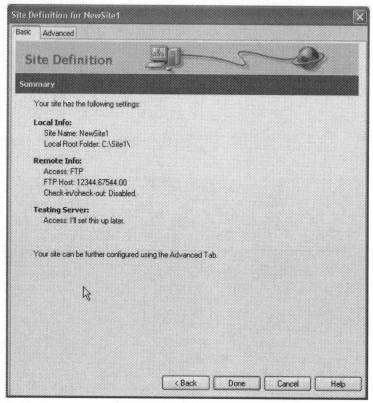

Fig.7.7 This window provides a summary of the selected options

sure you know what you are doing. Operate the Done button once you are satisfied that everything is correct. This completes the site definition and you are then ready to actually start building the new site.

When first using Dreamweaver it is probably best to use the wizard when defining a new site. This should ensure that no vital pieces of information are accidentally omitted. However, it is not essential to do things this way. Having launched the wizard, you can operate the Advanced tab and then go through each section of the Site Definition window using the menu in the left-hand pane. Operate the OK button when you have finished adding the information.

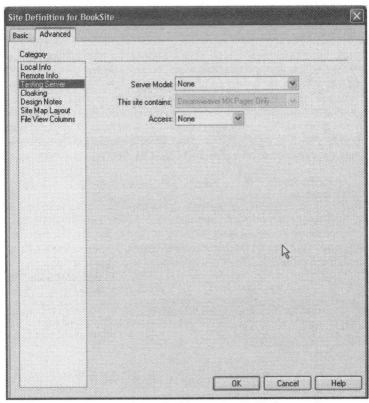

Fig.7.8 The Advanced tab makes it easy to edit settings

Preparation

It will be apparent from this description of the site definition process that
you must do a certain amount of preparation before using Dreamweaver
in earnest. While it is possible to produce a root folder for the new site
on the computer's hard disc during the definition process, in practice
things would not be done in this way. Making a folder "on the fly" is all
well and good when doing some initial dabbling, but when dealing with
the "real thing" you would normally have the root folder in place before
you start. In fact there would normally be a lot more than the root folder
if you were producing anything more than a very basic site. There would
be subfolders for images, sounds, or other files needed in the production
of the site.

You also need to sort out where on the Internet your site will be accommodated, and it is more than a little helpful if the necessary site address, password, or whatever is to hand when defining the site. The company providing the web space should be able to supply the information required by Dreamweaver. Of course, you may be producing material that will go onto a CD-ROM, and it is now quite common for catalogues and other information to be distributed as what is effectively a web site on a disc. In this case there is obviously no need to give details of where the site will be hosted. The completed site is copied from your hard disc drive to the CD-ROM, and it can then be accessed by an computer that has a standard CD-ROM drive and a web browser.

Edit Sites

An existing site can be edited by selecting Edit Sites from the Site menu. This produces the small window show in Figure 7.9. Of course, if no sites have yet been defined, there will be no sites listed in the left-hand section of the window. You must add one or two sites first if you wish to experiment with this feature. The buttons in the upper part of the right-hand side of the window provide six options:

New

This is used when you wish to build a new site "from scratch". It launches the Site Definition window where you can use the wizard or Advanced section to define the site in the normal way. This is effectively the same as choosing New Site from the site window.

Fig.7.9   Once sites have been created they can be edited via the Edit Sites window

Edit

Use this option to make changes to the settings for an existing site. You can use the wizard to repeat the original setting up process, making any necessary changes along the way, or operate the Advanced tab and sort things out for yourself.

Duplicate

This option clones the settings for an existing site.

Remove

A site can be deleted using this button.

Import

This facility enables a site to be imported in the form of an XML file.

Export

A site can be exported from Dreamweaver as an XML file using this facility.

Auto refresh

Initially you will probably prefer to use the wizard when producing a new site, but before too long it is probably best to delve into the Advanced sections of the Site Definition window. In the Local Info section (Figure 7.10) there is a checkbox labelled "Refresh Local File List Automatically", which is ticked by default. With this option selected Dreamweaver will automatically refresh the local file list whenever changes are made, such as moving or deleting files. The Local panel of the Site window will not automatically refresh if the tick is removed from this box, which will speed up operation of the program in some respects. The file list can be refreshed manually by operating the Site panel's refresh button (the one having a circular line with an arrowhead).

The HTTP Address textbox is used to enter the absolute address that the new site will eventually occupy. In other words, something like "www.robertpenfold.co.uk". It is not essential to use anything here initially, and when you are just making some initial experiments with Dreamweaver there is not much point in doing so. On the other hand, there is no harm in adding a web address here.

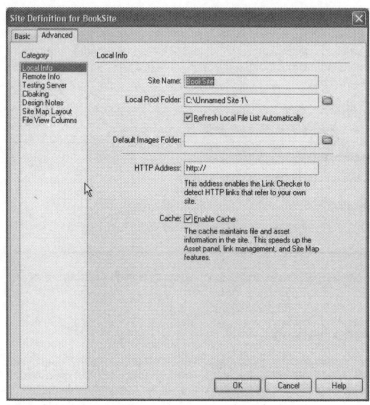

Fig.7.10 The Local Info section of the Site Definition window

The Cache checkbox is ticked by default, and a cache to help speed up link and other file management tasks will be produced. It is a good idea to use this option since the Assets panel will not work unless it is. With the Cache checkbox ticked you will sometimes get a message like the one of Figure 7.11 when exiting the Site Definition window. The message simply explains that the cache is being generated, and it is of no real significance.

Fig.7.11 This message explains that a cache is being generated

It is not essential to set a default image folder, but it is a good idea to do so. Either type the full path for the folder into the appropriate textbox, or operate the button beside this box and use the file browser to locate and select the appropriate folder. The obvious arrangement is to have a folder called "Images" as a subfolder of the root directory. Most of the other settings were covered earlier in the sections dealing with the New Site wizard.

Editing

When you have finished creating or editing a site, operate the Done button and then look at the Site window (Figure 7.12), which is a section of the files panel. Make sure that the correct site is selected in the left-hand menu, and that Local View is selected in the menu in the menu on the right. The new root folder will be shown in the main section of the window, beneath the menus. It is likely that only the root folder will be shown initially, but this can be expanded by left-clicking on the plus sign

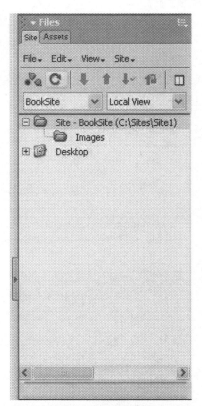

Fig.7.12 The new site should appear in the Site Window

just to the left of the folder's icon. Navigating your way around the site in the Site window is much the same as negotiating a folder structure using Windows Explorer, etc. The root folder is now in position and assigned to the new site, but it is still an empty site.

Next the Site window, which has its own menu system, must be used to add the files and folders that are needed for the site. Suppose that we wish to add a folder called "extra_images", and place some image files into it. First the folder must be created, and this is achieved by selecting New Folder from the File menu. Note that it is the File menu of the Site window that must be used (Figure 7.13) and not the File menu of the main document window. A new folder off the site's root directory will

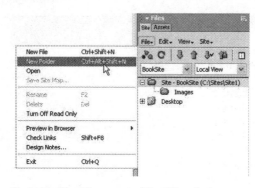

appear, and it will initially be called "untitled" (Figure 7.14). Type "extra_images" to rename the subfolder and then left-click in a blank area of the window to make the name change take effect. Alternatively, press the Return key to make the change take effect.

Fig.7.13 The File menu of the Site window

Now we need to add some files to the new folder. This can not be done using the Site window, because the files will be in folders outside the site at this stage. Therefore, use the operating system to copy files to the appropriate directory, and they should then appear in the appropriate folder if it is examined using the Site window (Figure 7.15). You can also generate files using a graphics program, word processor, etc., and then save them direct to the appropriate folder within the site. Once files are stored within the local site it is best to use Dreamweaver to undertake file management tasks such as moving or deleting files. Any links that are affected will then be changed automatically so that they are still correct. Changes made using the operating system could break links, and any damaged links would then have to be repaired manually.

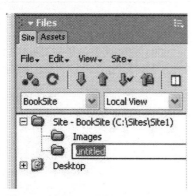

Fig.7.14 Files and folders are easily renamed

Here we generated a root folder and a subfolder using Dreamweaver and then added files into one of the folders. If preferred, you can generate the directory that will be used as the root folder, equip it with files, and then designate it as the root folder for your new site. The end result should be the same either way.

New HTML files

If you are going to use Dreamweaver to generate a new HTML file, a basic HTML file should be generated using the Site window first. With the Sites section of the Files panel open, start by left-clicking on the entry for the folder where the new file is to be placed. For the sake of this example left-click on the entry for the root folder. Next select New File from the Edit menu of the Site window, and a new file called "untitled.htm" will appear in the Local Folder panel. Edit the name to something more suitable such as "home.htm" and then press the Return key or left-click

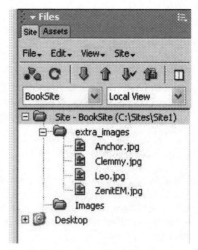

Fig.7.15 Newly added files appear in the Site window

on a blank part of the window. The entry for the new file will probably be at the bottom of the panel, well detached from the root directory, but it should appear in the Site window (Figure 7.16).

To open the new file simply double-click on its entry in the Site window. The file will then be opened in the usual Dreamweaver document window, enabling it to be edited in the normal way in design view, code view, or a mixture of both. Try typing some text into the document window when using design view, and then load in one or two of the image files stored in the "extra_images" subfolder of the local site. When you have finished, go to the File menu and select Save to save the modified version of the page.

Fig.7.16 A new file has been added

If you launch Dreamweaver and then start adding images into the document window and saving the results, it will almost certainly generate some error messages. These should be avoided by constructing a basic site first and then building up the web pages from the files it contains. This is not just of academic importance. With everything structured properly Dreamweaver can keep track of all the files and the links between them. This should ensure that everything in the site functions properly, with no blank spaces instead of images or links that lead to nowhere.

File management

The Site window can be used to handle various file management tasks such as moving or deleting files. These are undertaken in much the same way as when the same tasks are performed using the operating system. In order to rename a file, left-click on its entry to select it and then left-click on the entry again. Be careful to leave a reasonable gap between the two clicks or they will be construed as a double-click and the file will be opened. If all is well the text cursor will appear and the filename can be edited. Press the Return key or left-click on a blank area of the window to make the change take effect. If the file concerned is linked to another file

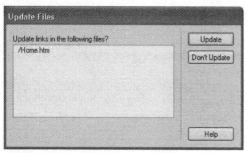

Fig.7.17 The option of automatically updating links will normally be taken

or files, a window like the one in Figure 7.17 will appear, asking for confirmation that the link should be modified to suit the change of name. Unless there is a good reason to do otherwise, operate the Update button. The site should then function as before.

New folders and files can be added, and this process was described previously. A file or folder can also be deleted by selecting its entry and either pressing the Delete key or selecting Delete from the File menu. If the file has a link or links to other files, a warning message similar to the one in Figure 7.18 will appear. Operate the Yes button to delete the file anyway, or the No button to abort the deletion process. Deleting a file that is used by a page in the site will result in the image disappearing from the page, and it will be replaced by a grey rectangle containing a question mark (Figure 7.19). It is then up to you to

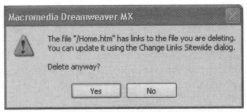

Fig.7.18 A warning is produced if you try to delete a linked file

delete the defunct image from the page or restore the missing file. Note that the image will not disappear immediately if the relevant page is currently open in Dreamweaver, but it will be absent the next time that page is opened.

Editing and deletion

As already pointed out, the main parameters for a site can be edited by going to the Site menu and selecting Edit Sites. Select the site you wish to edit from the list that appears, and then operate the Edit button. This

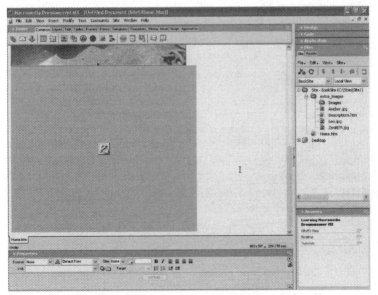

Fig.7.19 Space is still reserved on the page for the missing file

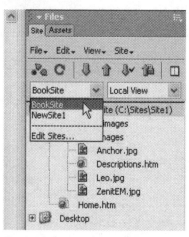

*Fig.7.20 This warning is produced
if you try to delete a site*

takes you to the Site Definition
window for the selected site,
where you can change its name,
the HTTP address, etc.

In order to delete a site, select
Define Sites option from the Sites
window to bring up the list of sites.
Select the site to be deleted and
then operate the Remove button.
This will produce the warning

message of Figure 7.20. If you are sure you wish to continue, operate
the Yes button to remove the site. You will then be returned to the list of
sites, which should no longer contain the one that has just been removed.

Note that the folders and files for the site are not deleted by this action,
and that everything will still be in place on the hard disc. The difference
is that Dreamweaver no longer considers those files and folders to
constitute a site. There is no one-click method of undoing the removal
of the site, but defining a new site based on the folders and files of the
old one can effectively reverse the process. If the files and folders are no
longer needed they must be deleted using the file management facilities
of the operating system.

Site selection

When two or more sites have
been defined, you can switch
from one to another using the left-
hand menu near the top of the
Site window (Figure 7.21). This
menu lists all of the available sites.
The currently selected site is
shown in inverse video in the
menu. To open a different site
simply left-click on its entry in the
menu, which will bring up the Site
window for that particular site.
You can then choose a file in the
site to open and edit, make an
"empty" HTML file and open it,
etc.

*Fig.7.21 The required site can be
selected from this menu*

Site map

A site map can be produced by selecting the Site Map option from the Site menu. However, initially this will probably produce the window of Figure 7.22, pointing out that

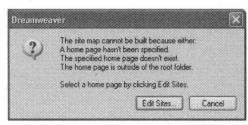

Fig.7.22 *This message is produced if a home page has not been specified*

a home page has yet to be specified. To specify a home page you must first operate the Edit Sites button. This brings up the familiar list of defined

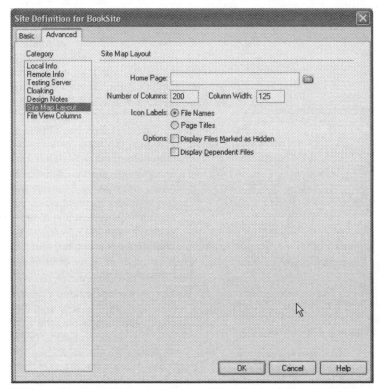

Fig.7.23 The Site Map Layout section of the Site Definition window

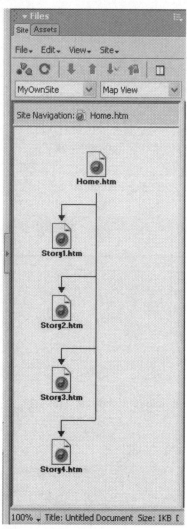

Fig.7.24 A simple site map

sites. The one to be edited is selected and then the Edit button is operated. This brings up the Site Definition window, and the Advanced tab should be selected. The Site Map Layout entry should be selected in the Category panel down the left-hand side of the window. This produces the window of Figure 7.23.

The full path and filename for the home page can be typed into the Home Page textbox, or operating the folder button to the right of this box will launch the file browser. If you use the second method, locate and select the home page HTML file and then operate the Open button. There are various options available that control the way the site map is displayed, but for the time being leave these as they are. Once the filename has been added to the Site Definition window, operate the OK button to return to the Define Sites window, and then operate the Done button to return to the main Site window. Close this window and select the Site Map option again, and this time a site map should be produced (Figure 7.24).

The difference between a normal view showing folders and files and a site map is that the map does not show the file and folder structure at all. It shows the pages in the site plus the main links between them. In most cases there will be additional links, and some pages could well link to dozens of other pages. Having hundreds of lines criss-crossing everywhere would be confusing and not very informative. Therefore, the minor links are shown as optional lists of linked pages. A list can be displayed by left-clicking on the "+" symbol displayed to one side of each icon that has additional links (Figure 7.25). Left-click on the "+" symbol again to retract a list.

Planning

With a small site that uses few files there is no necessity to resort to any subfolders at all. Even with everything in the root folder there will be no difficulty in finding any file you require. With larger sites a more planned approach is required. Dreamweaver should always be able to find the files it requires provided you always abide by the file management rules, and do not move or rename something while Dreamweaver's "back is turned". Getting the files and folders organised properly is more for your benefit, so that you can easily locate any file that you wish to work on.

Using a different subfolder for every page is one approach to things, with all the files needed for each page stored in the relevant

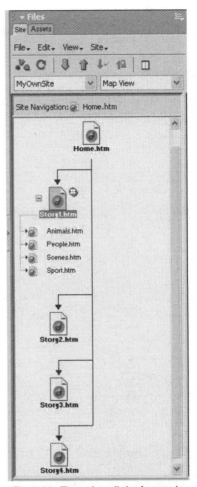

Fig.7.25 The minor links for each page can be shown

subfolder. With a large site this could result in a complex structure, with subfolders of subfolders of subfolders, and so on. Most users find it easier to have a separate subfolder for each section of a large site, rather than one per page. Where large numbers of image files, audio files, etc., are involved, each subfolder can have its own subfolder for storing these files. If few media files are involved, a single subfolder off the root folder is the more popular option. Presumably some general planning will be undertaken before starting work on anything other than a very basic site, with a sketch of the page structure being made. This should provide a good basis for working out a sensible file and folder structure for the local site.

Links

Adding links

It may be "love that makes the world go round", but it is that other four letter word beginning with "I" that makes the Internet go round. While using the Internet you click on one link after another. Links enable users to move around web sites with just a few clicks of the mouse, and move from site to site just as easily. People can and do surf the net for hours without typing in a single web address. Unless you put in links to enable users to easily move around your web sites they will probably give up and go elsewhere. Links that do not work properly are another "sure fire" way of getting rid of visitors to your site. It is the links from one page of the site to another that make it a web site rather than just a collection of separate pages.

Links to other sites are perhaps less important, and on the face of it there is no point in making it easy for people to leave your site and go elsewhere. However, if everyone took this attitude it would become much more difficult to navigate the Internet and find what you require. The secret of success with links to other sites is reciprocity, or "I'll scratch your back if you scratch mine" if you prefer. Provide links to other relevant web sites, but try to make sure that plenty of other sites have links that bring users to your site as well.

Relative links

Hyperlinks, or just plain "links" as they are often called these days, provide a quick way of directing a browser from one page to another. The page containing the link is the "referring" page, and the one that it is linked to is the "target" page. Obviously the link on the referring page must include the path and filename for the target page so that the browser knows exactly where to go. As we have seen already, web pages can be addressed using absolute or relative addresses. A link to another web site must use absolute addressing, while links within a site are relative, but relative to what? We have previously considered relative addressing using the site's root directory as the basis. With this method the path to the target file is given with the site's root directory acting as the starting point. Internal links can use this method of relative addressing.

Dreamweaver also supports document relative path names, which use the subfolder of the referring page as the starting point for the path. This is very convenient when linking to a page in the same subfolder, since no path is needed. To link to a page called "LondonBridge.htm" in the same folder as the referring page the target would simply be given as "LondonBridge.htm". Giving the path to somewhere lower in the directory structure is also very simple. Suppose that this target file was in a subfolder called "Tourism", and that this branched directly from the subfolder containing the referring page. The path and filename for the target would be "\Tourism\LondonBridge.htm".

Matters are a little more complex if the target is in a subfolder that is higher in the directory structure, or it is in a subfolder that has its origins higher in the directory structure. In either case it is still possible to use a document relative path, and two full stop characters (..) are used to indicate each move up one level in the directory structure. Consider these two paths and filenames:

../LondonBridge.htm

../../Bridges/LondonBridge.htm

In the first example the file is in the folder one level higher up the directory structure. This is indicated by the two full stops at the beginning of the path. In the second example there are two pairs of full stops, indicating that the file is two levels further up the directory structure. However, it is then down one level in a subfolder called "Bridges". Using this method it is possible to provide a path to anywhere in a local site, from anywhere within that site, but the site-root relative method is the simpler of the two systems. If you use a link that is relative to the referring page, always make sure that the page has been saved first. Until the page is saved there is nothing for the link to be relative to.

Making links

Adding links from one page of a site to another is very easy using Dreamweaver, using either text or images as the sources of links. To experiment with links make up a dummy site having two or three pages containing some text and an image or two per page. The Copy and Paste facilities enable a small amount of text to be repeatedly duplicated

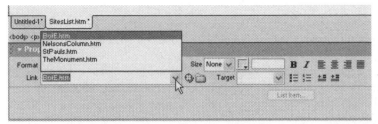

Fig.8.1 Some previously linked pages are available from a pop-down menu in the Properties Inspector

so that the dummy pages can be filled quite rapidly. In this example the word Parliament will be linked to a page containing a picture of the Parliament building, but for testing purposes you can link any word to any page. Even a blank page will do, but it is better if you add a few words to identify the page.

To use text as a link it must first be selected using the usual dragging technique. Drag the cursor over the text while holding down the left mouse button. If only a single word is involved, double-clicking anywhere on the word will select it. If the Properties Inspector is not already active it should be launched now. The name of the page to link to can be typed into the Link textbox in the bottom left-hand section of the Properties Inspector. When the filename has been entered, press the Return key to make the link active.

If a link to the same page has been used recently, an alternative method is to left-click on the downward pointing arrowhead at the right-hand end of the textbox. This will produce a pop-down menu showing the link pages that have been used recently (Figure 8.1), and the required page can then be selected by left-clicking on its entry. There is a third method available, which is to operate the Browse for File button (the one that uses the folder icon), and then use the file browser to locate and select the file for the correct page. The Relative To menu provides the option of using document relative or site-root relative paths.

Testing links

Once the link is active the selected text will be underlined and it will change colour. Left-click somewhere on the screen so that the link is no longer highlighted, and it should change to the default colour for linked text (Figure 8.2). The link can not be tested by simply left-clicking on the

Fig.8.2 The word "Parliament" is used as a link, and it is therefore underlined and in a different colour to the main text

Fig.8.3 When tested the link produced the desired result

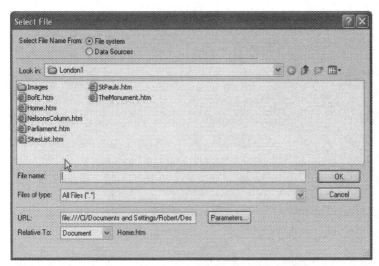

Fig.8.4 A file browser can be used to select the linked page

text in Dreamweaver's design view. As we will see shortly, there is a simple method of testing links using Dreamweaver.

The alternative is to test them using a web browser, either within Dreamweaver or externally. This subject has been covered previously and will not be considered further again here. Figure 8.3 shows the link being tested using Internet Explorer 5.5. It is being tested from within Dreamweaver, but the result should be the same if it is tested by running the browser outside Dreamweaver. The linked text has been left-clicked in Internet Explorer, and the correct page has been loaded.

A link can also be added by selecting the relevant text and then selecting the Make Link option from the Modify menu. This brings up a file browser (Figure 8.4), which is used to locate and select the link page. This is actually the same file browser that is produced via the Properties Inspector. Once the correct file has been selected, operate the Select button to return to the document where the linked text should be shown underlined and in a different colour. Yet another method of selecting the file for a link is to use the Point to File button, which is the one immediately to the right of the Link text box. In order to use this the Site window must be on view. If necessary, bring it to the fore by selecting the Site Files option from the Window menu. The Point to File icon is then dragged to the required file in the Site window (Figure 8.5).

*Fig.8.5 A page can be selected by pointing to its entry in the
Site window*

Here we have only considered relative links for use within the web site.
To make an absolute link the text is selected and then the full URL is
typed or pasted into the Link textbox of the Properties Inspector.

Removing links

If you change your mind and wish to remove a link, this is easily achieved.
One way is to select the linked text and the erase the entry in the Link
textbox of the Properties Inspector. Left-click on an inactive part of the
Properties Inspector or somewhere on the document to make the change
take effect. Another method is to select the linked text and then activate
the Modify menu. This menu changes to suit the situation, and with
linked text selected it will offer a Remove Link option (Figure 8.6).
Selecting this will immediately delete the link.

You will notice that the Modify menu also provides a Change Link option.
Selecting this brings up a file browser, and a new file to link to can then
be selected. The same thing can be achieved by selecting linked text
and then either editing the text in the Link textbox, or activating file browser

so a different file can be selected. In the Modify menu there is an Open Linked Page option, which gives a crude but effective means of checking that you have chosen the right page for the link. Once the linked page has opened, close it and return to the original page by left-clicking on the "X" icon in the top right-hand corner of the window.

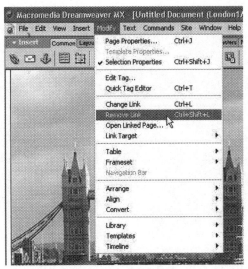

Fig.8.6 Links are easily removed .

Linking images

Images are linked in much the same way as text. Select the image and then use any of text linking methods described previously in this chapter. Note that as far as links are concerned there is no difference between an image and any border that is placed around it. When the page is displayed in a browser, left clicking on either the image or its border will move the browser to the target page.

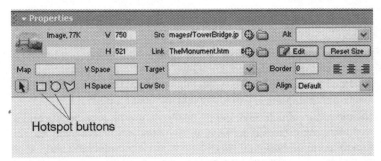

Hotspot buttons

Fig.8.7 The Hotspot buttons in the Properties Inspector

Fig.8.8 A rectangular hotspot has been added to Tower Bridge

Links from images have an interesting optional extra in the form of multiple links. In other words, rather than linking the entire image to one page, separate parts of the image can be linked to different pages. Hotspots and image maps are the key to this feature, and they are accessed using the buttons in the bottom left-hand section of the Properties Inspector (Figure 8.7). To try out this feature, load a page of the "dummy" site that has an image, and then select the image. In the Map textbox of the Properties Inspector add a name for the image map. Only use letters and numbers, and do not start the name with a number. Left-click on the hotspot button having the rectangular icon and then use the mouse to drag a rectangle somewhere on the image. The selected area will be filled in with pale blue, but the image will still show through to some extent. This gives something like Figure 8.8, where the central part of Tower Bridge has been used for the image map.

Next a target page is selected by operating the Browse for File button and then using the file browser in the usual way. Some text can be added to the Alt textbox if desired. With most browsers this text will be displayed below the pointer when it is positioned over the relevant part of the image. Where it will not otherwise be clear what the link actually

*Fig.8.9   The hotspot is not visible when the page is viewed in a
        browser, but the cursor changes and the Alt text appears
        to indicate its presence*

links to, this gives an opportunity to clarify things for users. In our Tower
Bridge example, the link could be to a page giving a brief history of the
bridge. The Alt text could then be something like "History of bridge"
(Figure 8.9).

Polygon hotspot

Now try another hotspot using the Polygon Hotspot Tool, which is
obtained using the button at the right-hand end of the row. Repeatedly
left-clicking on the image leaves square markers on the screen, and the
area between them is filled in with the pale blue mask to show the "hot"
area. Figure 8.10 shows part of the area occupied by HMS Belfast filled
in, and Figure 8.11 shows the completed job. This system is rather crude
by the standards of graphics programs, but it is good enough for this
application.

Fig.8.10 Adding a polygon hotspot

Fig.8.11 The completed polygon hotspot

Fig.8.12 Circular hotspots can also be used

Left-click the Arrow Tool when you have finished the polygon. The handles (the square markers) can be moved by dragging them around the screen, so "fine tuning" a hotspot is straightforward. If you make a mess of things, press the Delete key to remove the hotspot and then start again. When you have finished, select a target page and add the Alt text, as before. Note that you can return to a hotspot to change the link or edit other details. If you left-click on a hotspot, it is the hotspot that will be selected and not the image as a whole.

You might like to try the Oval Hotspot Tool as well (the middle of the three buttons). By left-clicking on the image and then dragging the pointer, a circle of the required size can be produced. It is difficult to get the circle exactly where you require it, but with a little resizing using the handles it is possible to edge the circle into the right position. You should then have something along the lines of Figure 8.12. The page and the links are then ready for testing using a browser.

Of course, when viewed in a browser the shading showing the hotspots is not shown, and there is nothing to indicate their presence other than the text that appears when the pointer is placed over a hotspot. However, the image can be edited to indicate the hotspots before it is loaded into Dreamweaver. The relevant areas can be shown paler than the rest of the image, tinted, or something of this nature. Once loaded into Dreamweaver, these areas then act as guides to help get the hotspots in the right places.

Link Checker

Ultimately you will probably wish to check all links by giving them the "acid test" using a browser, even if this takes a fair amount of time. Initially it is still a good idea to use Dreamweaver to search for problems with

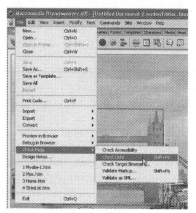

links so that they can be sorted out early in the proceedings. Then, hopefully, everything will be fine when your site is tested in practice. Dreamweaver's Link Checker can be used to test all the relative links of a page in a local site, but it will not check external links.

Fig.8.13 Launching the Link Checker

To launch the Link Checker go to the File menu and select the Check Links option from the Check Page submenu (Figure 8.13). This will produce a window like the one in Figure 8.14, and the Link Checker is actually part of the Results group. Therefore, selecting Results from the Window menu and then Link Checker from the submenu will also launch the Link Checker. This will not result in the check being run automatically, but activating the button near the top left-hand corner of the window will start one. This is the one that has the green triangular icon. It produces

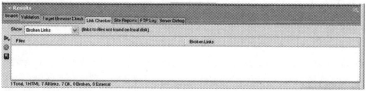

Fig.8.14 The Link Checker is part of the Results group

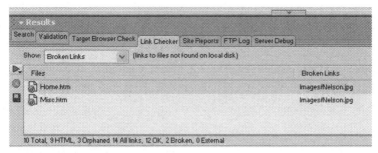

Fig.8.15 Any broken links are listed

a small window that permits the current document, the whole site, or selected items to be tested.

The main panel of the window lists any broken links that are found. In other words, it lists links to files that are not present on the local site, or are not in the right place. In the example of Figure 8.15 a file has been deliberately erased using the operating system instead of using Dreamweaver's file handling facilities. The entire site has then been tested for broken links. The erasure has resulted in two broken links, which have been duly listed by the Link Checker. A broken link can be repaired by reinstating the missing file, or the source of the link can be removed. In this example the erased file was reinstated from the Windows Recycle Bin, and a further check then showed that the broken link had been successfully repaired.

As pointed out previously, the Link Checker can be used to check links over selected files and folders or an entire local site. To check a site other than the current one, use the left-hand

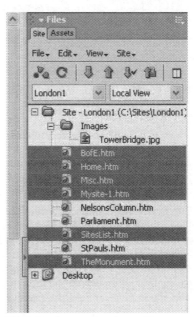

Fig.8.16 As usual, selected items are highlighted

menu in the Site window to select the appropriate site. If necessary, launch this window first by selecting Site from the Window menu. As before, you can then use the pop-out menu to check the current document, the whole site, or selected items. In order to check selected items, it is necessary to select something first using the local view of the Site window. To select a single item just left-click on it. To select several items, left-click on the first one and then hold down the Control key while left-clicking the other items. An object can deselected by left-clicking it while operating the Control key. As usual, the selected items are shown in inverse video (Figure 8.16)

The results can be saved to disc by operating the Save Report button in the Properties Inspector. This is the lowest of the three buttons on the left-hand edge of the window, and it produces the usual Save As file browser. This could be useful if a large number of problems are reported. Note that you can open a page by double-clicking on its entry in the list. The source of the link will then be selected automatically in the opened

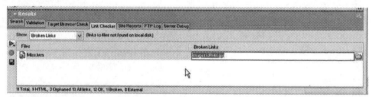

Fig.8.17 Broken links can be repaired by editing the appropriate text in the Link Checker

page. If you left-click on the entry for the missing or misplaced item, the text can be edited so that you can repair the link (Figure 8.17). The button at the right end of the text box launches the usual file browser so that a new target for the link can be selected. Simply delete the contents of the textbox if you wish to remove the link altogether.

The Show menu enables a search to be made for so-called "orphan" files, which are "unloved" files that are part of the local site but do not link to anything. It could be that any files listed are not supposed to be linked to anything at that stage in the development of the site, but it is useful to check the list to ensure that you have not forgotten to add links to any files. It is also a good idea to check the finished site. Remember that any non-linked files are effectively unavailable to users of the site.

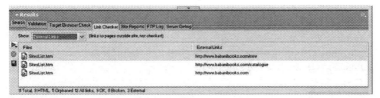

Fig.8.18 External links can be listed

External checking

Although Dreamweaver can not check external links, it can provide a list of them. Activate the Show pop-down menu at the top of the Link Checker window, and select the External Links option. A list of external links will then appear in the main panel of the Link Checker window (Figure 8.18). Although it is not possible to check an external link using Dreamweaver, you can copy a URL from the Link Checker to the address textbox of a browser. You can then check that the browser goes to the right page.

The point of this method is that it makes sure that the text used as the address in the browser is exactly the same as the text used for the external link. To copy a URL from the Link Checker, simply left-click on it and then press Control-C (Windows) or Command-C (Macintosh). It should then be straightforward to use the Paste facility of the browser to put the URL into the browser's address text box. Incidentally, the same method can be used to copy and paste a URL from the Link textbox of the Properties Inspector. If an error is found, it can be corrected by editing the textbox in the Link Checker or the Properties Inspector.

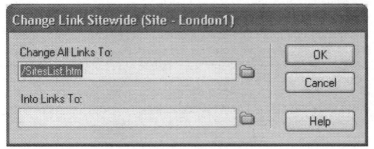

Fig.8.19 The Change Link Sitewide dialogue box

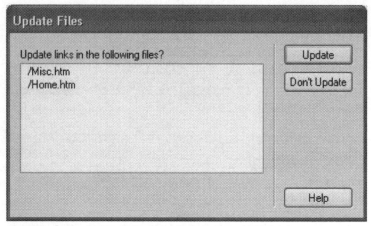

Fig.8.20 This window lists all the links to the old URL

Sitewise change

It is possible to simultaneously change all the links to a given page, be it internal or external. Suppose you have several pages in a site that link to a web page that is switched to a new site. One option is to go to all the affected pages and change the links one by one. The alternative is to first open the site by selecting it from the left-hand menu in the Site window. Then select Change Link Sitewise from the Site menu of the Site window (not the document window). This produces a window like the one in Figure 8.19 if one or more links are detected. In the Change All Links To text box type the URL of the existing link that you wish to change. By default this will start with the name of the currently selected document, but if necessary the existing text can be edited in the normal way.

In the Into Links To textbox type the name of the new URL that you wish to use for the links. Then operate the OK button, which will bring up another window, this time showing the links to the old URL that have been found (Figure 8.20). An error message will appear if Dreamweaver found no links to change. Assuming at least one link was found, operate the Update button to implement the changes or the Don't Update button to abort the operation. There will be an error message if the new link page can not be found, and you will have to try again. A file browser is available via the usual buttons, and this provides a reasonably foolproof method of selecting both the "before" and "after" documents.

Named anchors

The links covered so far are the most common type where the link takes the user to a new web page. There is another type that takes the user to a particular point on a page, and these are known as "named anchors". There is obviously little point in using a named anchor on a small page that can be viewed in totality on the average monitor, or which requires minimal scrolling in order to view the whole page. This type of link is used in long pages that have to be viewed bit by bit, with perhaps only about 10 percent of the page being visible at any one time. In general, this type of page is best avoided, and in most cases it is better if large amounts of material are broken up into separate pages of moderate size.

The long page option tends to be taken where there is not enough material to fully merit breaking things up into several separate pages, but there is too much material to be used easily as a single page. It is also popular where something like a series of news stories has to be put together and published on the web as quickly as possible. This could be done as separate pages, but one large page is easier to put together and test. A list of contents is used at the top of the page, with each item in the list linking to a named anchor in the relevant part of the page. By left-clicking on an item in the list a user is immediately taken to the relevant part of the page. Each section of the page normally has a link back to the top of the page, so that it is easy to return to the list to select another section of the document.

The single page method is slow initially because there is a large page to download. However, thereafter the system is very quick, and left-clicking on a link produces an almost instant response. This is due to the fact that there is nothing to load when a link is activated. The browser just has to move to a new point in the page that has already downloaded.

Anchors and links

To try out named anchors produce a document that is suitably long. The Cut and Paste functions can once again be used to repeatedly copy a small amount of text so that it soon fills a long page. Break the text into several sections, with a heading for each one. A named anchor consists of two parts, which are the link and the anchor. The link is much like any other link, except that it points to a named anchor rather than a page. When the link is activated, the browser jumps to the point in the page where the anchor is placed.

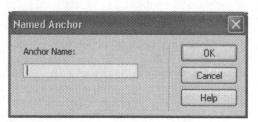

Fig.8.21 Use this dialogue box to name the anchor

An anchor is added at the current position of the text cursor, so left-click in the document at the position where the anchor is needed. To add an anchor, go to the Insert menu and select Named Anchor, which brings up the small window of Figure 8.21. A suitable name for the anchor is typed into the textbox. The name should only contain letters and numbers (no spaces, etc.), and should not start with a number. When the name has been entered, operate the OK button.

If Dreamweaver is set up to display anchors, as it probably will be, a small marker will be shown on the page at the point the anchor was added. In the example of Figure 8.22 the marker can be seen just to the left of the heading. If it is not, the warning message of Figure 8.23 will appear. Operate the OK button to remove the message window. The

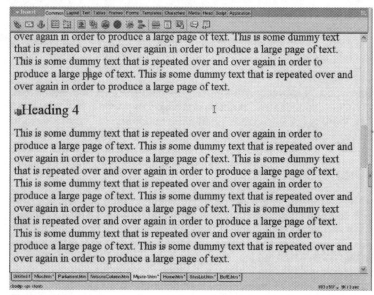

Fig.8.22 The anchor marker can be seen here next to the heading

anchor will still be added to the page, but it will not produce any visible result in the Dreamweaver document window. Of course, the anchors are never visible when the page is viewed using a browser.

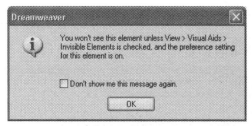

Fig.8.23 *A warning message is given if anchor markers are switched off*

Invisible elements

Which invisible elements are rendered visible is controlled via the relevant page in the Preference window. Select Preferences from the Edit menu to bring up the Preferences window, and then select Invisible Elements

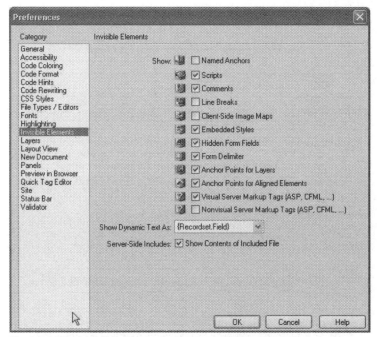

Fig.8.24 *The Invisible Elements section of the Preferences window*

over again in order to produce a large page of text. This is some dummy text that is repeated over and over again in order to produce a large page of text.

Heading 6

This is some dummy text that is repeated over and over again in order to produce a large page of text. This is some dummy text that is repeated over and over again in order to produce a large page of text. This is some dummy text that is repeated over and over again in order to produce a large page of text. This is some dummy text that is repeated over and over again in order to produce a large page of text. This is some dummy text that is repeated over and over again in order to produce a large page of text. This is some dummy text that is repeated over and over again in order to produce a large page of text.

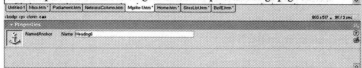

Fig.8.25 Editing the name of an anchor

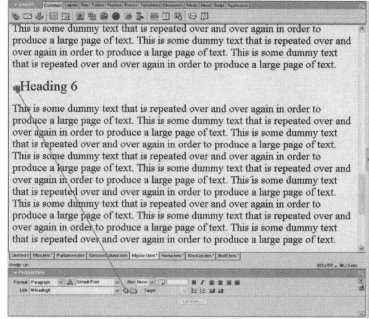

Fig.8.26 The pointing method can be used with named anchors

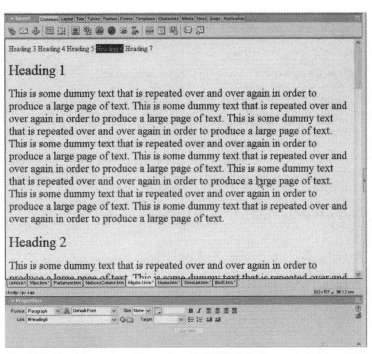

Fig.8.27 The screen scrolls to show the linked item

from the Category list down the left-hand side of the screen. This produces the Preferences page of Figure 8.24. Tick the checkbox for an element to make it visible, or remove the tick to render it invisible. If you wish to edit the name of an anchor it must be visible. Select its marker and the edit the name in the Properties Inspector (Figure 8.25). Left-click on the Apply button (the anchor symbol in this case) to make the change take effect.

Having added one anchor, add one or two more at substantially different places in the document. It is then time to add the links to them. One way of doing this is to use the Point to File button in the Properties Inspector. Select the text that will contain the link and scroll down to the appropriate anchor. Then drag the Point to File icon from the Properties Inspector to the marker for the anchor and release the mouse button (Figure 8.26). Obviously the marker must be visible for this method to work. The screen will automatically scroll up to show the text that contains the link, and this text will be underlined and in the default colour for

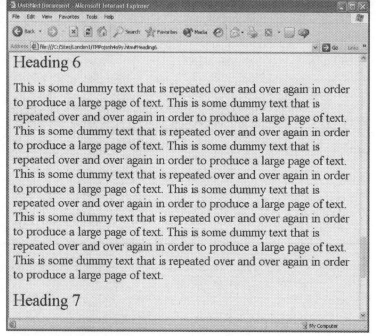

Fig.8.28   If everything is working well the anchor should be top line when the link is tested using a browser

linked text (Figure 8.27). The name of the anchor will then be added into the Link textbox of the Properties Inspector, but a hash (#) symbol will be added ahead of the name to indicate that the link is to an anchor and not a file.

An alternative method of adding the link is to select the text that will hold the link and then type the name of the anchor into the Link textbox. Remember to add the hash symbol ahead of the name. For example, for an anchor named "Specifications", it is actually "#Specifications" that would be typed into the Link textbox.

Having completed the links, save the file and then test the links using a browser. Figure 8.28 shows a link that has been tested using Internet Explorer. The line of text containing the anchor should appear at the top of the screen. In this example the link for "Heading 6" was activated at the top of the page, and things have clearly gone according to plan.

Email links

Even if you have not used the Internet very much you are likely to have encountered Email links on web sites. In order to contact someone at the site you click on the link and your Email program is launched, complete with the correct Email address already inserted. It is a good idea to include your Email address as well as a link, but a link of this type makes it easier for most users to contact you.

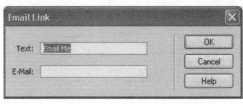

An Email link is easy to add using Dreamweaver. Start by highlighting the

Fig.8.29 The dialogue box for Email links

text you wish to use for the link. Next select Email Link from the Insert menu of the document window. A small window like the one in Figure 8.29 will then appear. The upper text box will show the text selected as

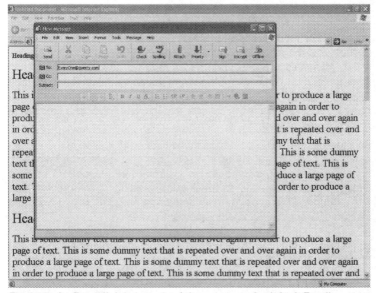

Fig.8.30 An Email link has caused the computer's default Email program to be launched

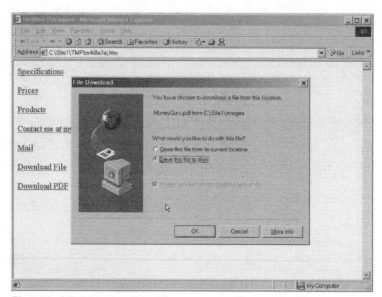

Fig.8.31 A link to something like a program file enables the user to download the file

the source of the link. The appropriate Email address is typed into lower textbox, and then the OK button is operated. The text used for the link will be shown as a normal link, so it is up to you to make sure that it is obvious to users that it is an Email type. If you try out an Email link in a browser you should get something like Figure 8.30, with the Email program launched within the browser, and the right Email address already present in the To field.

An Email link can also be added by selecting the source text and then typing the Email address into the Link textbox of the Properties Inspector. However, the address should be preceded with "mailto:" so that Dreamweaver knows it is an Email address rather than a normal link. For example, "mailto:myname@domainname.com" would be used instead of "myname@domainname.com".

Downloading

You may well have encountered web sites that have links to downloadable files. You click on the link, and the browser enables you to download the target file to a selected disc and folder under its original name or one of

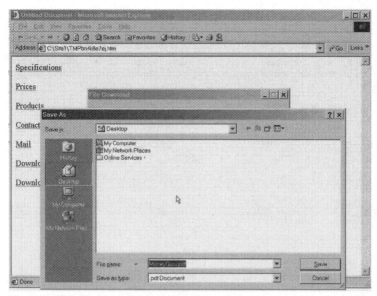

Fig.8.32 The file can be saved under a new name

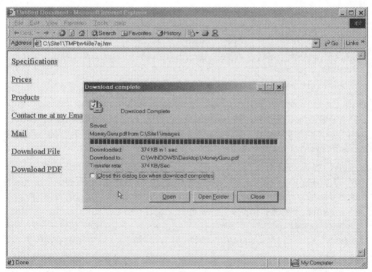

Fig.8.33 There is usually an indication of how things are progressing

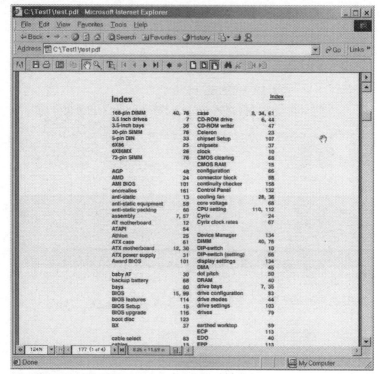

Fig.8.34 This PDF file is being displayed within Internet Explorer 5.5

your choosing. This type of thing is used for downloading programs, large documents in PDF format, or just about anything in the form of a ZIP or RAR file. A link of this type is added just like a link to an HTML page, but the browser will respond differently because the file will not have an HTML extension.

Figure 8.31 shows the link to a PDF file being tested in Internet Explorer 5.5. There is the choice of opening the file or saving it to disc. In most cases the file will be saved to disc, and choosing this option brings up a file browser (Figure 8.32). The destination folder for the file is then selected, and it can be renamed if required. Next the save button is operated, and the file will gradually be downloaded and saved to disc.

Of course, if you are testing the link on a local site the download will be almost instant. Most browsers show how things are progressing (Figure

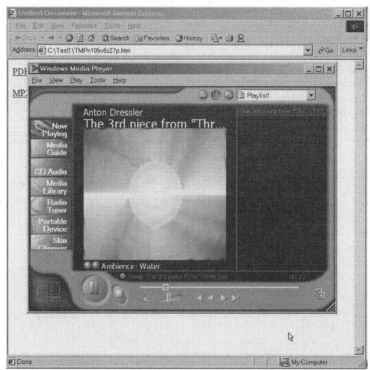

*Fig.8.35 Linking to an MP3 file results in the Windows Media Player
being launched to play the file*

8.33), which is important, because real downloads have been known to
grind to a halt. Once the file is downloaded the browser may be returned
to normal operation, or you might have the choice of opening the
downloaded file. In most cases the Download window is closed and the
file is checked out later. Note that this method only works with types of
file that the browser can not handle in the normal way. If you make a link
to something like a Jpeg image file, it will be displayed in the browser as
a web page.

Playing files

Links to some types of file will result in them being played or displayed
rather than saved to file. For example, if the user's PC has Adobe Acrobat
Reader installed and there is a link to a PDF file, with most browsers the

file will be displayed. Adobe Acrobat Reader augments the browser, with an additional tool bar appearing near the top of the screen. This provides the controls available in Adobe Acrobat Reader itself. Figure 8.34 shows a PDF file that is being displayed within Internet Explorer 5.5. Many multimedia files are handled in the same way, and Figure 8.35 shows an MP3 file being played by the Internet Explorer 5.5 media player. If you add links to files that need some form of player or plug-in for the browser to handle them properly, it is a good idea to include a link to a source of the plug-in or player.

Frames

What are they?

Frames are a feature of many web sites these days and they seem to be found on most commercial sites. Using frames a web page can be divided into sections, with each one containing a separate HTML document. In other words, you effectively have HTML pages within an HTML page. A common use of this feature is to have (say) the left-hand section of the screen devoted to a list of contents complete with links, and perhaps including a brief summary of each page. This is often referred to as the "navigation" frame.

The centre and right-hand section of the screen is devoted to an introductory document giving details of the company, organisation, or whatever. Frames can have independent scrollbars, so the navigation frame can be fixed while the introductory document can be scrollable. This keeps the entire navigation frame instantly accessible at all times, since scrolling down the main document leaves the navigation links in position.

In fact some sites have this arrangement for every page in the site, so that users always have easy access to every part of the site. The larger frames are often called the "content" frames, because they have the actual content of the site. With frames it is easy to produce sites based on this arrangement, with one HTML page (the navigation page) always visible. The reason for this is that links in the navigation frame can load new documents into the content frame. If you have something like 50 pages in the site, you only have to make an initial page having the two frames, plus 49 ordinary HTML documents. The 49 ordinary documents are loaded into the content frame, as and when necessary. This avoids having to make 50 pages with the navigation section included on every one of them.

Of course, with frames you are not limited to this basic two-page arrangement, and it is possible to have numerous frames per page. However, the more complicated the arrangement the greater the

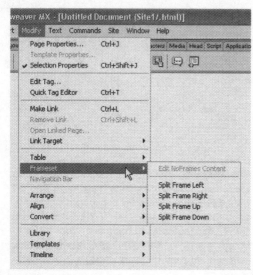

Fig.9.1 Framesets are available via a submenu

opportunity for things to go wrong, so it is best to settle for relatively simple arrangements at first.

It is only fair to point out that frames are not universally popular, and there are plenty of good sites that are totally frame-free. One advantage is that they are popular with users, since they can make site navigation much simpler. Frames also make it easier to update a site. There is just one navigation frame to update rather than having to alter what could otherwise be dozens of pages. On the downside, frames can be confusing if the site is not well designed, and many feel that frame based sites are aesthetically challenged. There can also be practical problems with frame based sites. For instance, in order to print out an entire page it is normally necessary to print the frames one by one. Like any facility of any program, frames should not be used simply because they are there. However, you should certainly learn the basics of using them and consider their use in web sites where appropriate.

Framesets

In order to understand the use of frames you have to understand framesets. In the example arrangement described previously there are three documents involved. The navigation and content documents constitute two of these, and the third is the page that contains the two frames into which the other two documents are fitted. This third document that contains the other two is the frameset. To experiment with framesets have a blank document open in Dreamweaver. If necessary, open a new document by choosing New from the File menu of the document window

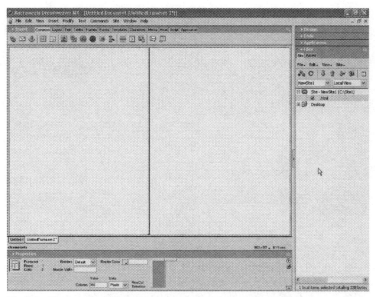

Fig.9.2 The result of selecting the Split Frame Left option

or add a new page to an existing test site. Next go to the Modify menu and choose Frameset, which will produce a submenu like the one in Figure 9.1.

There are four options available, and Figures 9.2 and 9.3 respectively show the result of selecting the Split Frame Left and Split Frame Up options. The Split Frame Right option gives a result that looks the same as Figure 9.2. Similarly, the Split Frame Down option produces a split screen that looks the same as the one of Figure 9.3. Select one of the options to produce two frames in your test document. The dividing line between the two frames can be dragged to a new position, as in Figure 9.4.

Another way of making frames is to go to the View menu, select Visual Aids, and then choose Frame Borders from the submenu. This produces a frame border around the page, but does not divide the page into two frames (Figure 9.5). However, you can drag one of the borders into the window to provide a split, as in Figure 9.6. In fact two or more of these drag operations can be used to split the page into four or more frames (Figure 9.7). Drag the lines back to the borders again in order to remove them.

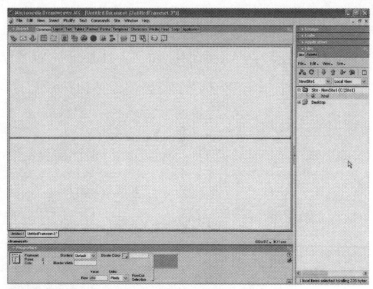

Fig.9.3 The result of selecting the Split Frame Up option

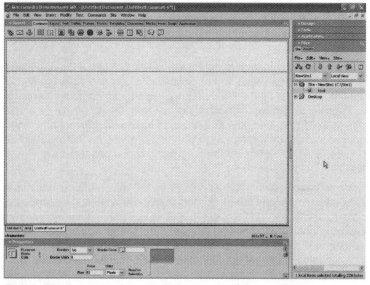

Fig.9.4 The frame borders can be dragged to new positions

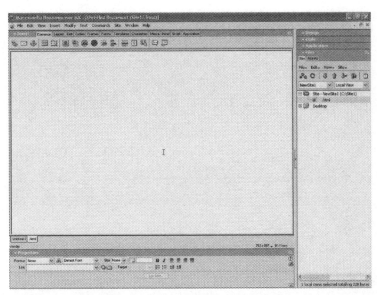

Fig.9.5 Adding a frame border to a page

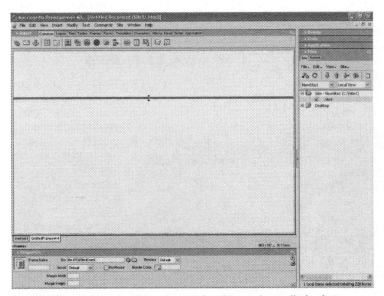

Fig.9.6 The newly added border can be dragged to split the frame

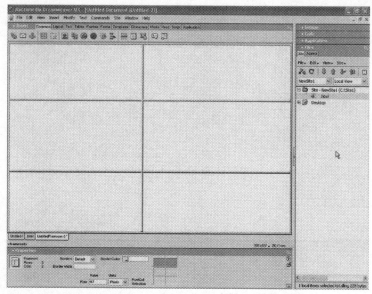

Fig.9.7 Further dragging permits more splits in the border frame

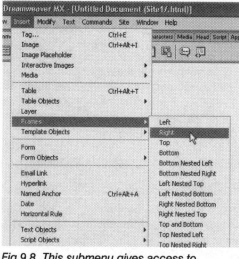

Fig.9.8 This submenu gives access to preset frame structures

Quick and easy

There is a quick and easy method of adding preset frames available from the Insert menu. Selecting the Frames option brings up the submenu of Figure 9.8. This gives 13 preset frame structures, and the example of Figure 9.9 shows the Left Nested Top frameset. A little experimentation will soon reveal all the

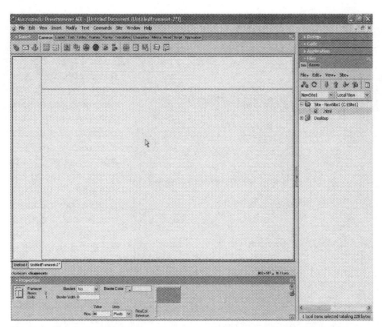

Fig.9.9 The Left Nested Top frameset. This is one of the 13 preset framesets that are available

available options. The same facilities are available from the Frames section of the Insert palette, and this makes things much easier because the icons show the frame arrangements that are available (Figure 9.10). The frames look different when produced using these methods, but this is simply because the frame borders are switched off. They are standard frames that can be altered using the normal methods. Changing the frame parameters is covered later in this chapter.

Fig.9.10 The Frames section of the Insert toolbar has buttons that show the available framesets

Frames window

The Properties Inspector can be used to show the properties of an individual frame or a frameset, but you have to make sure that what you

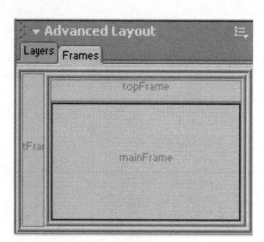

have selected and what you think you have selected are one and the same. It is possible to see what is currently selected, and alter the selection, using the Frames window (Figure 9.11). If this is not already on the screen it can be launched by going to the Window menu and selecting the Frames option from the Others submenu. By default the Frames window is grouped with the Layers

Fig.9.11 The Frames window

window. If this group is already on the screen, left-click on the Frames tab to bring this window to the fore.

The Frames window shows a thumbnail version of the current document, complete with borders for the frames. It also shows the name for each frame, and they will all be given sensible names such as "Mainframe". However, the names can be changed to more appropriate ones if preferred. The frameset will probably be selected initially, but you can switch to any frame simply by left-clicking within its section of the Frames window. Holding down the Alt key and left-clicking within a frame in the design view has the same effect. A broken line that is added just inside the normal frame markers highlights the border of the selected window. In Figure 9.12 the large frame is selected. To switch back to the frameset, left-click on the outer border in the Frames window.

Nested frames

A frameset can have either columns or rows, but not both. On the face of it this is rather limiting, but arrangements having rows and columns

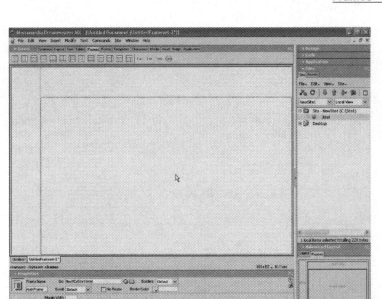

Fig.9.12 The large frame has been selected using the Frames window

can be produced using nested frames. In other words, by inserting one frameset into another frameset. Try editing the frames of your test document so that the page is split into two halves with a left-right arrangement. Left-click on the left half of the design view and then from the Modify menu select Frameset and Split Frame Up. This should give an arrangement like the one in Figure 9.13. Next select the frame in the bottom left-hand corner by left-clicking in its area of the Frames window. If you look at the tag selector in the bottom left-hand corner of the screen you will notice that its reads "<frameset><frameset><frame>", indicating that the selected frame is within a frameset that is itself within a frameset. The same is true for the frame in the top left-hand section of the screen, but not the large frame to the right.

Saving

Saving your work is a little more complicated when using frames, and you need to take care to save everything correctly. The normal Save and Save As functions are not present in the File menu when the current document uses frames. If you left-click in one of the frames to place the

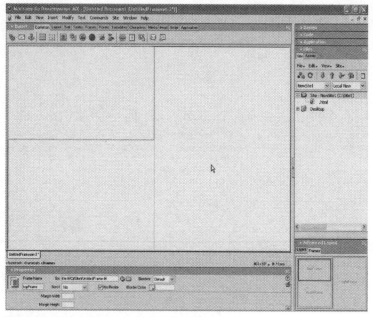

Fig.9.13 A simple example of nested framesets

text cursor there, the File menu offers Save Frame and Save Frame As options. These save the HTML document in the appropriate frame, much like Save and Save As when not using frames. If you select the frameset and then go to the File menu, Save Frameset and Save Frameset As options are available. Again, these operate much like the normal Save and Save As commands, but they save the HTML document that contains the frameset.

There is also a Save All Frames option, which is a quick and easy way to save changes to any frames that have been altered since the previous save operation. Initially, most users prefer to select each frame and save it under a suitable name. Suppose that the page is about rocks, and that it is split into upper and lower frames. These could be called "rocktop.htm" and "rockbottom.htm" respectively. The frameset could be saved as just "rock.htm", but it is helpful to add an "f" to the beginning or end of a frameset file to help distinguish them from ordinary HTML documents. The frameset would therefore be saved as either "rockf.htm" or "frock.htm". This method ensures that each part of the page is saved under a suitable name, and that none of the names are accidentally swapped over. Having successfully saved everything to disc, the Save All Frames command provides a quick and easy way of saving all the frames and the frameset.

Naming

Returning to frames and the Properties Inspector, when used with frames there are two versions of the Properties Inspector. The one for framesets is shown in Figure 9.14, and the one for individual frames is shown in

Fig.9.14 The Properties Inspector for framesets

Figure 9.15. In both cases the Properties Inspector must be in its expanded form in order to show all the parameters. We will consider the frame version first. As pointed out previously, by default each frame is called something appropriate such as "TopFrame", and this is not altered

Fig.9.15 The Properties Inspector for an individual frame

by saving the frame to disc. The Src textbox contains the name of the file used for the contents of the frame, but the frame has a separate name. This enables alternative contents to be targeted at the frame by a special form of link. If you are not satisfied with the default frame name type a more appropriate one into the Frame Name textbox and then operate the Apply button to make it take effect. In this case the Apply button is the large blue one in the top left-hand corner of the Properties Inspector.

Borders

The menus in the top right-hand corner of the Properties Inspector control the border colour and type. Matters are less than straightforward when dealing with borders, since adjacent frames share a common border or borders. Consequently, a change to the border setting of one frame may affect the border of another. Try altering the border colour and you will soon see what I mean. This colour control works in standard Dreamweaver fashion incidentally. The Border menu offers three settings, which are On, Off, and Default. Some designers prefer to switch off borders or merge them into the background colour in order to make the use of frames less obvious. Although the appearance of the site might be improved, hiding borders could also make things more confusing for users.

With the Default setting, borders are switched on or off depending on the default setting of the browser used to view the page. Note that borders are displayed or hidden in Dreamweaver's design view depending on the View setting used. Borders are toggled on and off by selecting Visual Aids from the View menu, and then selecting Frame Borders from the sub-menu. This just controls the way in which borders are displayed in Dreamweaver's design view. It is the border settings that determine whether the borders are switched on or off in the document.

Scroll and resize

The Scroll menu determines how horizontal and vertical scrollbars will be used by the frame. These are the four options:

Yes

Scrollbars will always be displayed, even if they are not necessary. If they are not required, the scrollbars will still be present, but it will not be possible to adjust them. The use of unnecessary scrollbars is not of great importance, but it does waste screen space.

No

Scrollbars are never used for the frame, even in situations where only part of the contents can be displayed. This setting might have its uses, but it could leave users with no means of viewing anything other than the top left-hand section of the document. Do not use this setting unless you are sure you know what you are doing.

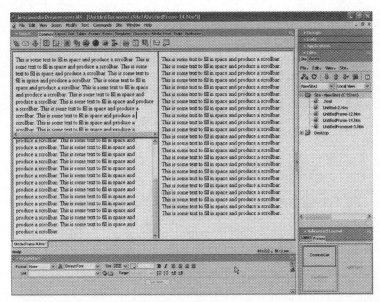

Fig.9.16 Where appropriate, scrollbars are shown in the design view

Auto

This is the option normally used, where scrollbars are used only when they are actually needed. In other words, if a frame is not large enough to display the full contents, horizontal and (or) vertical scrollbars will be added so that the full content is accessible.

Default

The browser's default setting for scrollbars is used. In most cases this will be the same as using the Auto setting.

If in doubt it is best to use the Auto setting. This avoids the use of unnecessary scrollbars, and ensures that users can access all the content of the document. Where appropriate, Dreamweaver's design view will display the scrollbars (Figure 9.16). There would have to be a very good reason for using the No option, which could easily leave important content inaccessible to many users.

By default the No Resize checkbox is ticked, but you might prefer to remove the tick. Users are then able to drag the frame boundaries in the

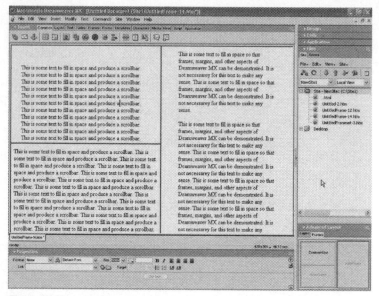

Fig.9.17 The margins are individually adjustable for each frame

same way that they can be moved around in the Dreamweaver document view. An advantage of being able to do this is that users can minimise frames that they are not using and thereby have more material on view in the other frames. In doing so they will make a mess of your beautifully designed layouts. Despite the potential advantages of the resizing capability, many designers prefer to "play safe" and suppress resizing.

Width and height

The margin width and height sets an exclusion zone for the contents of a frame around the frame edges. The figures entered into these textboxes set the margin sizes in terms of pixels. By default settings of 0 and 0 are used, enabling the content to go right out to the frame border. This is the setting used in the bottom left-hand frame in Figure 9.17. In general, pages look much better if a margin is used. The top left-hand frame of Figure 9.17 uses width and height settings of 20 and 40 respectively, while the right-hand frame has these settings at 40 and 20. A little experimentation with the margin settings should soon produce the effect you desire.

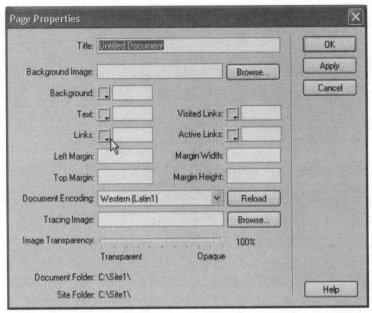

Fig.9.18 The page can be named using the Page Properties window

Frameset settings

The Properties Inspector has border controls when the frameset is selected, and these provide a convenient way of changing to a different set-up for all the borders. Note though, that these settings can be overridden by the border settings for the individual frames. There is no name textbox in the frameset version of the Properties Inspector, but a name for the page can be set in the usual way by selecting Page Properties from the Modify menu. This produces the window of Figure 9.18, where the new name for the page is entered in the Title textbox. Bear in mind that the name used here will appear in the title bar at the top of the browser when the page is displayed. If you require individual title bars for the frames, these must be added like any other content in the frames.

Note that some of the parameters in the Page Properties window do not have any effect when a frameset is selected. In particular, the colours must be changed for the various frames individually. It is quite possible

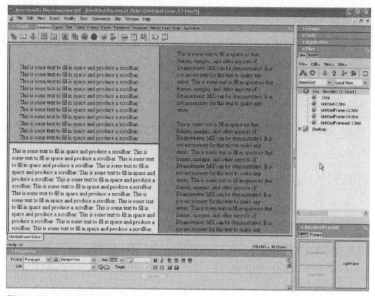

Fig.9.19 A different background colour can be used for each frame

to have a different background colour for each frame, as in Figure 9.19. To change the settings for a frame, select that frame and place the text cursor somewhere within it. Then go to the Modify menu, select Page Properties, and change the settings in the usual way.

Adding content

To add content directly to a frame, place the text cursor in the right frame by left-clicking within the frame, and then type in text, add images, etc., in the usual way. Things like text size, font, and colour are also edited in the normal fashion. The contents of an HTML file can be placed in a frame by placing the text cursor in the appropriate frame and selecting Open In Frame from the file menu. This brings up the usual file browser so that the desired file can be located and opened.

Targeting

Using links with frames is inevitably more complicated than using them with ordinary HTML pages. The link leads to an internal or external

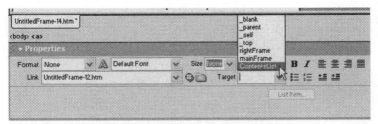

Fig.9.20 The Target menu of the Properties Inspector

document in the normal way, but there are various options governing where the new document is opened. The link to the document is made in the usual way, and then the Target menu in the Properties Inspector (Figure 9.20) is used to determine where the linked document is opened. These are the first four options in the menu and the methods of displaying the document that they select:

_blank

This opens another browser window and displays the document in the new window. The original browser window and page are left intact but "underneath" the new browser window.

_parent

This opens the new document in the parent frameset. Where nested framesets are not in use this means that the new document will occupy the browser's entire window area. Where nested framesets are used, the document will only occupy the part of the window that does not contain any child framesets. As you will probably have gathered, in frameset terminology the main frameset is the parent, and any smaller framesets it contains are its children.

_self

With this option the new document is opened in the frame that contains the link. This is the default option incidentally.

_top

The new document occupies the full browser window, and replaces the existing document in the usual way.

Additionally, the names of any frames currently on view in the document window will be listed in the menu. This enables documents to be opened

Fig.9.21 The initial version of the frames demonstration

in the desired frame, and it is a feature that is used a great deal with frame based sites. It is an essential part of sites that use the navigation frame and content frame arrangement. Pages selected in the navigation frame are opened in the content frame.

Targeting a link is pretty straightforward, but it is a good idea to try out some simply dummy sites to check that things work as expected. It is certainly worthwhile making a dummy site that has a navigation frame and some simple pages for the content frame. Start by making the page having the frames, and use a simple left-right split with a narrow frame on the left. Name the frames "leftframe" and "mainframe". In the left-hand frame put four lines of text to use as links. It is best to keep it simple by using something like "Page One", "Page Two", etc. In the large frame add some suitable text, such as "This Is Page One". Save the document in the left frame as "navigation.htm", and the document in the main frame as "pageone.htm". Remember to save the frameset as well.

Fig.9.22 Operating the "Page Two" link has had the desired effect

You now need to make three ordinary HTML pages called "pagetwo.htm", "pagethree.htm", and "pagefour.htm". These should respectively contain text saying "This Is Page Two", "This Is Page Three", and "This Is Page Four". Obviously you can add further content if you wish, but use the text labels to make it perfectly clear which page is which. Next you need to return to the frames page so that the four pieces of text in the left frame can be linked to their respective documents. Select the "Page One" text string and use the Properties Inspector to link it to "pageone.htm". Use the Target menu of the Properties Inspector to set "mainframe" as the target. Repeat this process to link the three remaining pieces of text to their respective HTML documents, and in each case set "mainframe" as the target.

Having saved everything to disc, the dummy site is ready for testing in the browser. Initially you should get something like Figure 9.21. The navigation links are displayed in the left-hand frame, and the content for page one of the site is in the main frame. Left-clicking on the "Page Two" link should leave the left-hand frame unchanged, with the content for page two of the site loading into the main frame (Figure 9.22). Operating

Fig.9.23 This page has correctly opened in the entire window

any of the links should result in the appropriate page appearing in the main frame while the left-hand frame remains the same. Left-clicking on the link for a page that is already loaded into the main frame will cause it to be reloaded.

You may like to return to the navigation page in Dreamweaver and try some different target settings for some of the pages. In Figure 9.23 page three of the site has been opened via a link that has _top as the target. It has correctly been opened to use the entire window of the browser. The _blank target was used the target for page four of the site, which has resulted in this page opening in a new browser window in Figure 9.24.

Frame-free

A major problem with frames when they were first introduced was that a fair proportion of the browsers in use at the time did not support frames. Unfortunately, without support for frames the contents of frame pages is

Fig.9.24 The _blank option has resulted in this page opening in a new browser window

not displayed. This is less of an issue these days because practically everyone uses a browser that can handle frames. You might still prefer to include some material that can be accessed with a browser that can not handle frames, even if it the non-frames content is nothing more than a message apologising for the fact that the user can not access the site properly. This makes the situation clear to users who have a browser that can not handle frames, or to visually impaired users running software that is not fully compatible with frames.

One solution is to have a splash page that makes it clear to users that a frames-compatible browser is needed to use the site. A splash page is simply an initial page that gives some brief details of the site before users enter the main pages of the site. It is only fair to point out that splash pages are not universally popular with web users, and splash pages that take a long time to download are a good way to get people to make an early exit from your site. The neater solution to the frames problem is to include some content that is accessible using any browser. In Dreamweaver terminology this is called "NoFrames" content. To add NoFrames content go to the Modify menu, select the Frameset option, and then choose Edit NoFrames Content from the submenu (Figure 9.25).

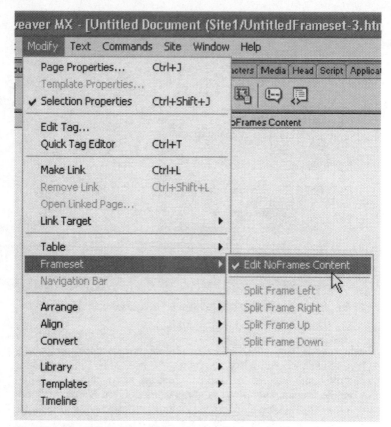

*Fig.9.25 The Edit NoFrames Content option is available from the
Modify menu via a submenu*

The frames will disappear from the screen and will be replaced by a
window headed "NoFrames Content" (Figure 9.26). Material is added
into this window in the normal way. You can add a simple message of
apology, or put in material to take the place of the framed version of the
site. To switch back to the normal page, go to the Modify menu and
select Frameset and Edit NoFrames Content again. Testing this feature
is likely to be problematic, since any modern browser will display the
pages with frames and ignore the alternative non-framed content.
Presumably it can only be done using an old browser that does not
support frames, if you can find one.

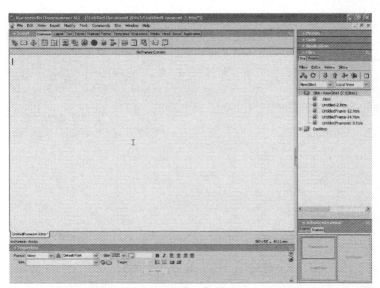

Fig.9.26 The screen with the NoFrames Content selected. Text, etc., is added in the usual way

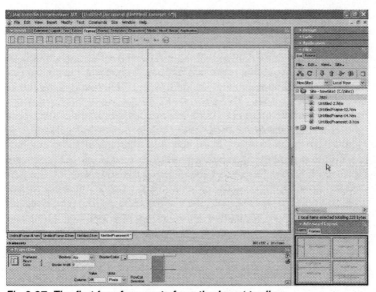

Fig.9.27 The first four framesets from the Insert toolbar

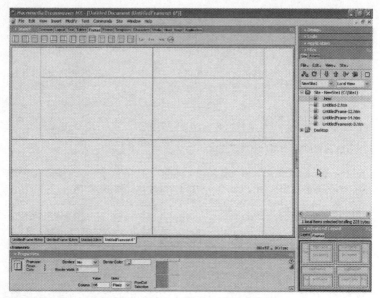

Fig.9.28 The last four framesets of the Insert toolbar

Keep it simple

It is easy to get carried away with frames, probably ending up with an over-complex layout that users find baffling. In general it is best to use the simplest arrangement that will do the job. This reduces the risk of errors when building the site, and should make matters more straightforward for users of the site. For most purposes the preset frame arrangements available from the Insert palette are all that is needed. In Figure 9.27 the screen has been split into quarters, with the first four preset frame arrangements shown in the four sections of the screen. Figure 9.28 follows the same basic scheme of things with the last four preset frame arrangements. These are probably the eight preset arrangements that are the most useful. Do not forget that the borders of these framesets are adjustable in the normal way, and that a frameset can be nested within another frameset.

Tables

Rows and columns

Tables were originally introduced into HTML as a means of displaying things like scientific and financial data in tabular form. However, the use of HTML tables has expanded beyond basic functions such as these, and tables can be used for aligning images and other tasks. Therefore, even though tables may seem to be irrelevant to the types of web site you will be producing, it is as well to learn something about them. They might actually be very useful to you if used in the right way. In fact you will probably use them a great deal.

Producing a table is a two or three stage process. First the basic parameters for the table are set and it is added to the document. Where necessary, the table is then "fine tuned" to get it exactly as required. Once any modifications have been completed the data or other content for the table is added.

In order to add a table to a document, go to the Insert menu and select the Table option. Alternatively, select the Tables section of the Insert palette and then operate the Insert Table button (the button at the left end of the palette). Either way, the Insert Table window of Figure 10.1 will appear. The first thing to decide is number of rows and columns in the table. In the example of Figure 10.2, there are

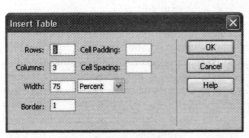

Fig.10.1 The Insert Table dialogue box

five columns and seven rows. The boxes in a table are called cells, and there are some 35 of them in this case. It is not essential to carefully plan

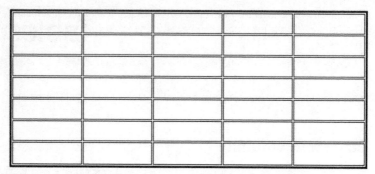

Fig.10.2 A table structure having five columns by seven rows

the table so that it is the perfect size right from the start. Once a table has been inserted into a document it can be freely edited using the Properties Inspector. It can also be resized using the handle dragging method, and the cell "walls" can also be dragged into new positions. It obviously helps if you can make an intelligent guess about a suitable size for the table, but the table can evolve if you get things wrong or the requirements change.

Properties Inspector

For some initial experiments with a table, increase the row and column settings to produce a slightly larger table and then operate the OK button to insert the table into the current document. Next the table is selected so that it can be manipulated using the Properties Inspector. To select

Fig.10.3 The Properties Inspector with a table selected

the table, position the cursor over the table's outer border or a cell wall so that the cursor changes to one consisting of a cross with arrowheads at the end of each line. Left-clicking with this cursor present will select the table. Incidentally, the cursor will not give the desired change if it is positioned over the left or top borderlines of the table. With the table selected the Properties Inspector should then look something like Figure 10.3.

To select a single cell of a table it is merely necessary to left-click within the cell. You can select an entire row by positioning the cursor over the left-hand borderline for the row, and the cursor will then change to a black arrow pointing to the right. Left-clicking with this cursor showing

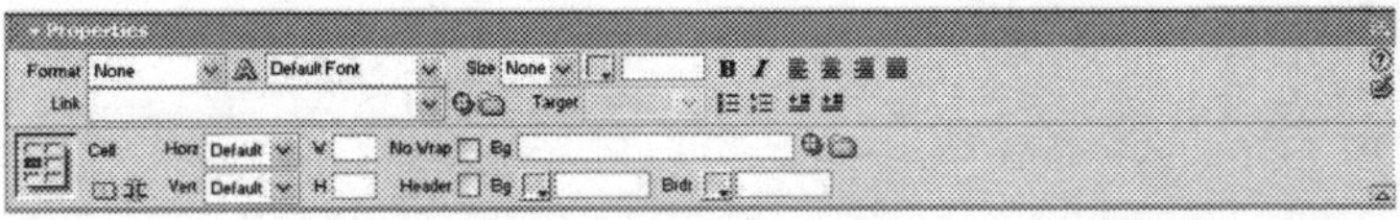

Fig.10.4 The Properties Inspector with a single cell selected

will select the row of cells. Similarly, to select a complete column, position the cursor over the top borderline for the row so that the cursor changes to a black arrow pointing downward. Left-clicking will then select the complete column of cells. With a single cell selected the Properties Inspector looks like Figure 10.4. It looks much the same with a row selected, but a row of cells is shown in black on the Apply button. With a column selected, a column of cells is shown in black on the Apply button.

When it is applied to tables, many aspects of the Properties Inspector are the same as when it is used with text and (or) images. Some of the other parameters are fairly obvious and do not merit an explanation here. A few are worthy of some amplification though. As already pointed out, you can select the table and then use the three handles to resize it, just like resizing an image. It is also possible to drag the wall for an entire column or row of cells. If you try this you may soon end up with a table that has a lot of uneven cell spacing. This may be what you require, but where things get out of hand the Clear Row Heights and Clear Column Widths buttons can be used to restore uniformity. The table will probably shrink somewhat when either of these is used, but it can be dragged back to a more suitable size.

The Properties Inspector enables a specific height and width to be set for the table as a whole, or for a selected row or column. If a height is set for a single cell, that height will be used for all the cells in the same row. Similarly, the width setting for a single cell will be used for all the cells in the same column. By default the sizes are set in pixels, but a percentage

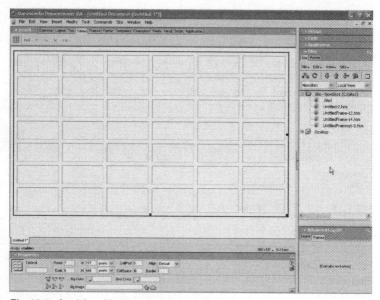

Fig.10.5 A table with the spacing set at 10

option is available. Percent in this case means so many percent of the browser window at its initial size. Incidentally, the table will not be resized if the browser's window is resized.

Padding and spacing

The cell padding parameter in the table version of the Properties Inspector enables the contents of the cell to be kept away from the cell outline. This is rather like the margin setting for a frame. The spacing parameter controls the amount of space between the pairs of lines used for the cell walls. The default spacing setting is 2. Figure 10.5 shows a table with the value raised to 10.

Merging and splitting

Merging two or more cells into one large cell is very straightforward. First select the cells you wish to merge by holding down the Control or Command key and left-clicking on the cells. Alternatively, drag the cursor

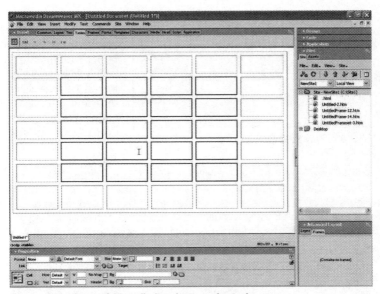

Fig.10.6 A block of 20 cells has been selected

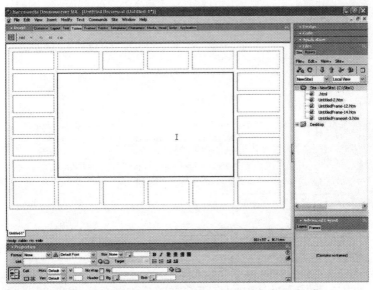

Fig.10.7 Here the cells have been merged into one large cell

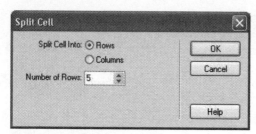

across the cells you wish to select. The selected cells will then appear highlighted, as in Figure 10.6. To merge the cells either operate the cell-merging button in the Properties Inspector (just to the right of the Apply button), or

Fig.10.8 The Split Cell window

select Table from the Modify menu, followed by the Merge Cells option from the submenu. The cells will then be merged, as in the example of Figure 10.7. A complete row or column can be merged in this way if desired. The selected cells must form a rectangle, and cell merging will not work with "T" shaped arrangements, "L" shaped arrangements, etc.

A cell can be split by selecting it and then choosing Table from the Modify menu, and Split Cell from the submenu. This produces the window of

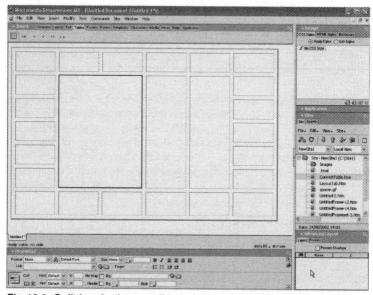

Fig.10.9 Splitting the large cell into three columns has not provided the desired result as one column is wider than the others

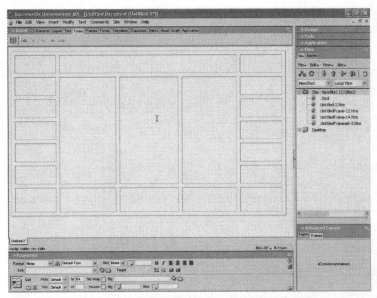

*Fig.10.10 Some manual editing and a few compromises have
produced an acceptable result*

Figure 10.8. Select rows or columns as appropriate, and set the number
of rows or columns required. Then operate the OK button and the cell
will be split. This command does not always provide the exact effect
you require. In the example of Figure 10.9 the splitting of the large centre
cell into three columns has resulted in two narrow cells and one wide
one. However, a little dragging of the cell walls will usually set things
exactly as required, but in some case it will be necessary to edit additional
cells in order to get things just right. The table structure imposes some
limitations on the layout, so you may have to compromise. Figure 10.10
shows the table adjusted to give the final arrangement that I required.

Deleting and inserting

Deleting a row or column is very easy. Simply select a cell in the row or
column you wish to remove, and then select Table from the Modify menu,
followed by Delete Row or Delete Column from the submenu that appears.
A complete table can be removed by first selecting it and choosing Cut
from the Edit menu. Selecting the table and pressing the Delete key
also removes it.

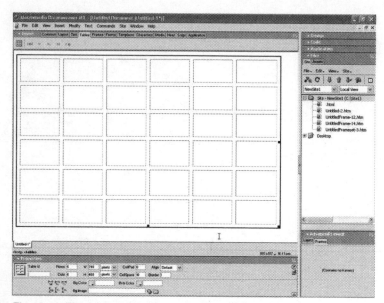

Fig.10.11 The table before the new column was added

To add a column, place the cursor in the column you wish to duplicate, select Table from the Modify menu, and the select Insert Column from the submenu. Figure 10.11 and 10.12 show "before and after" versions of a table that has been given an extra column. The table has not been made larger to accommodate the additional column. Instead, the existing columns have been reduced in size to make way for the new column. If this is not what is required, the table can of course be resized. A row can be added using the same basic method. Place the cursor in the row that must be duplicated and then select Insert Row from the Table submenu.

It is possible to add more than one row or column at once. Go to the Modify menu, select Table, and then select Insert Rows or Columns from the submenu. This produces the window of Figure 10.13. Use the two radio buttons at the top to select rows or columns, set the number to be added, and then use the lower radio buttons to choose where on the table they will be added. Operate the OK button and the new rows or columns will be added to the table. Do not forget that the number of columns and rows in a simple table can be altered by editing the Row and Column figures in the Properties Inspector. The complete frame must be selected in order to do this, and not just a cell or group of cells.

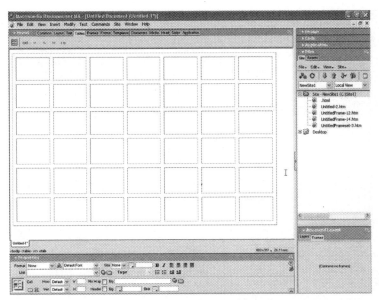

Fig.10.12 The "after" version of the table, with another column added

Header cell

Tables often have a single large cell to take a label that states exactly what the table is for. This cell is usually at the top, but it can be placed elsewhere if desired. A cell of this type is called a "header" cell. Where appropriate, merge several cells to

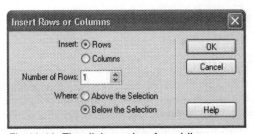

Fig.10.13 The dialogue box for adding multiple rows or columns

produce a single cell of adequate size to take the legend that will be used in the cell. To designate the cell as a header type, left-click in it and then tick the Header checkbox in the expanded version of the Properties Inspector. Any text added into the header cell will be displayed in bold type and will have centre alignment (Figure 10.14). The exact way in

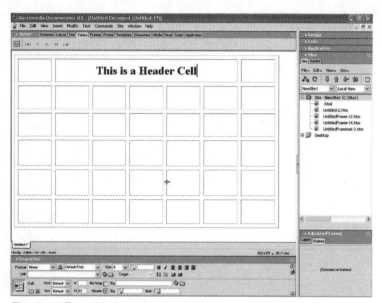

Fig.10.14   Tex added to a header cell has centre alignment and is in bold type

which the text is displayed in a browser will vary somewhat from one browser to another, but it will normally be centred and fairly prominent.

No Wrap

With one or several cells selected, the Properties Inspector has a No Wrap checkbox. By default this is left unchecked, and text entered into the cell then has the usual word-wrap function, like text typed into a document in the normal manner. With the No Wrap option selected, text is not wrapped at all, and is all placed on one line unless it contains any carriage returns. Figure 10.15 shows some text added to two cells of a table. The text in the top left-hand cell has been added with the No Wrap option enabled, and the text is all on one line. This cell, and the others in its column, has automatically widened to accommodate the text. The text in the cell below was added without the No Wrap option selected, and the text has wrapped to fit the existing width of the cell. Because there is more than one line of text the height of the cell, and the others in its row, has been automatically increased to accommodate the extra lines.

This Is The Header Cell		
This cell uses the No Wrap Option		
This cell does not use the No Wrap option so word wrapping has been used		

Fig.10.15 Cells that do and do not use the No Wrap option

This Is The Header Cell		
This cell uses the No Wrap Option		
This cell does not use the No Wrap option so word wrapping has been used		

Fig.10.16 Changing the No Wrap option can cause changes to any text in the cell

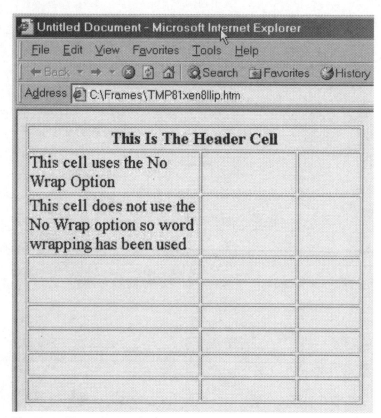

Fig.10.17 The table looks much the same when it is viewed in a browser

The No Wrap setting can be altered after a cell has been given some content. Simply select the cell or cells you wish to change and then alter the Word Wrap setting in the Properties Inspector. This may cause some changes to the cell and the existing arrangement of text. In Figure 10.16 the table used in the previous example has had the No Wrap option removed from the top left-hand cell, which has resulted in a slight narrowing of that column. As a result of this, the line of text in the cell has word-wrapped onto the next line. The Dreamweaver WYSIWYG design view does a good job of showing things as they will look when viewed using a browser, but as always, results should always be checked using a browser or two. In this case (Figure 10.17) there is a slight

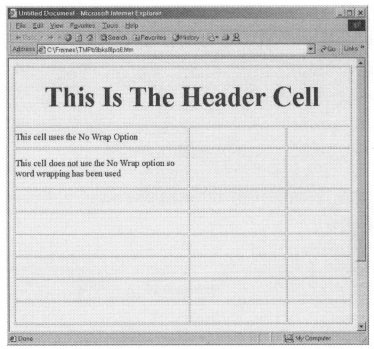

Fig.10.18 Here the table has been expanded to fill the page

difference in the upper cell as viewed using Internet Explorer, but nothing too drastic has happened.

Full-size tables

Tables can be a small part of the page or they can be set at the full-page width and used to hold all the contents of a page. Remember that cells can be as large as you require, and that they can contain images and other objects in addition to text. Laying out a number of images neatly on a page is a common use of tables. In order to use a table as a full page, select the table and then set the width to 100 percent in the Properties Inspector. To make sure that the table also fills browser windows vertically, repeat this process with the height setting. Figure 10.18 shows the same table as the one shown in Figure 10.16, but it has

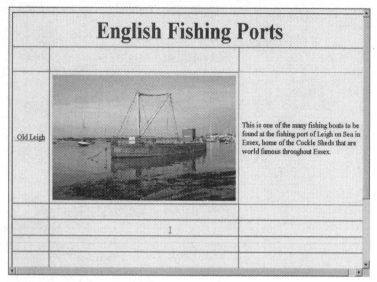

Fig.10.19 A table used to position an image

been stretched to fill the browser window. The text in the header cell has also been enlarged.

Adding content

Adding, text, images, etc., to a cell in a table is much like adding the same objects straight onto the page. Once in a cell, the content can be edited in the usual fashion as well. By dragging on its cell borders an image can be positioned at the desired point on the page, with text being added around it (Figure 10.19). It is not possible to switch off the cell borders, but making them the same colour as the background, as in Figure 10.20 can effectively eliminate them. The title at the top of the page is in a header cell, and its borders are still visible, but none of the other borderlines are visible. Remember that the border colour for each cell can be set independently. Select the cell and then change its border colour using the Properties Inspector. Figure 10.21 shows three cells with the borders made visible, and the others (apart from the header cell) hidden from view.

Fig.10.20 The page as it appears in a browser

Incidentally, if you use the table method to lay out a page, this does not prevent a "proper" table being used on that page. It is possible to have a table in a table cell. Simply place the cursor in the cell where the table is required. Then select Table from the Insert menu, put the appropriate settings in the Insert Table window, and operate the OK button. The table will then appear in the selected cell, as in Figure 10.22. It seems to be possible to have a table within a table, within a table, although this probably has limited practical applications.

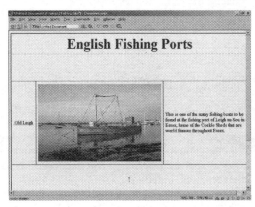

Fig.10.21 The borders can be shown or hidden

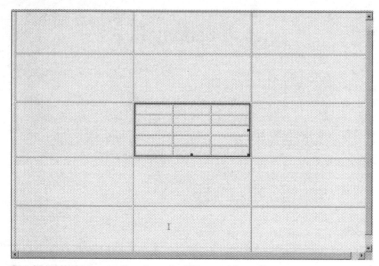

Fig.10.22 A table can be placed within a table cell

Layout view

The table method of laying out pages is better suited to some types of page than it is to others. Within reason, practically any layout could probably be produced using this method, but with many layouts a lot of splitting, merging, and other editing is needed to produce the required layout. Dreamweaver MX has an alternative method of producing table layouts that makes life a lot easier when dealing with arrangements that are not easily achieved using conventional tables. This feature is not available prior to version four of Dreamweaver incidentally. In order to use layout tables Dreamweaver must have the Design view displayed. If necessary, select Design View from the View menu before trying to produce this type of table.

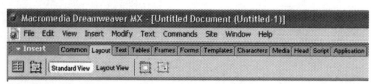

Fig.10.23 The Layout section of the Insert toolbar

Next select the layout tab of the Insert palette, which will then look like Figure 10.23. The two large buttons enable Dreamweaver to be switched between the Standard and Layout modes. As one would expect, the default is Standard mode. You must therefore start by using the Layout button to switch to the Layout mode. The message box of Figure 10.24 will probably appear,

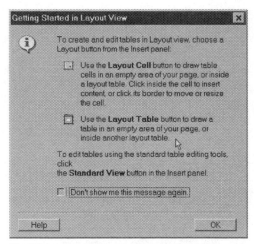

Fig.10.24 This message box explains the differences between the two modes

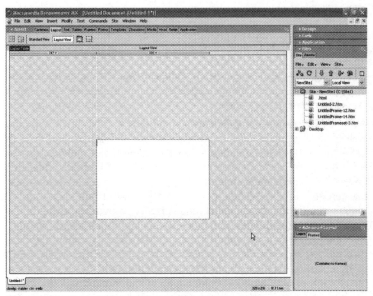

Fig.10.25 A layout table and cell added to the page

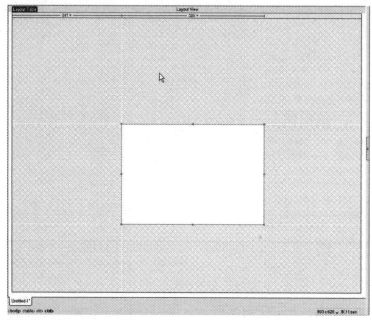

Fig.10.26 A layout cell can be resized using the eight handles

explaining the two options available in this mode. The two buttons at the right end of the Insert palette are used to switch between drawing a layout table and a layout cell.

What makes the Layout view different to the Standard view? With the Layout view you can draw cells straight onto the screen and then fill them with text, images, tables, or whatever. A layout table is used to hold the layout cells. To experiment with layout cells, operate the Draw Layout Cell button in the Objects palette, and draw a cell somewhere on the screen. To draw a cell, position the pointer at one corner of the required cell, hold down the left mouse button, move the pointer to the opposite corner of the cell, and then release the mouse button. In other words a rectangle is dragged onto the screen, and you should end up with something like Figure 10.25. A layout table has been made automatically, and the new cell has been added to it. If you require the layout table to occupy less than the full page, operate the Draw Layout Table button and draw the table outline before adding layout cells to the screen.

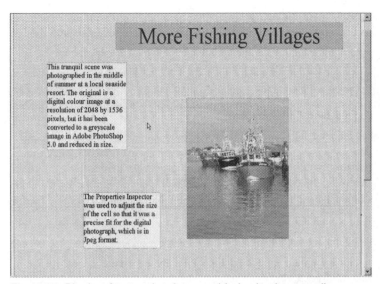

Fig.10.27 Blocks of text and an image added using layout cells

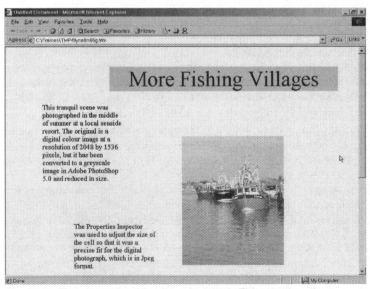

*Fig.10.28 The page viewed using a browser. This matches the
Dreamweaver WYSIWYG display quite accurately*

To add more cells, operate the Draw Layout Cell button and draw another cell, operate the button and draw a third cell, and so on until all the required cells have been added to the table. Dragging one of its borders to a new position will move the entire cell to a new location. This does not resize the cell, but instead moves the whole thing to a new position. To resize a cell, first left-click on its outline to select it. This produces eight handles on the outline (Figure 10.26), and these can be dragged to resize the cell.

Figure 10.27 shows three layout cells added to the screen with some dummy content in each cell. The layout has been deliberately made a bit haphazard to emphasise the point that with this method you can easily add cells that do not conform to a regular table structure. Figure 10.28 shows the page viewed using Internet Explorer 5.5, and it matches the Dreamweaver layout very accurately. The cell guide markers are not shown in the Internet Explorer version of course, but in other respects everything is very much where and as it should be.

Autostretch

The Properties Inspector can be used to examine and control some settings of a layout cell. With the Properties Inspector on the screen, left-click on the outline of the layout cell and the Properties Inspector should then look like Figure 10.29. Most of this is the same as for an ordinary table cell, but there is one additional property in the form of an Autostretch facility. To use the Properties Inspector for the layout table, left-click on a blank area of the table or on its outline to select it. The Properties Inspector should then look something like Figure 10.30. Again this is all fairly straightforward apart from the Autostretch option.

Normally the width parameter is set as a specific number, such as 250 pixels. With Autostretch the width automatically resizes to suit the size of the window in which it is displayed. The usual width figure in the

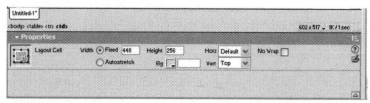

Fig.10.29 The Properties Inspector when used with a layout cell

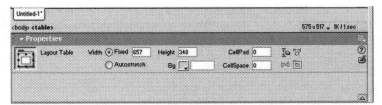

Fig.10.30 The Properties Inspector when used with a layout table

appropriate box of the Properties Inspector is then blanked out. All the cells in the same column will be affected by selecting the Autostretch option, and only one column per page can use this facility. If you set a column to Autostretch operation, any column that is already in this mode will be switched back to normal fixed width operation.

A typical use of Autostretch would be with a page having a menu bar down the left-hand side of the screen and the main content on the right. The menu cell would be set at a fixed width in pixels to ensure that it always had sufficient space to display the menu correctly. The right-hand cell would be Autostretched so that it made full use of whatever window space was left. A real-world layout would be probably be much more complex than this, with other elements that needed to be at a fixed size or automatically adjust to suit the window. However, this very basic example demonstrates the difference between the two types of sizing.

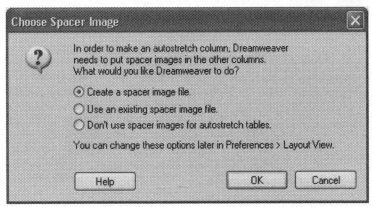

Fig.10.31 This window may appear when the Autostretch option is selected

When the Autostretch option is selected for the first time in a site, the window of Figure 10.31 will appear. The radio buttons offer these three options:

Create a spacer image file

Empty cells can have a tendency to collapse rather than retaining their set size. The standard ploy to avoid this is to fill such cells with a small GIF image that is transparent. Because of the image's transparent property the cell looks exactly the same as if it were empty. The image is stretched to fill the cell so that it prevents it from shrinking when the page is viewed using a browser. Incidentally, this method is often used with troublesome cells in conventional tables. Non-breaking spaces are sometimes used as a simple if less neat alternative.

Use an existing spacer image file

This option can be used if there is already a suitable spacer image file for Dreamweaver to use.

Don't use spacer images for Autostretch tables

With this option no spacer image is used. A warning message will be produced, explaining that without the spacer image the cells may collapse.

The easy and safe option is to accept the default setting, which will get Dreamweaver to create and use a spacer file. When the file browser appears, accept the default file name and operate the OK button.

To try out the Autostretch option, make a page having a narrow layout cell on the left and a wider cell on the right. Add some words to form a dummy menu in the left-hand cell. One way to set the width of the narrow cell is to select it and then edit the value in the Properties Inspector. A little trial and error should soon locate a figure that gives a suitable width. The alternative is to set a ridiculously low value, which will produce an error message stating that the selected width is too narrow. Operate the OK button and Dreamweaver will then substitute

Fig.10.32 A cell can be made to Autostretch

the narrowest width setting that will accommodate the contents of the cell. This will not always give the desired result, but it usually works well with something simple like a menu.

The right-hand cell can be set to Autostretch mode via the Properties Inspector, or via the pop-up column menu. In order to bring up this menu, left-click on the width figure at the top of the

Fig.10.33 No text is lost off the right-hand side of the window

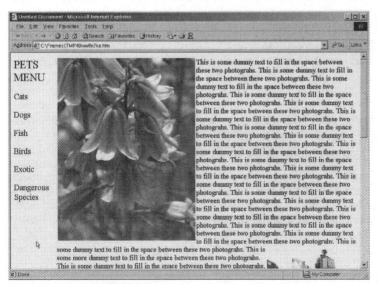

Fig.10.34 The text has reformatted to suit the wider window

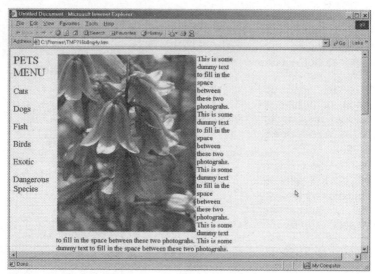

Fig.10.35   The effect of switching off the Autostretch option is clearly apparent here

right-hand column (Figure 10.32). Select the Make Column Autostretch option. The width figure at the top of the column should change to a wavy line to indicate that the Autostretch option is in operation.

Now add some dummy content into the right-hand cell and save the document. Use the browser preview facility to view the page, and try varying the width of the window. Compare the dummy page of Figure 10.33 with the wider version shown in Figure 10.34. In Figure 10.33 there is no material that can not be seen because it is beyond the right-hand limit of the window. Similarly, in Figure 10.34 there is no empty space down the right-hand side of the window. As the window is made wider or narrower, the content of the Autostretched cell is reformatted to suit the new shape. Compare Figure 10.35, where the Autostretch option has been switched off, with Figure 10.34. The narrow and fixed page width is wasting screen space in Figure 10.35, but not in Figure 10.34 where the Autostretch facility is in use. The Autostretch option is not appropriate to all types of material, and in some cases the reformatting could produce some rather poor results, with the automatic reformatting spoiling a carefully prepared layout. It generally works well with a cell that only contains text, or is predominantly filled with text.

Tables to layers

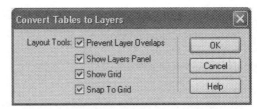

Using layers is covered in the next chapter, so it is a subject we will not consider in detail here. Suffice it to say

Fig.10.36 The Table to Layers dialogue box

that layers enable precise placement of objects within a page, but they do not work with old versions of browser programs. Layers require Netscape 4 or Internet Explorer 4, or later versions of either. Presumably most web users now use suitable browser programs. Dreamweaver can convert a normal table into a group of layers, and the first step is to select the table. Then select Convert from the Modify menu, and Tables To Layers from the submenu that appears. This should produce the window of Figure 10.36, offering four options via checkboxes. If you wish to make some preliminary experiments with layers, accept the default settings and operate the OK button to convert the table to layers.

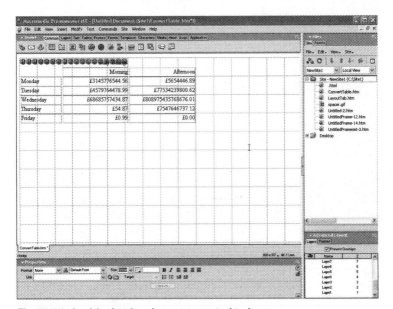

Fig.10.37 A table that has been converted to layers

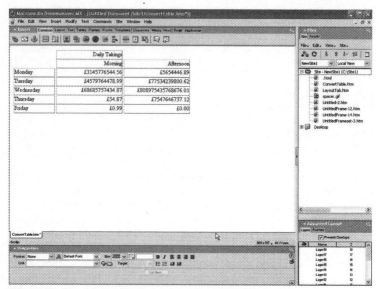

Fig.10.38 The table with invisible elements switched off

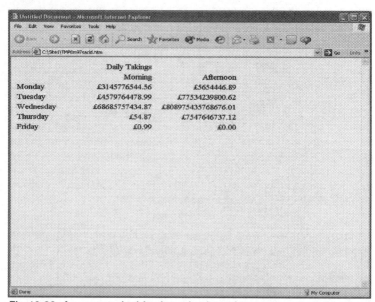

Fig.10.39 A converted table viewed using a browser

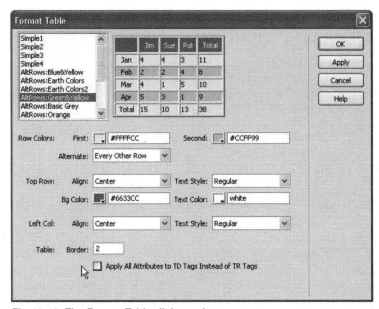

Fig.10.40 The Format Table dialogue box

You should end up with something that does not look too far removed from the original table. There will be a grid of lines on the screen and some other marks (Figure 10.37). The grid can be toggled off by going to the View menu and selecting Grid, and then choosing Show Grid from the submenu. The grid lines are only an aid to laying out pages anyway, and they will not appear when the page is viewed using a browser. The marks along the top left-hand section of the table can be switched off by first selecting Preferences from the Edit menu, and then selecting Invisible Elements from the menu. Then remove the tick in the Anchor Points for Layers checkbox. The screen should then look much cleaner (Figure 10.38), and should little different to the non-converted version.

The Layers window will be activated, and it will give details of the new layers generated by the conversion process. If you try viewing a converted table using a suitable browser you should find that it accurately matches the version seem in Dreamweaver's design view (Figure 10.39).

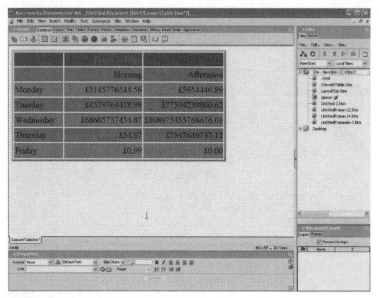

Fig.10.41 A table based on a preset format

Preset format

There are a number of preset formats that can be applied to tables, and these control things like colours, alignment, and the cell borders. The preset formats enable a data table to be almost instantly formatted to give attractive and readable results. To format a table, start by placing the text cursor somewhere within the table and then select the Format Table option from the Commands menu. This brings up a window like the one in Figure 10.40. The preset formats are listed in the menu at the top left-hand corner of the window, and the dummy table to the right of this shows the colour scheme, etc., for the formatted table. Operate the Apply button to apply the format to your table so that you can see exactly what it will look like in the design view. You are not forced to accept the preset values, and a number of parameters can be edited in the lower section of the window. Figure 10.41 shows a table produced using a preset format, edited to enlarge the border width but otherwise unchanged.

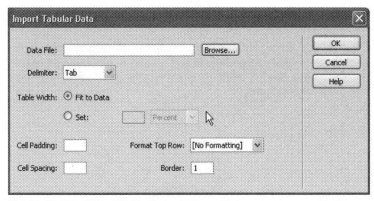

Fig.10.42 The Import Table Data dialogue box

Import/export

If you already have the data for a table it will probably be possible to import it into Dreamweaver rather than having to type it all in again. In order to bring the data into Dreamweaver it must be saved in text format from the spreadsheet or other program used to originate the data. To import data select the table, go to the File menu and then select Import. Next select Import Tabular Data from the submenu, and the dialogue box of

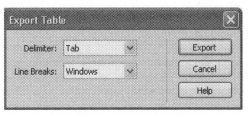

Fig.10.43 The Export Table dialogue box

Figure 10.42 will appear. The name of the data file is typed into the Data File text box, or the file can be selected using the Browse button and the file browser. The delimiter must be specified, and this will often be a tab character, but an alternative can be selected.

To export data select the table containing the data, and then go to the File menu and select the Export option. Next select the Export Table option from the submenu which will produce the dialogue box of Figure 10.43. If necessary, alter the delimiter, and make sure that the correct operating system is chosen in the lower menu. Operating the Export button will bring up the usual file browser, which is used to name the new file and save it in the appropriate folder.

Being realistic about matters, it will probably take some experimentation in order to get the import and export functions working as desired. However, with a little trial and error this sort of thing can usually be made to perform satisfactorily.

Layers

Adding a layer

Layers enable the precise placement of objects on a web page without the need for complex tables. One slight problem with layers is that older browsers cannot handle them. With more and more people switching to modern browsers this is a diminishing problem, but provided one or two restrictions are met, Dreamweaver can convert layers into tables if required.

Adding a layer is very simple, and one method is to select Layer from the Insert menu. This will insert a box to represent the new layer, and it will be added at the current cursor position. For most purposes the better way of adding a layer is to operate the Draw Layer button in the Common section of the Insert palette. This is the fifth button from the left end. You can then drag a rectangle onto the design view where the new layer is required (Figure 11.1). Note that it is only possible to draw layers in standard view, and that this facility is disabled in layout view.

The newly added layer can be moved around by dragging the tab in the top left-hand corner (when the layer is selected), or by dragging anywhere on the layer's outline. It is best to use the tab, as otherwise it is very easy to accidentally select the contents of a layer rather than the layer itself. The crossed-arrows pointer will appear when the layer can be dragged. Left-clicking when this pointer is present selects the layer. When a layer is created, an invisible element marker is added to the page. Unless this type of marker is switched off, you can hardly miss the arrival of this yellow marker on the screen. Left-clicking the marker is another way of selecting the layer.

Once selected, eight handles appear on the layer's outline (Figure 11.2). These can be dragged to resize the layer. The pointer changes to a single line with arrowheads at each end when it is correctly in position over one of the handles. If they are not already active, launch the Layers and Properties windows. The Properties window is launched by selecting Properties from the Window menu. To bring up the Layers window first

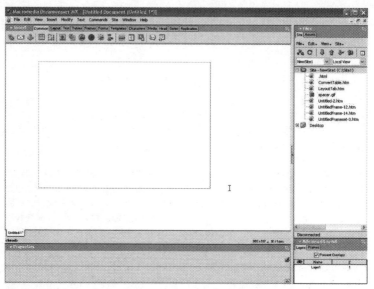

Fig.11.1 A layer drawn onto the screen via the Insert toolbar

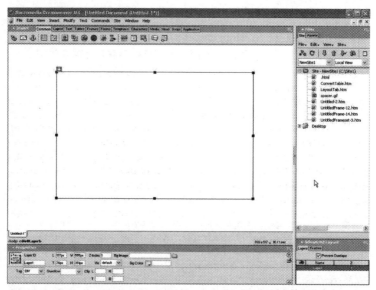

Fig.11.2 Eight handles appear on the layer when it is selected

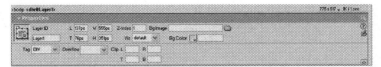

Fig.11.3 The Properties Inspector with a layer selected

select Others from the Window menu, and then left-click Layers in the submenu. Figure 11.3 shows the Properties window with a layer selected.

The Layers window (Figure 11.4) will show the selected layer highlighted. In this case there is only one layer, so this is the only one shown. By default the layers are called "Layer1", "Layer2", etc., but you can rename a layer by double-clicking on its name in the Layers window and then editing the text.

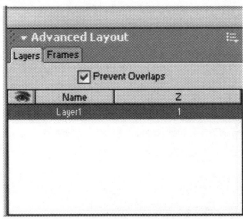

Fig.11.4 The selected layer is highlighted in the Layers window

Well stacked

The right-hand column in the window is labelled "Z", and with only one layer there will only be a "1" in this column. When using tables it is not possible to have overlaps, but layers live up to their name and they can be stacked one on top of the other. Layers have X and Y dimensions that determine their size, and a Z dimension that gives their position in the stack. The layer having a Z value of 1 is the bottom layer, the one having a Z value of 2 is the next layer up, and so on. The top layer is the one having the highest Z index value.

If you are experienced with graphics programs you should already be familiar with layers in one guise or another, but do not worry if you have not encountered them before. The concept is very easy to grasp. Try drawing some more layers on to the screen, and see if you can get them

Fig.11.5 Layers live up to their name and can overlap

to overlap. This will not be possible unless the tick is removed from the Prevent Overlaps checkbox in the Layers window. If you will need to convert layers to tables it is advisable to leave this box ticked. Tables can not accommodate overlaps, so layers can only be converted to tables if there are no overlaps present.

Unless overlapping layers are used, the Z value is not usually of great importance. If you intend to stack layers then it is clearly of great importance, and the final appearance of the page can be changed radically by altering the Z values. Figures 11.5 and 11.6 show the same page but with the Z values of the two layers first set one way around and then reversed. One way of altering the Z values is to drag the name of a layer up or down in the Layers window. The layers are always listed with the highest number at the top, going in reverse order down to the lowest number at the bottom of the list. This is logical, since the one having the highest value is the top layer when the page is viewed using a browser. You may get some strange renumbering if you use this method of manipulating Z values. You may find that you end up with something like values of 2 to 5 instead of 1 to 4. This does not really matter, but use the alternative method or renumbering if you would prefer to avoid this, or would like to correct it.

Fig.11.6 Here the Z index values of the two photographs have been swapped

The alternative method is to edit the Z index value in the Properties Inspector, having selected the layer first (Figure 11.7). You can also double-click on a Z value in the Layers window and then edit the value. It has to be pointed out that a selected layer and its contents will be shown on top of any other layers in the design view. However, this does not affect the way the layers will be displayed in a browser. The one having the highest Z value will always be on top, the next highest will be one lower in the stack, and so on. One slight oddity is that you can give two or more layers the same Z value. If the numbering is left to Dreamweaver it will give each layer its own Z value, but you can edit the

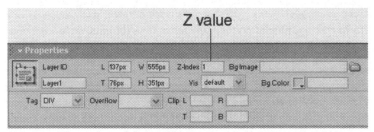

Fig.11.7 The Z value can be edited in the Properties Inspector

Fig.11.8 One layer can exist totally inside another

values so that some or all are the same. This is perfectly valid in HTML code. If two layers have the same Z index value, the one that appears first in the HTML code has precedence, but it is better to make sure that stacked layers have unique Z values.

Nested layers

There is no restriction that says one layer can not exist totally within another layer. In the example of Figure 11.8 the photograph is in the original layer. The caption was placed into a second layer that was drawn outside the first one. The required background colour was set using the Properties Inspector and then the caption layer was dragged into position. Of course, the Prevent Overlaps checkbox in the Layers window must not be ticked when doing this type of thing.

It is also possible to have layers within layers, or nested layers as they are termed. When the parent layer is moved, the child layer moves with

it. This does not happen if you
simply position one layer over
another, as in the example of
Figure 11.8. In order to nest
existing layers go to the Layers
window, and then drag the name
of the child layer over the name
of the parent layer while holding
down the Control key. Figures
11.9 and 11.10 show the Layers
window before and after an
operation of this type. In Figure
11,10 the child layer is indented
to make it clear that it is a child of
the parent layer above. When
nesting layers some shifting of
their positions may occur, but this
can be corrected by dragging
them back into suitable positions.
When using layers it can be
difficult to select the one that is
required. The most reliable
method is to select the required
layer by left-clicking on its name
in the Layers window. A layer can
be un-nested by dragging its
name away from the parent name
in the Layers window.

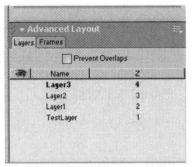

*Fig.11.9 The initial version of the
Layers window*

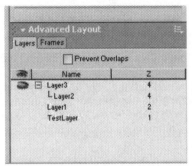

*Fig.11.10 The Layers window with
two nested layers*

Visibility

When using large numbers of layers it can sometimes be easier to work
with one or more of the layers switched off. This renders the layer and all
its contents invisible in the Dreamweaver design view. The setting used
in the first column of the Layers window controls the visibility of layers.
There are three options available, and all three are shown in Figure 11.11.
With the closed eye icon the relevant layer is switched off, and with the
open eye icon it is switched on. With neither present the layer is switched
on or off depending on the visibility setting of the parent layer. If there is
no parent layer, the document itself becomes the effective parent. Since
the document is always visible, with no parent layer this setting is
effectively the same as having the layer switched on. Repeatedly left-

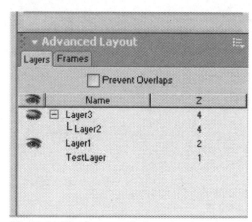

Fig.11.11   The Layers window showing the three visibility options

clicking in the visibility column cycles through the three settings. To select the one that is required just keep left-clicking until it appears.

It is important to note that the visibility setting does not only affect the way a layer is displayed in Dreamweaver's design view. If a layer is switched off in the Layers window, it will not appear when the page is viewed using a browser. In Figure 11.12 the caption layer is still present, but it is still switched off. Consequently, it has failed to appear when the page is viewed using a browser. If you switch any layers off, it is clearly essential to switch them back on again before uploading the page to the server. Incidentally, left-clicking on the eye icon at the head of the visibility column will switch on all the layers.

Fig.11.12   The caption layer is still present but it has been switched off

Content

Content is added to a layer in much the same way as it is added direct to a page or into a table cell, etc. Most types of content are permissible, including text, images, tables, and forms. The one major exception is that frames are not permitted within a layer. To add content

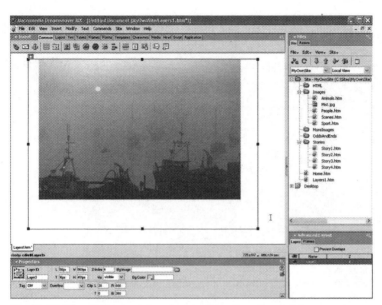

Fig.11.13 The photograph has been clipped on three sides

to a layer, start by left-clicking within its perimeter to place the text cursor within the layer, and then add text, images, or whatever in the usual fashion.

Layer properties

Some of the parameters in the layers version of the Properties Inspector are straightforward, but a few require some explanation. The four Clip settings enable a clipping area to be defined. If you try adding some content to a layer you will soon notice that the size you set initially is regarded as no more than a starting point, with the layer outlines expanding to fit whatever you put in them. In this respect they are like cells in a table, but unlike cells a clipping area can be set. In other words, you do not have to display (say) a complete image even though the layer expands to accommodate the image. An image can be cropped to the required size using a suitable graphics program, or the clipping area can be used to provide the same effect.

Fig.11.14 When viewed in a browser there is nothing to indicate that the photograph has been clipped

The figures used in the Clip boxes control the amount you wish to clip, and the unit of measurement is pixels. However, if you need to remove a 50 pixel-wide strip from the bottom of an image it is no use specifying a B figure of 50. The clipping system operates in a slightly less than obvious fashion with measurements that are relative the top left-hand corner of the layer. In the example of Figure 11.13, nothing had to be clipped from the top of the photograph, so a T value of 0 was used. If 20 pixels had to be removed, then a figure of 20 would have been used. Matters are equally simple with the clipping on the left-hand side. It was necessary to clip 30 pixels, so an L value of 30 was used.

The R setting is not an amount in from the right-hand side, but is instead the distance from the left-hand side of the layer to the right-hand edge of the visible picture area. A value of 600 was found to give the desired effect, with about 60 pixels being clipped from the right-hand side of the picture. Similarly, the B value does not directly set the amount that is clipped from the bottom of the photograph. It sets the depth of the visible part of the photograph, but also includes any clipped section along the top. In this example a setting of 380 gave the desired effect. It results in about 100 pixels being clipped at the bottom of the picture. The layer remains the same size incidentally, and clipping the picture governs how much of it is visible, not the size of the layer. The outline of the layer is

Fig.11.15 The non-clipped photograph

not visible when the page is viewed in a browser (Figure 11.14), and all the viewer sees is the non-clipped part of the image. For comparison purposes, Figure 11.15 shows the non-clipped version of the photograph.

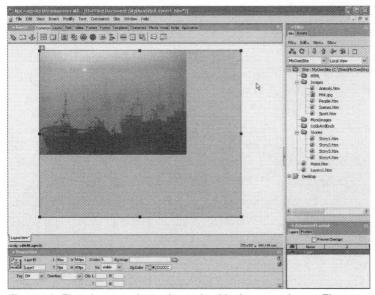

Fig.11.16 The photograph can be resized in the normal way. The layer's background colour has also been changed

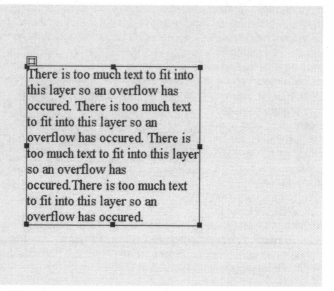

Fig.11.17 The test layer as it appears in Dreamweaver's design view

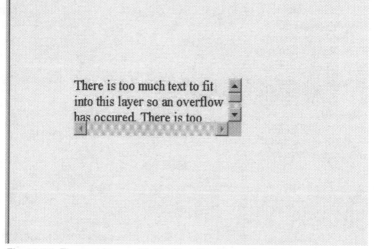

Fig.11.18 The test layer with the Scroll option selected

If you need to make an image smaller without any clipping, it is just a matter of selecting the image and resizing it in the normal way. This has been done in Figure 11.16. Also, the Bg Color button in the Properties Inspector has been used to add a darker background to the layer. As one would expect, this background is visible in the unoccupied part of the layer along the bottom and on the right-hand side. The background is not visible elsewhere because it is effectively covered by the image.

Size and position

The L (left) and T (top) parameters set the position of the layer relative to the top left-hand corner of the page. In the case of a nested layer, these values set the position relative to the top left-hand corner of the parent layer. The W (width) and H (height) values set the width and height of the layer. In many cases it is easier to set these by moving and resizing the layer onscreen, but the ability to set these values in the Properties Inspector can be useful when very precise sizing and positioning is required.

Overflow

The overflow setting governs how excess content will be treated if the layer is too small to display the entire contents simultaneously. When content is added to a layer it expands to suit, but the dimensions of the layer can be reduced using the Properties Inspector. In Figure 11.17 the height of the layer has been reduced, but this produces no visible effect. However, when the page is

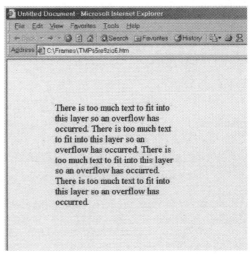

Fig.11.19 The test layer using the Visible setting

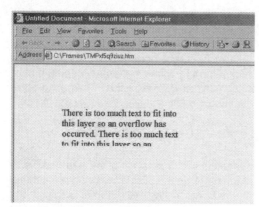

Fig.11.20 The Hidden setting can result in some content being inaccessible

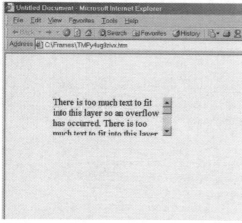

Fig.11.21 With the Auto settings, scrollbars are only used if they are needed

viewed using a browser (Figure 11.18) the reduced height of the layer is apparent. In this example the Scroll option has been selected from the Overflow menu in the Properties Inspector, and scrollbars have been produced so that all the content of the frame is accessible.

In Figure 11.19 the Visible setting has been used, and the full content of the layer has therefore been displayed by the browser. The width and height values set using the Properties Inspector have been overridden by the browser so that the full content has been made visible. The Hidden setting is used in Figure 11.20, and the excess content is hidden from view. Not only is it hidden from view, but also there is no way for the user to access it. This option should only be used if there is a good reason for doing so. Finally, in Figure 11.21 the Auto option has been used. With the Auto setting a scrollbar will only be used if it is needed. In this case a vertical scrollbar is needed, but there is no need for a horizontal type. Consequently only the vertical scrollbar is included. Compare this with

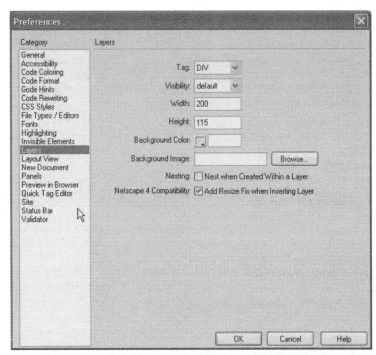

Fig.11.22 The Layer defaults are set in this section of the Preferences window

the Scroll version of Figure 11.18, where a horizontal scrollbar has also been included even though it serves no useful purpose.

Layer preferences

When a layer is added via the Insert menu a default layer is added at the current cursor position. Some of the characteristics of a default layer can be adjusted by way of the Layers section of the Preferences window. Select Preferences from the Edit menu to launch the window, and then left-click on Layers in the Category menu down the left side of the window. This will give the window of Figure 11.22. Apart from the size settings, the defaults set using the Preferences window will also be used for layers added using the Insert palette.

The Tag menu gives four tag options for layers, but simply leave this at the DIV setting unless there is a good reason to do otherwise. The next five options set things like the size and background colour, and these operate in the same way as their equivalents in the Properties Inspector. A background image can be added, and this operates in much the same way as adding a background image to a page. The background image will be tiled if it is too small to fill the layer, or clipped if it is too large. With the Nesting checkbox ticked, a new layer will be automatically nested if it is created within another layer.

When selected, the final option results in a resizing fix being added so that the layers operate properly with Netscape Navigator 4 and later. Without this fix layers might shift out of position when the size of the window is adjusted.

Layers to tables

In the previous chapter the subject of converting tables to layers was covered briefly. Dreamweaver can make the opposite conversion provided none of the layers on the page overlap. To make this conversion select the Convert option from the Modify menu, and then choose the Layers to Table option from the submenu. This will produce the Convert Layers To Table dialogue box (Figure 11.23). It is likely that everything will be converted properly if you simply accept all the default settings, operate the OK button, and proceed with the conversion. Figure 11.24 shows a simple layout using three layers, and Figure 11.25 shows the result of the conversion to a table. The layout was reproduced accurately when viewed using a browser (Figure 11.26). These layout options are available:

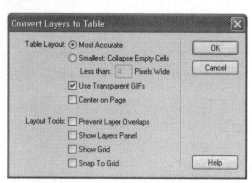

Fig.11.23 The Convert Layers to Table dialogue box

Most Accurate

By default the Most Accurate checkbox is ticked, and this results in every layer being converted into a table cell, and any other cells that are needed

Fig.11.24 A simple layout that uses three layers

Fig.11.25 The table structure produced by the conversion

Fig.11.26 The converted layout shows good accuracy when viewed using Internet Explorer

Fig.11.27 A deliberately awkward layout

Fig.11.28 The simplified layout produced by the conversion

are then added around them. This does not necessarily give the simplest conversion, but the table should mimic the layers as accurately as possible.

Smallest

With this option, rather than putting in very narrow columns or rows only a few pixels high, Dreamweaver adjusts the layer boundaries to align them. This simplifies the table layout, but obviously accuracy will be lost to some extent. The minimum acceptable cell width and height have to be specified. The higher the number used the greater the loss of accuracy that can result. Figure 11.27 shows a layout produced using layers, and it has been designed to avoid having everything neatly aligned. In fact it has been designed to have things almost aligned but not quite. Figure 11.28 shows the result of letting Dreamweaver make compromises during the conversion. The design has been closed up slightly in addition to some aligning of layer boundaries. It would presumably be possible to use this feature to tidy up a slightly haphazard design.

Use Transparent GIFs

As pointed out previously, transparent GIF image files can be used to fill otherwise empty cells to prevent them from collapsing and probably ruining the layout.

Centre on Page

By default the completed table is left-aligned. If this option is selected the new table will be centred on the page instead.

Layers clearly provide a neat way of accurately placing practically any type of content on a page, and you need to become reasonably fluent in this aspect of Dreamweaver. It is certainly worthwhile spending some time experimenting with layouts based on layers. Remember that most layouts designed using layers can be converted to tables so that they are compatible with older browsers. Make sure overlapping layers are avoided if you intend to convert them to a table.

Forms and
Flash

Form problems

Forms are undoubtedly a very useful component for web pages. They can be used to collect various types of user input, permitting two-way communications between a site owner and the users. Dreamweaver makes it easy to add forms to a page, and then add radio buttons, text boxes, menus, etc., to the forms. Unfortunately, adding forms to pages using Dreamweaver is one thing, and actually getting those forms to do anything useful is quite another. In order to use information from a form it is necessary to have a program to transfer the information to a database on the server. With free or very low cost server space this may not be possible, but most rented server space comes complete with a range of facilities to support this type of thing.

However, it is a subject that goes beyond the scope of this book. If you need to use forms to gather information from site users it will be necessary to learn some programming, or to learn how to use the "off the shelf" scripts that are available on the Internet. Alternatively, you can hire someone to properly integrate your web site with the server. You also need to make sure that the server you use supports the facilities you are trying to implement and the methods of implementation you intend to use.

Here we will only consider the use of forms to provide jump menus. A jump menu is a pop-down menu that enables the user to go to a selected page in the site. An ordinary menu can be made by having a list of words on the page, with each word linked to the relevant site. A jump menu provides a more compact alternative and is often preferred where links to a large number of pages are required.

Adding a form

A form is added by placing the cursor at the point in the page where the form is required and then selecting Form from the Insert menu.

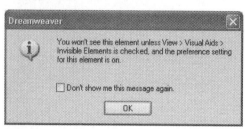

Alternatively, operate the Form button in the Forms section of the Insert palette. If the warning message of Figure 12.1 appears, forms are switched off in the Invisible Elements section of the Preferences window. This can be corrected by selecting

Fig.12.1 A warning is issued if form outlines are switched off

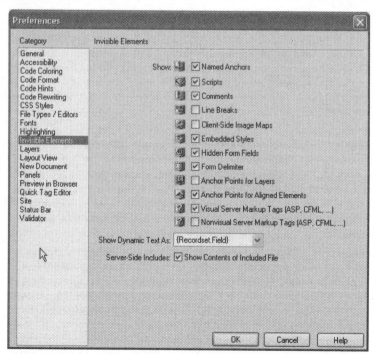

Fig.12.2 Make sure that the Form Delimiter checkbox is ticked

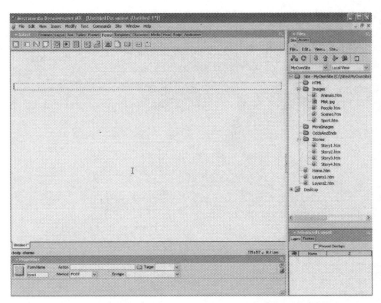

Fig.12.3 The newly added form is visible near the top of the page

Preferences from the Edit menu, and then selecting the Invisible Elements category in the Preferences window (Figure 12.2). Make sure the Form Delimiter checkbox is ticked and then operate the OK button. With the form added to the page you should have something like Figure 12.3, with a broken red line representing the outline of the form.

If it is active, the Properties Inspector will show the form's properties. Left-clicking on its outline will select a form, incidentally. With a form selected the Properties Inspector will only show three parameters. I would not worry too much about these for the moment, but you will probably wish to change the default name to something more appropriate.

Ordinary objects such as text, tables and images can be added to a form, as well as the objects that are designed specifically for use in forms. You will find nine of these on the Forms section of the Insert palette. In most cases it will be necessary to add text so that users of the form know exactly what they are supposed to do. Remember that what is obvious to you will probably be far from obvious to some visiting the site for the first time. Try adding some text and an image to a form. The form starts out at the full page-width but only one line of text high. However, as you

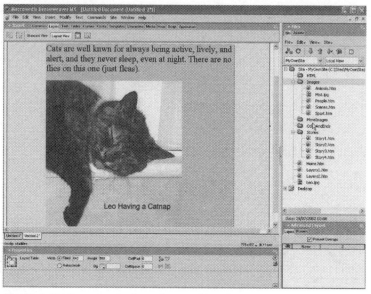

Fig.12.4 Ordinary content can be used in a form

add more objects to a form it expands to take the new material. If a narrower form is required, simply make a table cell of the required size and put the form into it. Altering the background colour of the cell can effectively change the background colour of the form.

Figure 12.4 helps to illustrate these points. The form has been placed inside a layout cell, and it has been expanded vertically by adding some text and a bitmap image. The background colour of the cell has been changed to mid-grey. Of course, the various guide lines in Figure 12.4, including the red outline of the form, do not appear when the page is viewed using a browser (Figure 12.5).

Jump menu

A jump menu is a good place to start when using forms because no scripting or other programming is needed to make it work. It is not used to obtain information from users and store it on a server. A jump menu simply provides a means of moving to one of several pages listed in a menu. To try out a jump menu, make a small layout cell and add a form

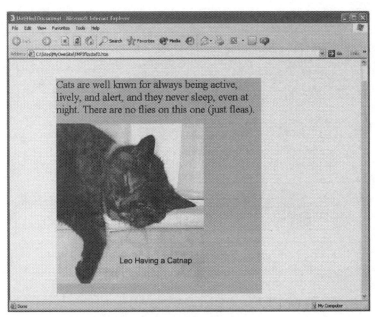

Fig.12.5 The form as it appears in a browser

in it. Next place some text at the top of the form and press the Return key to move down to the next line. Now add the jump menu by operating the appropriate button in the Insert palette, or by selecting Form Objects from the Insert menu, and then choosing Jump Menu from the submenu that appears. This will produce the dialogue box of Figure 12.6.

The first task is to add the list of menu items and the link for each one. There is a default entry, and this is edited to produce the first entry in the menu. The Text field is the text that will be displayed for that item in the menu. Edit this to the text you require and then left-click on the entry in the Menu Items list. The text here should change to match the text you have just put into the Text field. Next left-click on the Browse button and choose a file for the menu item to link to. This operates in the same fashion as choosing a normal link, for the very good reason that it is a normal link. Now operate the + button to add a new menu item, edit the text field, left-click on the new entry in the Menu Items list to change the text there, and select the URL for the new entry. Repeat this process a few times until you have added all the entries you require.

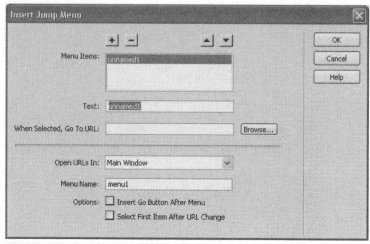

Fig.12.6 The Insert Jump Menu dialogue box

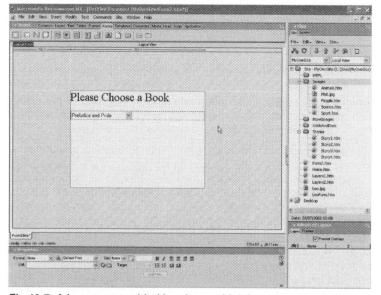

Fig.12.7 A jump menu added in a form, which has in turn been placed
         in a layout table cell

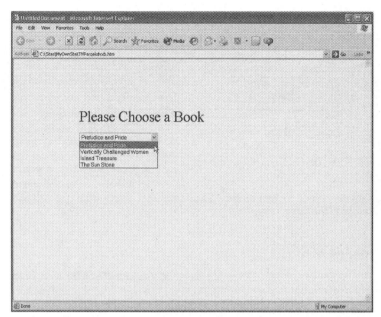

Fig.12.8 The expanded version of the jump menu

When you have finished adding entries operate the OK button, and the main screen should then show the form complete with the newly added menu (Figure 12.7). The pop-down menu will not operate in the Dreamweaver document view, so you must use the browser preview facility to try out the menu. Placing the cursor on the downward facing arrowhead should activate the menu (Figure 12.8), and left-clicking on an entry should switch the browser to the appropriate page in the site.

Go

In the Insert Jump Menu window there is a checkbox that enables a Go button to be added to the menu. With the standard version of the menu it is not necessary to press a button to confirm your selection. Left-clicking on an entry immediately moves the browser to the linked page. With the Go button added (Figure 12.9), left-clicking on an entry closes the menu and the selected item is displayed in the menu's textbox. Left-clicking the Go button activates the link and moves the browser to the

Choose one of these books

| Lady Lovellies chatter | ▼ | Go |
| Lady Lovellies chatter |
| The big sheep |
| How green was my valet |
| Done with the wind |

Fig.12.9 The menu plus Go button

selected page. An advantage of the Go button is that it gives the user a chance to change their mind, or to reselect the page if they make a mistake the first time.

The Open URLs In menu will only offer one option unless you are using frames. This is the Main Window option, which means that the linked page will replace the existing page in the current browser window. If frames are in use, the names of the frames will appear in the menu. With one of these selected the linked page will be opened in the selected frame.

Menu editing

The Properties Inspector permits a limited amount of editing on a jump menu after it has been added to a form. To select a jump menu simply left-click on any part of it. The Properties Inspector should then look something like Figure 12.10. The name of the menu can be edited in the

Fig.12.10 The jump menu version of the Properties Inspector

textbox at the left end of the window. The item to be shown initially can be selected from the list of menu entries. Usually the item at the top of the menu is the one that is displayed before the menu is expanded, but this facility enables a different entry to be selected if desired.

Operating the List Values button brings up the dialogue box of Figure 12.11. This enables the existing entries to be edited. The + and – buttons permit entries to be added or removed. There is no file browser facility available from this window, so any URLs have to be added or changed by editing the text for their entries in the list.

The two radio buttons in the Properties Inspector give the option of using a menu or a list. Using the default settings there is actually no difference

between a menu and
a list. However, with
the list option selected
the Height textbox
becomes active
(Figure 12.12). In this
case the height
setting is the number
of items that will be
shown in the list. If
this number is less
than the actual

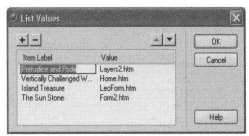

*Fig.12.11 Menu entries can be edited using
the List Values window*

number of items in the list, you get
a sort of cross between a list and
a menu. With eight items in the
menu and a height setting of four,
four items would be displayed at
once, but the others could be
displayed by scrolling the list up
and down. In Figure 12.13 there

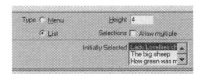

Fig.12.12 Setting the height of a list

are four items in the menu, and a height setting of 4 has been used so
that all four are visible at once, and a true list has been produced.

If you left-click on the Go button
the Properties Inspector will show
its parameters, as in Figure 12.14.
The Label textbox enables the
lettering on the button to be
changed. The button will be
enlarged if a longer text string is
used, as in the example of Figure
12.15. There was too little space
for the enlarged button in its
original position, so it has been
moved onto the next line.

*Fig.12.13 A simple list having
four items*

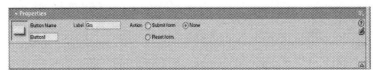

Fig.12.14 The Properties Inspector for the Go button

*Fig.12.15 The Go button with
added text*

Flash text

As many readers will be aware, Flash is a graphics and animation program produced by Macromedia. In order to produce sophisticated Flash graphics and animations you have to buy the program, but basic Flash text and buttons can be produced using Dreamweaver. You do not need to have Flash installed on your computer in order to add these objects using Dreamweaver, but note that versions prior to Dreamweaver 4 do not support this function.

Flash text has a few advantages over normal HTML text. Perhaps the most important is that it is possible to use any TrueType font that is installed on your computer. Furthermore, anyone viewing the text does not need to have that font installed on his or her computer. Another important

*Fig.12.16 This error message appears if the
current page has not been saved*

factor is that Flash text can handle larger sizes than normal HTML text. A further advantage is that anti-aliasing can be used on the text. This feature helps to give smooth edges to text, giving a much neater appearance. This can work on most sizes of text, but it is particularly effective with large sizes that can otherwise literally look a little rough at the edges. Flash text can also be made to change colour when the pointer is placed over it, giving a simple rollover effect.

To add Flash text select Interactive Images from the Insert menu, and then select the Flash Text option from the submenu that appears. Alternatively, operate the Flash Text button in the Media page of the Insert palette. An error message appears (Figure 12.16) if the current page has not been saved yet. If this happens, operate the OK button, save the current document, and then try again. When all is well the dialogue box of Figure 12.17 will appear instead of the error message.

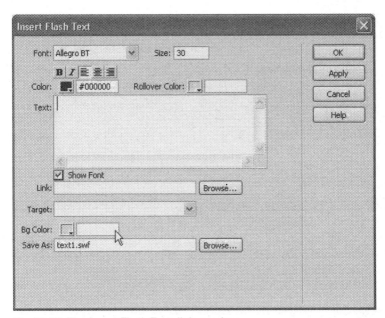

Fig.12.17 The Insert Flash Text dialogue box

The required text is typed into the Text textbox, and multi-line text can be used. The Font menu is used to choose the required font from the compatible types, and the required size is typed into the Size textbox. In this case the text size is in point sizes incidentally. If the Show Font checkbox is ticked, the text you type into the Text field will be shown in the correct font, but not at the correct size. You can see exactly what the text will look like by operating the Apply button. The text will then appear in the main document window at the correct position (Figure 12.18). You can keep making changes to the text and settings, operating the Apply button each time to check its appearance. If the rollover effect is required, choose a rollover colour from the appropriate menu. Simply leave this blank if ordinary text is required.

Most of the other settings are fairly straightforward, and are the type of thing that has been covered previously. One exception is the Save As field. Unlike ordinary HTML text, the Flash text is saved to disc as a Flash movie file having a "swf" extension. You can use the default name or choose something more appropriate if preferred. When the text is exactly as required operate the OK button and it will be added into the

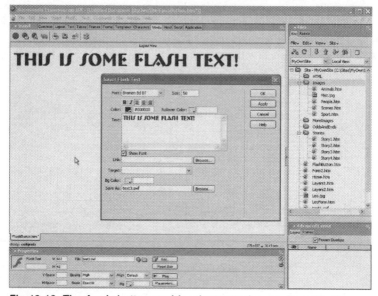

Fig.12.18 The Apply button enables the text to be previewed in the document window

document. Incidentally, if you use the Apply button, the Flash text will not be erased from the document if you change your mind and exit from the dialogue box using the Cancel button. However, the text is easily removed by selecting it and pressing the Delete key or selecting Cut from the Edit menu.

Flash Properties

With the Flash text selected the Properties Inspector can be used to show its properties and edit them. For Flash text the Properties Inspector will look like Figure 12.19. If the rollover effect was selected, one way of testing it is to view the page in a browser. The quicker alternative is to

Fig.12.19 The Properties Inspector for Flash text

Fig. 12.20 The Flash text in its normal guise

operate the Play button on the Properties Inspector. Positioning the
pointer over the text should then produce the rollover effect in
Dreamweaver's design view. Figures 12.20 and 12.21 show "before and

*Fig. 12.21 The Flash text in its alternative colour scheme. The
background does not change colour incidentally*

after" views of a Flash text rollover. The Play button in the Properties
Inspector will change to a Stop button, and operating this will switch off
the rollover effect.

It is possible to resize the text using the three handles that appear when
the text is selected, or by editing the W (width) and H (height) values in
the Properties Inspector. Using either method it is possible to produce
enormous text (Figure 12.22). Operating the Reset Size button in the
Properties Inspector returns stretched or compressed text to its original
size. Operating the Edit button brings back the Insert Flash Text dialogue
box so that the text and its parameters can be changed.

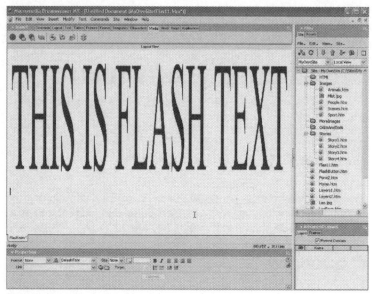

Fig.12.22 It is possible to produce enormous text in a range of styles using Flash text

Flash buttons

Dreamweaver comes complete with a number of Flash buttons in a variety of styles. The buttons can be used for navigation menus, and they give a more professional looking result than simply having words on the screen that are used as the sources for the links. Flash buttons can be added using the Insert palette (the second button from the left), or by selecting Interactive Images from the Insert menu and then Flash Button from the submenu that appears. Either way, the Insert Flash Button dialogue box (Figure 12.23) will appear. The first task is to choose the required button from the Style menu. The Sample box shows the appearance of selected buttons, so it is quick and easy to go through the buttons looking for something suitable for your requirements. Placing the pointer over the Sample button will show the change that will occur when the real thing is used, as will left-clicking on it. Typically, the button appears to light up when the pointer is placed over it, and it gets even brighter when it is left-clicked.

Operating the Get More Styles button will connect the computer to the appropriate page of the Macromedia web site where more designs are

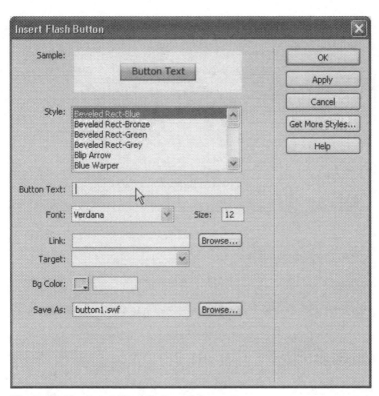

Fig.12.23 The Insert Flash Button dialogue box

available. Of course, this will only work if your PC has an active connection to the Internet at the time, so where necessary activate the Internet connection before trying this option.

By default buttons are not marked with any text, and for most applications a suitable label must be entered into the Button Text textbox. Note that some buttons are marked with symbols and that no text can be used on these. The Size textbox enables the size of the lettering to be set in point sizes. In practice it is not possible to use large sizes as they will not fit on the button. Operating the Apply button enables you to see the button in place on the page (Figure 12.24). The rest of the dialogue box is pretty straightforward, and is the same as for Flash text. When a suitable button has been selected, together with the desired settings, operate the OK button.

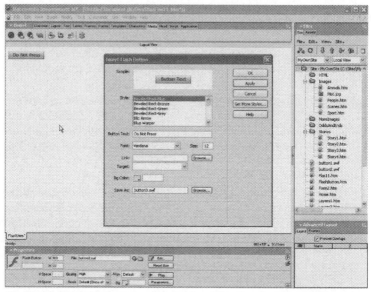

Fig.12.24 Flash buttons can be previewed in the document window

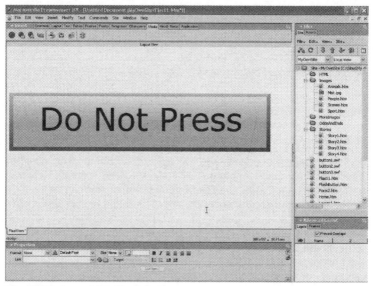

Fig.12.25 An outsize Flash button

Fig.12.26 The version of the Properties Inspector for Flash buttons

When selected, the button has three handles that enable its size and aspect ratio to be adjusted. Dragging the button to a suitably large size can produce an outsize button (Figure 12.25). If a button with large text is required, use small text that will fit onto the button initially, and then stretch the button and text to the required size. This avoids having the text bursting out of the button.

The Properties Inspector for a Flash button is much the same as the one for Flash text (Figure 12.26). To test the button in Dreamweaver, first operate the play button on the Properties Inspector. Then place the pointer over the button and also left-click on the button to check that the correct changes are produced.

Behaviours

Behaviour modification enables objects on a web page, or the web page itself, to do clever things with the aid of JavaScript programs. This is a fairly involved subject, and here we will only consider the use of behaviours to play a sound file when the mouse pointer is placed over an image. In this example the image is of a robin, and the sound file contains the song of a robin.

Fig.12.27 The Behaviors window

You can obviously try the same general scheme of things using any image file in a standard web format and any sound file that is reasonably small (about 20 to 80 kilobytes). For test purposes the sound does not have to be an appropriate one for the image. If you do not have a suitable sound file there are plenty of them available on the Internet. In fact there are probably a large

Fig.12.28 The Actions menu

number of short sound files already on your computer, because the operating system and probably other programs use them. The search facilities of the operating system should be able to locate a WAV file that can be copied to the local site you are using for test purposes.

There are three parts to an action added using behaviours. First there must be an object that is used to trigger the action. In this example it is an image, but practically any object including the page itself can be used as the source. Next something must happen to trigger the action, which in this instance is the mouse pointer being positioned over the image. Other methods of triggering include the object being loaded onto the page, the object being left-clicked or double-clicked, etc. Finally, there is the action itself, and here we are playing a sound. There are other possibilities, such as a message being displayed on the screen or an image being swapped for another one. The options available depend to some extent on the object used as the source of the action.

Adding behaviours

Start by adding the source object to the web page and then making sure it is selected. Next select Behaviors from the Windows menu, which will launch the Behaviors window of Figure 12.27. This is part of the Design group of windows. Operate the + button to produce a pop-up menu giving a list of the available actions that can be applied to the object (Figure 12.28).

In this case we wish to play a sound, so it is the Play Sound option that is chosen. This will produce the dialogue box of Figure 12.29, and the filename for the sound file can be typed into the textbox or it can be selected via the Browse button and the usual file browser. Once this has been completed the OK button is

Fig.12.29 This dialogue box is used to specify the sound file

operated. The screen should then look something like Figure 12.30, with a new entry in the Behaviors window but no change in the appearance of the image or document.

If you wish to delete an entry in the Behaviors window, simply select it and operate the – button. In order to edit an entry it should first be selected. The entry in the Events column might be one you require, but

Fig.12.30 A new entry has appeared in the Behaviors window

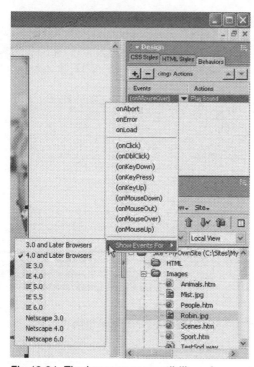

it will probably have to be altered. Left-clicking on the arrowhead between the Events and Action columns produces a menu of available events. The number of options depends on the browser compatibility setting selected. To change this compatibility, move the pointer down to the bottom entry in the menu, which is Show Events For (Figure 12.31). This produces a submenu with various browser options.

If you require compatibility with older browsers the list of available events will be quite short. Opting for compatibility with just one recent browser gives a much greater range to choose from. Choosing the 4.0 and Later Browsers option is a good compromise that gives a good range of events to choose from while giving compatibility with most of the browsers currently in use. The On Mouse Over event we require to run the sound file.

Fig.12.31 The browser compatibility submenu

When viewed using a browser the test page looked like Figure 12.32. A lot of sites that have clever features leave users "in the dark" about accessing them. It is best to give some onscreen instructions, as in this example, or users might leave the site without discovering the clever features. Obviously it is not possible to see from the screen dump that the sound file played successfully (which it did), but you can see that the pointer has changed from the normal arrow to a hand, showing that the image is not a passive part of the page.

Fig.12.32 The test page viewed using a browser

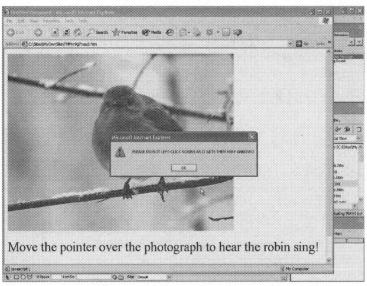

Fig.12.33 A pop-up message produced by left-clicking on the robin image

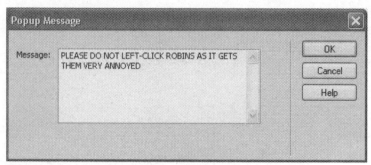

Fig.12.34 The dialogue box for adding the pop-up message

You might like to try experimenting with some of the other events and actions. Note that it is not necessary to remove one entry in the Behaviors window in order to add another one. Several behaviours can be assigned to a single object. In the version of the page shown in Figure 12.33 a Popup Message action has been used in conjunction with an On Click event. The message box is primarily to provide a warning message when an On Error event occurs, but it can be used for other purposes. When this option is selected a dialogue box like the one in Figure 12.34 appears. Simply type the required message into the textbox and then operate the OK button. The Set Text action is another simple one to experiment with. It can be used to display a message in the status bar when the appropriate event occurs.

Style sheets

Cascading what?

Cascading style sheets, or just CSS as this system is better known, enable designers to define the appearance of text in a more flexible fashion than is possible with standard HTML. As the style part of the name implies, a style is imposed on the selected text. Normally if all the links on a page needed to be in bold text, each link would have to be manually changed to a bold setting. Using the style method the link tag would be modified to include the bold setting so that all the links in the page would be automatically set to bold text.

If you did not like the look of the finished page it would not be necessary to change each individual link back to normal. The link tag would be altered and all the links would then return to normal. Using Dreamweaver it is not necessary to get deeply involved with the code in order to use styles and style sheets, and everything can be handled using the menus, dialogue boxes, etc.

It has to be pointed out that style sheets are still relatively new and only work with newer versions of browsers. It would perhaps be more accurate to say that they do not work with old versions of browsers. Microsoft Internet Explorer 4 and later or Netscape 4 and later are suitable. Once again, it is something that is gaining in popularity as the older browsers fall out of use, but it is still not safe to assume that all browsers will work properly with style sheets.

Types

Matters are slightly confused by the fact that there are four different types of style sheet. The simplest variety is the type described previously, where an HTML tag is modified so that is has additional properties. With this type of style sheet, or just plain style as it is better described, the tag gains new properties, but the original ones are retained. In our link

Fig.13.1 The CSS Styles window

Fig.13.2 The pop-up menu of the CSS Styles window

example, it may have other properties added, but it will always remain a link. This is adequate for many purposes, but does limit the possibilities.

The second type of style is termed a "class", and you use it to name and define a new style. Once defined, the new style can be applied to text in the standard fashion. Select the text and then apply the style by name, much as you would set the font or put the text in Italics. Using the new style it is possible to set the font, colour, and other aspects of formatting in one operation.

The third and fourth style types are the imported and linked varieties. In both cases the style is defined by creating a separate document, and both the redefining and class types can be included. These are true style sheets rather than just styles, because you generate documents (the style sheets) that define the styles. Having created a style sheet, the styles it contains can be applied to several or even all the pages in a site.

Style creation

To create a new style, launch the CSS Styles window by choosing CSS Styles from the Window menu. This window is part of the Design group, so it can be selected by operating the CSS Style tab if this group is already displayed. Either method should produce something like Figure 13.1. The main area of the window lists the defined styles, but as no styles have been defined at this stage it will simply say "No CSS Style". Next launch the New Style window by selecting

Fig.13.3 The New Style dialogue box

New Style from the pop-out menu (Figure 13.2), or by operating the appropriate button at the bottom of the window. This is the second button from the left in the row of four buttons.

Either way, the dialogue box of Figure 13.3 should appear. Operate the Redefine HTML Tag radio button in the middle section of the window, and the This Document Only radio button in the bottom section of the window. Next select a tag from the menu (Figure 13.4) or type a tag name into the text box. At this stage do not worry too much about the functions of the various tags. For initial experiment one of the heading style tags will do, such as the h6 tag.

Operate the OK button and the style

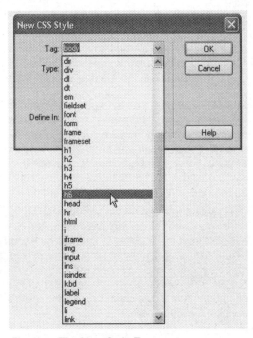

Fig.13.4 The New Style Tag menu

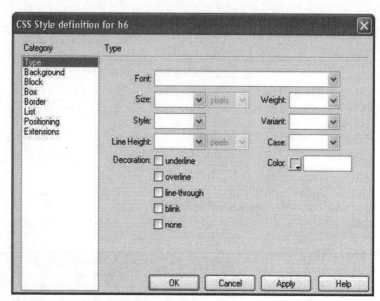

Fig.13.5 The Style Definition window is used to set the required parameters. This is one of eight pages

definition dialogue box will appear (Figure 13.5). There are plenty of settings to choose from on the first section of this dialogue box, but several other categories are available from the list on the left. In this respect it operates in a manner that is very much like the Preferences window. For an initial experiment, stick with the initial category and make some changes to the font, size, colour, etc. When you have finished making the changes operate the OK button.

Now place some text on the screen, select it, and apply the new style to it. In this case the h6 tag has been altered, so Paragraph Format is selected from the Text menu, followed by Heading 6 from the submenu. Figure 13.6 shows some text in the new style, plus some text in heading styles 1 and 5. Heading style 6 was originally the smallest heading style, but the new version is actually bigger than heading style 1. The other changes made to the style such as the underlining and colour change are also readily apparent.

If you look at the CSS Styles window you will notice that the new style is not listed. However, it will be listed in the Edit Style Sheet dialogue box. Select CSS Styles from the Text menu, and then Edit Style Sheet from

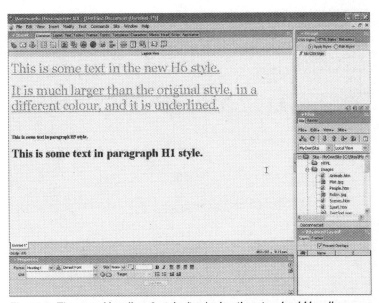

Fig.13.6 The new Heading 6 style (top) plus the standard Heading 1 and 5 styles below

the submenu, and this dialogue box will appear (Figure 13.7). The main panel lists the existing styles that have been defined, which in this case is just "h6". If you select this style its settings will be shown in the Style Definition panel. If you operate the Edit button the Style Definition window will appear so that the settings can be altered. The style can be deleted by operating the Remove

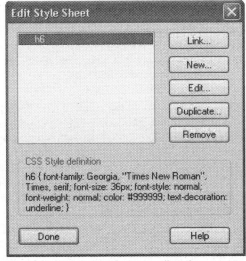

Fig.13.7 The new style is now listed

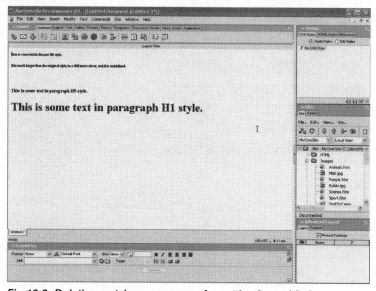

Fig.13.8 Deleting a style removes any formatting it provided

Fig.13.9 Operate the New button to create a style class

button, but this will cause any text formatted with the new style to return to normal (Figure 13.8).

Style class

To create a new style class, start by launching the Edit Style Sheet dialogue box (Figure 13.9), which is accessed via the pop-up menu of the CSS window. Operate the New button and the New Style dialogue box will appear. Using the upper set of three radio buttons select the Make Custom Style (class) option, and in the lower set select This Document Only. A name for the new style must be typed into the textbox at the top of the window. Use lower case letters with no spaces or other

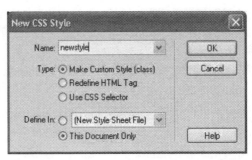

Fig.13.10 Setting up and naming a new class

punctuation marks. You should then have something like Figure 13.10. Left-click the OK button to continue.

This brings up the Style definition window (refer back to Figure 13.5). Next go through the eight pages of parameters selecting the ones that you wish to apply to the new style. The functions of most of the settings

on the first page are fairly obvious, and the more obscure ones on the later pages are mostly optional. Quickly go through the pages adding in the main parameters and operate the OK button when you have finished. This takes you back to the Edit Style Sheet window, which should now show the new class selected in the main panel at the top of the window, and the selected characteristics in the panel beneath this (Figure 13.11).

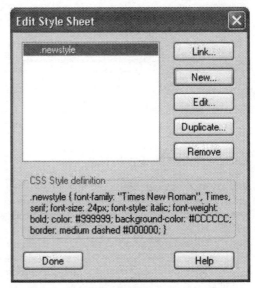

Fig.13.11 The new class shown in the Edit Style Sheet window

Fig.13.12 The new class in the CSS Styles window

Operate the Done button to exit the Edit Style Sheet window and then look at the CSS window. The newly defined class should now be listed in this window (Figure 13.12). Try typing a line of text into the document window, and then with the text cursor still on the same line as the new text, select the new style in the CSS window. The text should then take on the characteristics of the new class, as in the example of Figure 13.13. Try selecting the "none" option in the CSS window. This should set the text back to its original settings.

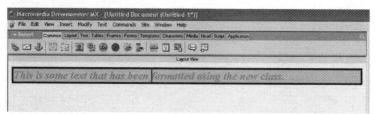

Fig.13.13 Some text that has been formatted using the new class

Linked and imported

The styles described so far are strictly for use with the current page. If you try making a new class in the manner described previously and then move to another page, the new class will disappear from the CSS window when the new page is opened. Return to the original page and the new class will appear again. The new class is effectively part of page, and is not available to other pages even if they are in the same site. This is also true of redefined tags. In some cases this may be all that you require, but often a style will be needed in several or even all the pages in a site. This can be achieved using imported or linked style sheets, which differ in the way that the new style is applied to pages.

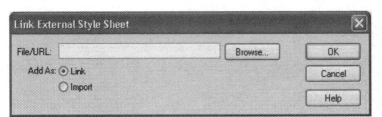

Fig.13.14 The linked style sheet must be given a filename

To produce an imported or linked style sheet, start by launching the Edit Style Sheet window in the normal way and then operate the Link button. This produces the window of Figure 13.14 where the new style sheet must be given a filename. The name used should conform to the normal file naming conventions and should be given a CSS extension (e.g. Style15.CSS). Use the radio buttons to select either a linked or imported style sheet. Linking is the more tried and tested method incidentally, and is the one that we will use here. Operate the OK button to return to the Edit Style Sheet window, where the new style sheet should now be listed (Figure 13.15).

This produces a new style sheet, but as things stand it does not contain any styles. In order to save and use a style sheet it must contain at least one style. Operate the Edit Styles radio button at the top of the CSS Styles window

Fig.13.15 The Edit Style Sheet window lists the new style sheet

and then double-click on the entry for the new style sheet. This produces the new window of Figure 13.16. Left-click on the new button to bring up what is more or less the same New Style window that we have encountered previously in this chapter. One difference is that the This Document Only option is not available (Figure 13.17), and it is clearly inappropriate in this case. In other respects things are much the same as they were before, and a new style is defined in standard fashion.

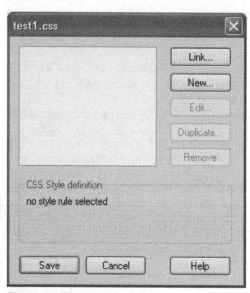

Redefine one of the heading tags and it will then appear in the window for the new style sheet (Figure 13.18). The Save button is now enabled, but before saving the file operate the New button and define a new class. Operating the Save button will move things back to the New Style Sheet window. Left-click the Done button to return to the document, which will then be linked to the newly created style sheet.

Fig.13.16 The style sheet has been created, but it does not contain any styles

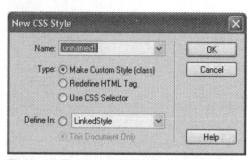

Fig.13.17 The New CSS Style window for the style sheet

As a first step in using the new style sheet, put a line of text or a paragraph into the document and format it in the new version of the heading style. Then add another line or paragraph, and with the text cursor still within that block of text select the new class from the CSS

Styles window. Both sets of text should then reflect the new formatting, as in Figure 13.19. So far this is nothing more than could be achieved by simply redefining a tag or creating a new class. The next step is to use the new style sheet with another document, so go to the File menu and select New to create a new document. The newly created class will then disappear from the CSS Styles window, and text

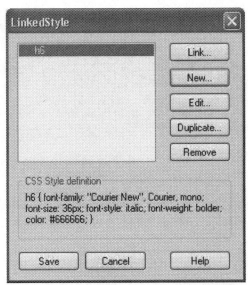

Fig.13.18 The redefined tag listed in the style sheet's window

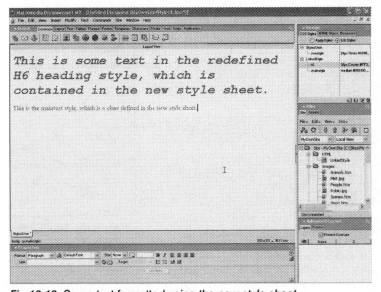

Fig.13.19 Some text formatted using the new style sheet

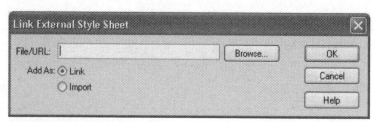

Fig.13.20 Specifying the style sheet that will be linked to the page

formatted using the redefined heading tag will have the normal heading style.

In order to use the style sheet with the new document the style sheet must be linked to the document. Go to the pop-up menu of the CSS Styles window and select the Edit Style Sheet option. Next operate the Link button to bring up the new window of Figure 13.20. The name of the style sheet's file can be typed into the textbox, or it can be located and selected using the browse option. Using the file browser is usually the easier and more reliable method. There are two radio buttons that provide Link and Import options, and here we are using the link method so make sure that this button is selected.

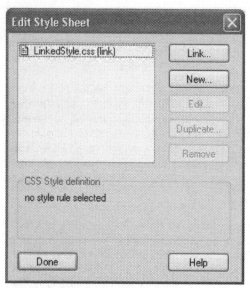

Fig.13.21 The linked style sheet listed in the Edit Style Sheet window

With everything set up correctly, operate the OK button to return to the Edit Style Sheets window, which should now show the name of the style sheet (Figure 13.21). Left-click the Done button to return to the document, where the CSS Styles window should now show the new

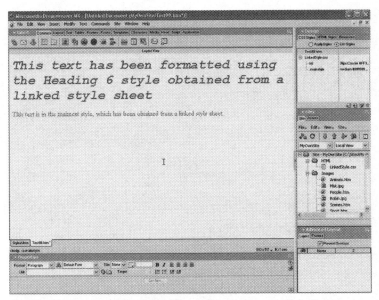

Fig.13.22 The class linked from the style sheet is now listed

class obtained from the style sheet (Figure 13.22). There is nothing obvious to show that the heading style has been successfully redefined, but if you use the relevant tag and the new class the text should be formatted accordingly. This has been demonstrated in Figure 13.22 where some suitable formatted text has been added to the document window.

Style sheet editing

The styles held within a style sheet are not "set in stone", and it is possible to edit or delete the existing styles or add new ones. Any changes made to an existing style will affect all instances of that style in documents. If you wish to change some instances and not others, a new style must be defined and applied to only pieces of text that need to be changed. To edit a style sheet start by opening the Edit Style Sheet window using the pop-up menu of the CSS Style Sheets window. Select the style sheet you wish to edit and then operate the Edit button. In the new window that appears select the style that you wish to alter and then operate the Edit button.

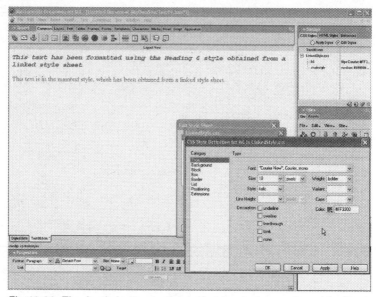

*Fig.13.23 The Apply button enables changes to be previewed in the
document window*

This brings up the usual Style Definition window where any settings for
the style can be altered as required. Note that if you operate the Apply
button, any changes that have been made will be applied to appropriate
blocks of text in the document window, giving a useful preview facility.
Compare Figure 13.23 with Figure 13.22 for example. The Heading 6
style has been decreased in size from 36 points to 18 points and then
the Apply button has been used. When the necessary changes have
been made, operate the OK button to return to the previous window
where the Save button can be used to save the changes to disc.

Other editing is possible from this window, and a style can be deleted by
selecting it and then left-clicking the Remove button. Of course, any
formatting provided by the deleted style will be removed. Operating the
New button enables a new style to be defined, and this is just a matter of
repeating the processes used to produce the existing styles. The
Duplicate option enables a new style based on an existing one to be
produced. This avoids having to go through dozens of settings when
there are only one or two that are different from an existing style. By
"borrowing" all the settings from an existing style, only those that are
different in the new style have to be altered.

Suppose that a new heading style is required, and that it is the same as the modified heading 6 style except that the size parameter is to be 24 point instead of 18 point. First the h6 style is selected and then the Duplicate button is left-clicked. This brings up the Duplicate Style window (Figure 13.24), which is essentially the same as the window that appears

Fig.3.24 Duplicating a style

when producing a new style. The tag that is selected is h6, but the new style must be based on one of the others, and the h5 tag is the obvious choice. This one is therefore selected from the Tag menu. If the new style were based on a class rather than a tag, the textbox would have the name of the existing style with "CopyOf" added ahead of it. This would be changed to a suitable name for the new style.

Having selected a new tag or name, operate the OK button to return to the previous window where the new style will be shown in the list (Figure 13.25). The new style still has the same characteristics as the one it was cloned from, but it can be edited in the normal way. Figure 13.26 shows some text in the original style at the top, and in the edited (24 point) clone version below.

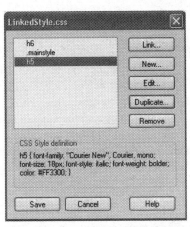

Fig.13.25 The cloned style added to the list

Removing classes

If you apply a class to some text and then try to use an ordinary paragraph style instead, the original formatting will be retained. The class style will override formatting applied using an ordinary paragraph style, but this does not mean that once a class has been applied it can not be removed again. Select the text that you wish to change and then left-click on the "none" entry in the CSS Styles window. This will remove the class style,

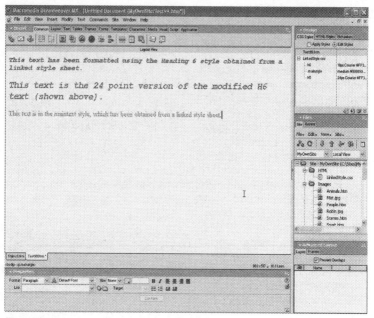

*Fig.13.26 The top line paragraph is in the original style and the second
one is the modified (24 point) version*

and conventional paragraph formatting can then be applied. If any
formatting of this type has already been used on the text, it will assume
the new format as soon as the class style is removed.

With a class in use you may find that trying to alter some of the
characteristics of the text has no effect. There is one setting in the class
and another set via the Properties Inspector or menu system, and the
winner will be whichever places its tags closer to the text in the HTML
code. Style sheets work best with the blanket approach to formatting,
which is the type of formatting normally needed. If "bits and pieces"
formatting is required it will probably be necessary to do it the hard way,
formatting each piece of text individually. This can be done using the
Properties Inspector, or by defining numerous classes if formatting
beyond the capabilities of the Properties Inspector is required. Remember
that a class does not have to be applied to a complete paragraph. The
dragging method (also known as spanning) can be used to select a
block of text and a class or paragraph style can then be applied to that
text.

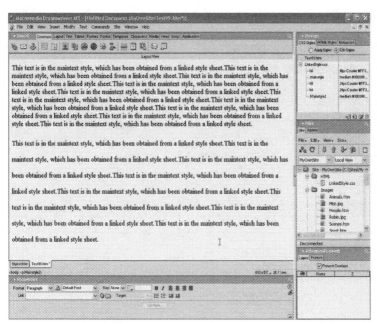

Fig.13.27 Text with the standard line height (top) and increased line height (bottom)

Attributes

Having looked through the various pages in the Style Definition window you will have noticed that it is possible to apply a lot more attributes using styles than the usual size, font, colour, etc. Most of the settings in the initial page (Type) are straightforward text attributes that do not merit any further explanation. There are a couple of exceptions, one of which is the Line Height setting. In Figure 13.27 the text in the top paragraph has the Medium text size and a line height of 20 points. All the settings are the same for the lower paragraph except the line height has been increased to 40 points. By experimenting a little with the line height it is possible to have the lines of text bunched together, spaced well apart, or anything in between.

The case menu enables the text to be set as all lower case, all upper case, or capitalised. The latter means that the first letter in each word is set as a capital letter. The capitalise and upper case options are good for headings and short captions. Of course, a normal option is also available.

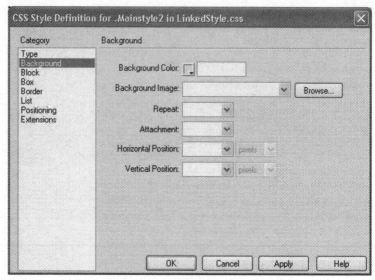

Fig.13.28 The style definition settings for backgrounds

Background

This is similar to setting the background colour or image for a page, but there are more tiling options for images. Figure 13.28 shows the background version of the Style Definition window. The Repeat option provides normal tiling, and the No-Repeat setting switches off tiling. If the image is too small, with no tiling selected it will only occupy the top left-hand section of the screen and the rest will have the normal background colour. The X and Y versions of repeat tiling only provide this facility in the horizontal and vertical directions respectively. Figure 13.29 for example, shows a background image that uses the Repeat-X version. The horizontal and vertical offsets enable the background to be offset from the top left-hand corner of the screen. In Figure 13.30 respective horizontal and vertical offsets of 100 and 50 have been used.

The attachment menu offers Fixed and Scroll options. Scroll is the normal method, whereby the background image scrolls together with other content on the page. With the fixed option, if the browser supports this feature, the background image remains fixed when the other content is scrolled.

Fig.13.29 A background that uses the Repeat X option

Fig.13.30 An offset background image

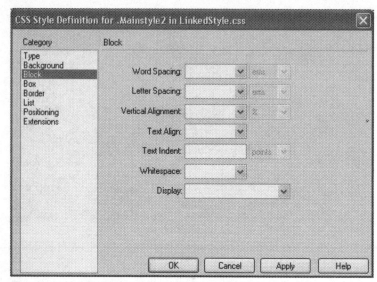

Fig.13.31 The Block section of the Styles Definition window

Block

The block section of the Style Definition window (Figure 13.31) provides control over various typographical settings that can be used to alter the appearance of the text. In most cases the defaults give text having a very neat appearance, and it is not essential to alter any of these settings. The word and letter spacing, as one would expect, simple adjust the spacing between words and characters in a word. In Figure 13.32 these have deliberately been set very large at 2 millimetres and 4 millimetres in order to illustrate the range of control available.

Options in the Text Alignment menu include the usual left, right, and centre justifications, but it is worth noting that full justification is also available. This is not a normal HTML alignment option, and it is not available by way of the Properties Inspector, etc.

Using the Text Indent option it is possible to indent the first line of each paragraph by a specified amount. In Figure 13.33 this facility has been combined with the full justification option. The amount of indentation in Figure 13.33 is a nominal 10 millimetres incidentally, but a very wide range of settings can be used.

Whitespace governs spacing within the text. With the No-Wrap option any soft returns are ignored and each paragraph is forced onto a single line.

Cascading style sheets, or just CSS as this system is better known, enable designers to define the appearance of text in a more flexible fashion than is possible with standard HTML. As the style sheet part of the name implies, a style is imposed on the

Fig.13.32 Word and letter spacing are adjustable

Box

The box page of the Style Definition window is shown in Figure 13.34. The padding option enables a "no-go" area to be placed around the selected text, and this operates much like the similar facility for table cells. This facility is very effective when used in conjunction with the Float menu. The float facility enables a block of text to effectively be set aside from the main flow of text. It can be left or right aligned, with the rest of the text flowing around it. In Figure 13.35 the main body of the text is in the normal text (size 5), but some of it has been formatted using a style that includes floating with right alignment, plus 20 pixel padding

Cascading style sheets, or just CSS as this system is better known, enable designers to define the appearance of text in a more flexible fashion than is possible with standard HTML. As the style sheet part of the name implies, a style is imposed on the page. If all the links on a page needed to be in bold text, each link would have to be manually changed to a bold setting using ordinary HTML. Using the style method the link tag would be modified to include the bold setting so that all the links in the page would be automatically set to bold text. If you did not like the look of the finished page it would not be necessary to change each individual link back to normal. The link tag would be altered and all the links would then return to normal. Using Dreamweaver it is not necessary to get deeply involved with the code in order to use style sheets, and everything can be handled using the menus, dialogue boxes, etc.

It has to be pointed out that style sheets are relatively new and only work with newer versions of browsers. Microsoft Internet Explorer 4 and later or Netscape 4 and later versions are suitable. Once again, it is something that is gaining in popularity as the older browsers fall out of use, but it is still not safe to assume that all browsers will work properly with style sheets.

Fig.13.33 These paragraphs have full justification and indents

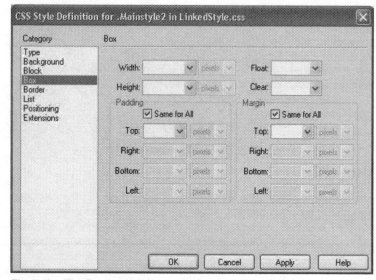

Fig.13.34 The Box section of the Style Definition window

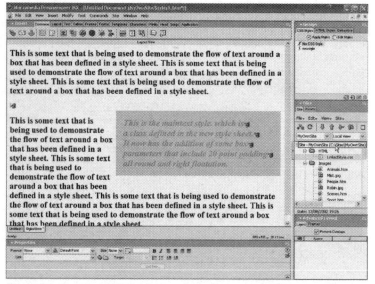

Fig.13.35 Dreamweaver's design view gives reasonable accuracy

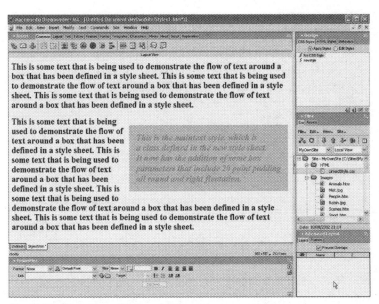

Fig.13.36 The page displayed using a browser

on all sides. Some soft returns have also been added to the text to break it up into lines of a similar length.

With earlier version of Dreamweaver the design view could not show a fair percentage of the style sheet attributes, including the ones used here. Matters are much improved in Dreamweaver MX though, and the formatting is produced properly when viewed from within Dreamweaver. Figure 13.36 shows the page viewed using Internet Explorer, and the version in Figure 13.35 is clearly quite close to this. The design view in Dreamweaver can be made more accurate by making the anchor points for aligned elements invisible using the Preferences window. Figure 13.37 shows the design view with the anchor point rendered invisible.

On the face of it there is no difference between the padding and margin facilities. The difference seems to be that padding is placed between the border of the element and its content, while the margin is placed outside the perimeter of the content. In other words, under some circumstances the margin option will reduce the amount of space available to other elements rather than constraining the content of its own element. The margin setting is of most use when a border and (or) a different background colour is used for the floating text. The margin

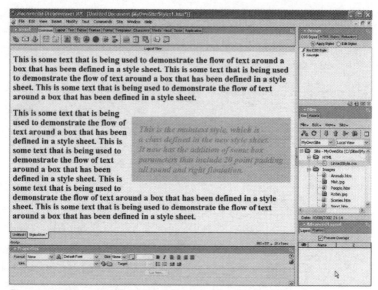

Fig.13.37 The accuracy of Dreamweaver's design view can be improved by making the anchor points invisible

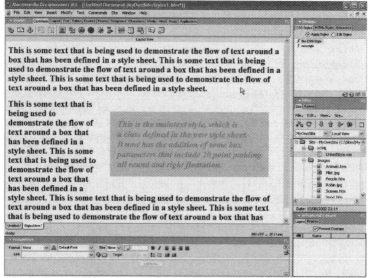

Fig.13.38 The effect of adding margins around the box

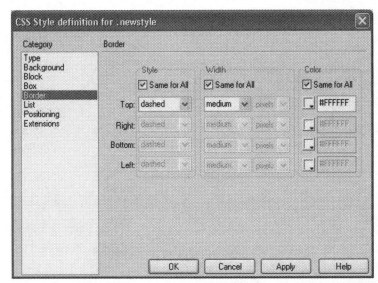

Fig.13.39 The Border section of the Style Definition window

setting can be used to keep the other text a certain distance away from the border or background, as in Figure 13.38 where a margin value of 30 has been used on all sides.

Border

The page for border settings is shown in Figure 13.39 and fairly straightforward. Each section of the border is individually adjustable for thickness and colour, and there are numerous styles available. In the example of Figure 13.40 the Dashed border style has been used with a medium line thickness. The dashed line style does not display properly in Dreamweaver's design view, but the box will be displayed properly in a browser (Figure 13.41).

List

This page, which is shown in Figure 13.42, is only relevant if a list is being formatted. Various bullet styles are available, and there is a useful facility that enables an image to be used for the bullets. Figure 13.43 shows a list that uses a 50 by 50 pixel Jpeg image for the bullets. Here

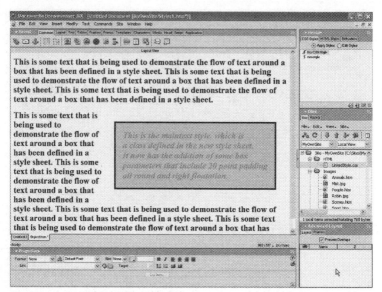

Fig.13.40 The dashed border does not display properly in Dreamweaver's design view

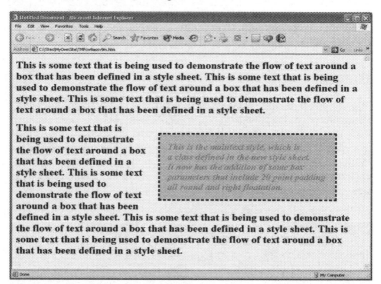

Fig.13.41 The border does display properly in a browser

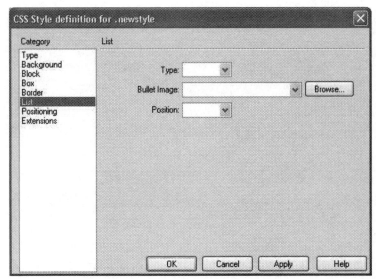

Fig.13.42 The List section of the Style Definition window

the formatting has been applied to the complete list, but it can be applied to a single line using the dragging method to select the line. It would presumably be possible to have a different image for each line by creating and applying a different style to each one.

Positioning

The positioning settings (Figure 13.44) are used with layers, and they should look familiar if you have read through chapter 11. Although for use with layers, the positioning properties can be applied to other objects such as

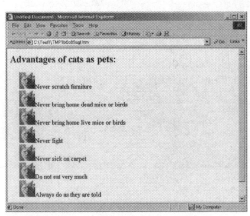

Fig.13.43 Small images used as bullets

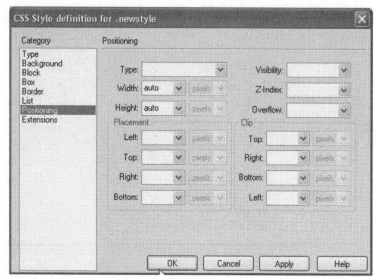

Fig.13.44 *The Positioning section of the Style Definition window*

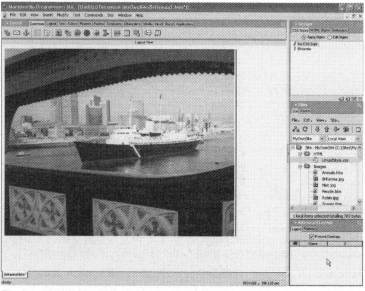

Fig.13.45 *An image placed on the page in the normal way*

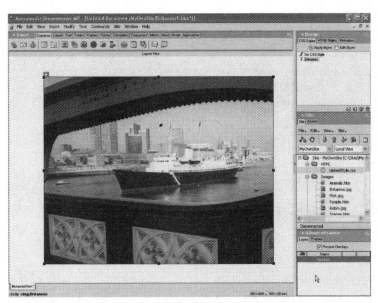

Fig.13.46 The image has been placed in a layer by applying a style

images and blocks of text, which are then placed in new layers. The placement parameters are worthy of some amplification, since they provide a means of positioning objects on the page with high precision. When used with absolute positioning, the placement parameters set the layer so that its top left-hand corner is offset from the equivalent corner of the parent object by the specified amount.

Figure 13.45 shows an image placed on the page in the top left-hand corner. In Figure 13.46 the image has had a style applied, and this has moved it 100 pixels to the right and 70 pixels down from the parent object. Of course, the parent object is the page itself, so the offset is from the top left-hand corner of the page. The tab of the newly generated layer can be seen at the top left-hand corner of the image. Next some text was typed onto the page and then moved into position just above the image using another style. The Apply button plus some trial and error soon found the optimum position for the text. When viewed using a browser the image and text were perfectly positioned (Figure 13.47).

Note that it is possible to position objects by selecting them and placing the pointer on the border of the frame. They can then be dragged to the

Fig.13.47 The image and caption are perfectly positioned when the page is viewed using a browser

Fig.13.48 Items can be dragged to new positions

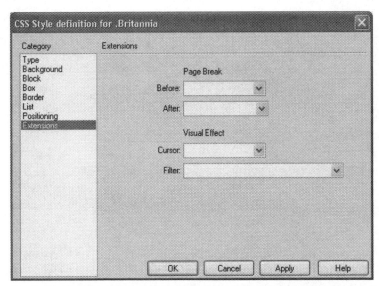

Fig.13.49 The Extensions page of the Style Definition window

required position, and the position figures in the Style Definition window will alter to suit the changes made. In Figure 13.48 the photograph has been moved up the page and the caption has been placed beneath it. In both cases they were dragged into position and there was no conventional editing of the two styles.

Extensions

Figure 13.49 shows the Extensions page of the Style Definition window. It is possible to apply clever effects using these options, although the majority of browsers do not necessarily support them. The mouse pointer can be made to change when it is over the object to which the style has been applied (Figure 13.50), and various filter effects are available. Figure 13.51 shows the Invert effect applied to a photograph.

Finally

From this quick look at styles and style sheets it should be clear that they enable pages to be set out in ways that would be difficult or impossible using ordinary HTML. If you need to design complex pages

Fig.13.50 The pointer changes to a hand when placed over this image

Fig.13.51 The Invert filter applied to the image

then styles are well suited to the task. They are also very good where there are numerous pages to be produced and a uniform style is needed. Using style sheets it is possible to quickly format the pages. It is certainly well worthwhile spending some time exploring their possibilities.

13 Style sheets

Uploading

Look and learn

In a book this size it is not possible to cover all aspects of Dreamweaver, but with the information in the previous chapters it is possible to produce some quite sophisticated sites using this program. If you do a tour of the web looking at a variety of sites you should now be able to see how most of the sites are put together. Using the methods described previously you can add text to a page and format it in various ways, add images, sounds, jump menus, frames, flash text and buttons, link to files for downloading, and a great deal more. It is a good idea to experiment with methods available in Dreamweaver, making up some dummy pages and sites so that you become reasonably fluent with their use before going on to the real thing.

It is also well worthwhile looking at a good range of sites and casting a critical eye over them. It is good to learn from your mistakes, but it is much better to learn from the mistakes of others. For example, if you find some methods of site navigation easy to use and others very confusing, it is quite likely that others will concur with your findings. Use the methods you feel work well and ignore the rest.

Uploading

Having completed your web site there is the minor matter of uploading it to the server. If your computer is connected to the server via a LAN (local area network) you will presumably know how to upload it, or whoever looks after the system will be able to do it for you. For most of us the connection to the server is via a modem and a telephone line. It does not matter too much whether the connection is via a standard telephone modem or a DSL type, and uploading web sites is much the same either way. If you are dealing with a large web site or sites the extra speed of a DSL connection is clearly an advantage though.

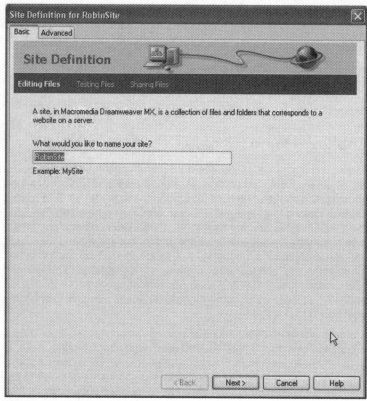

Fig.14.1 The Site Definition window

Bear in mind that most Internet connections provide upload rates that are slower than the download rates. A 56.6k modem for example, uploads at a maximum of 33.6k, and a 512k ADSL connection has an upload rate of 256k. An upload rate of 256k is still very respectable, but uploads using a 56k modem are unlikely to proceed at more than about three kilobytes per second. Uploading a large site at this rate can be very time consuming, as can subsequent site maintenance.

There are programs available that can be used to upload a site to a server, but one of these is not essential with Dreamweaver as it has built-in facilities for uploading sites. The method described here utilizes Dreamweaver's integral uploading facilities. In order to upload the files in your site you need to give Dreamweaver the information it will require

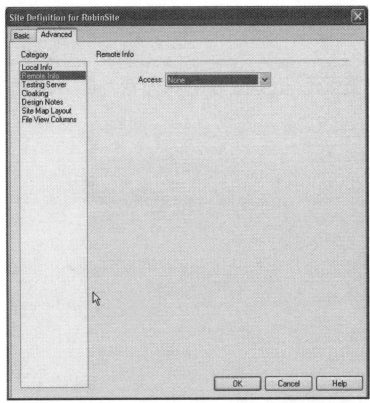

Fig.14.2 The Advanced section offers an alternative to the wizard

to make the transfer. It is presumed here that the site has been defined, but that the information needed to transfer the site to the server has not yet been entered.

Start by selecting Edit Sites from the Site menu, which will bring up a list of existing sites. Select the appropriate site from the list and then operate the Edit button. This will bring up the Site Definition window (Figure 14.1), but this is not the page that is required. One option is to stay with the wizard version of this window, working through the pages until the right one is reached. The quicker alternative is to operate the Advanced tab at the top of the window, followed by the Remote Info option in the Category list on the left. This produces a rather empty looking page (Figure 14.2). Choose FTP (file transfer protocol) from the Access menu,

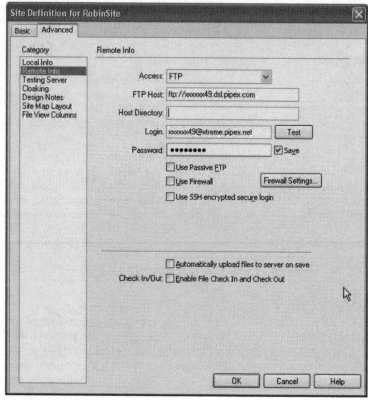

Fig.14.3 The FTP option produces several textboxes

which will result in several textboxes being added to the window (Figure 14.3).

The host directory can sometimes be left blank, but the other three text boxes must be filled with the relevant information. The web space provider should have supplied this information when you first hired space from them, or when you opened an account with a free web space provider. If you are using free server space provided by your ISP it is possible that this information was not provided when you opened your account, but it should be available on request. Most ISPs have FAQ (frequently asked questions) facilities on their sites, and the information you require will usually be found there. Here is a brief explanation of the significance of each of the four settings.

FTP Host

This is the web address of the host, and it will usually be similar to the initial part of your new site's web address. However, it will start "ftp" rather than "http".

Host Directory

This is the particular directory on the host's server that the new site will occupy. This is not always needed, because the server will often be able to find the right directory from the other information provided.

Login

This is also known as the User Name and User ID. Obviously the server does not give free access to anyone who would like to upload a site, and the Login name is a means of identifying the user to make sure they have authorisation to use the server. With free space provided by an ISP this will normally be the same as the user name you use to logon to the Internet.

Password

The password is used to verify that you are who you say you are. The login and password operate in the same way as their equivalents when signing on to an ISP. Get either of them wrong, even in a very minor way, and you will not get gain access to the server. Dreamweaver will remember your password if you leave the Save checkbox ticked, and it will then be unnecessary to enter it again. Note though, that the password is saved as a simple text file on the hard disc, and that it is not encrypted. If you are using free space provided by an ISP, the password used here will usually be the same one you use when logging on to the Internet.

Some web space providers, and particularly ISPs, have their own way of handling things. It may be necessary to be logged into the host ISP before the uploading can take place, which will only be of importance if you use more than one ISP. You may then have to use somewhat non-standard entries in some of the fields in order to access the server. Although web space is free with many ISPs, you may have to register before the space is made available. It pays to read the connection information provided by the host before attempting to upload your files. Where the host provides software for uploading sites it might be better to use this instead of the built-in facilities of Dreamweaver.

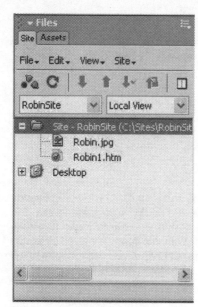

Fig.14.4 The Site window showing the files for the site

Connecting

In order to upload your site it is necessary for the computer to have an active Internet connection, so make sure the PC is connected to the Internet before you start the uploading process. Uploading is done from the Site window for the relevant site. The right site should already be selected if you have just edited its settings to insert the correct FTP address, etc. On future occasions you might have to select the right site before uploading, and it is then a matter of choosing Edit Sites from the Site menu, followed by the appropriate site from the menu in the Edit Sites window. Operate the Done button to return to the main Dreamweaver screen. This should produce the Site window, complete with the files for your site. Figure 14.4 shows the Site window for the simple one-page dummy site used for this demonstration.

Put and Get

Fig.14.5 This message is obtained while a search is made for the host

There are two buttons on the toolbar that have arrow icons. The one having the upward pointing arrow is for uploading files, and the one with the downward pointing arrow is for downloading files from your site to the hard disc. In Dreamweaver terminology these are the Put and Get commands respectively. In this case it is uploading we require, so operate the Put button. If these buttons are greyed out and inoperative, your

Internet connection is probably absent. Try selecting Connect from the Site menu of the Site window or operate the Connect button on the Site window's toolbar.

Once the Put button has been activated you will probably see a message on the screen saying that Dreamweaver is trying to connect to the host site (Figure 14.5). If the FTP settings are incorrect you will get an error message, and the settings will have to be checked. If all is well, you will probably get a message asking if you are sure that the entire site should be uploaded. Obviously there is no existing site to update in this case, so the entire site must be uploaded.

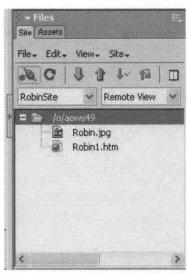

Fig.14.6 The uploaded files are present and correct

Having uploaded the site, select Remote View from the right-hand menu near the top of the Site window. This should look something like Figure 14.6, with the uploaded files and folders all present and correct. You can view a log of the actions that occurred during the uploading process by launching the Results group of windows and operating the FTP Log tab

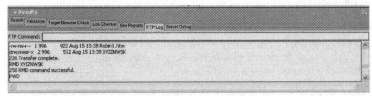

Fig.14.7 A log of the upload process is available

(Figure 14.7). This could be useful if things have not gone entirely according to plan. It is possible that additional messages will be obtained before the uploading takes place. You have to use some common sense

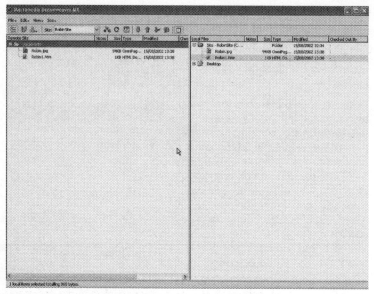

Fig.14.8 The expanded version of the Site window

here, but in general it is just a matter of answering Yes. You should then avoid problems with blank spaces left in some pages, blind links, etc.

When uploading and downloading from your site it is helpful to switch the Site window to its expanded version. It is toggled between the expanded and collapsed views via the button at the right-hand end of the toolbar in the Site window. The expanded version is split into two sections with the remote site shown on the left and the local one on the right (Figure 14.8). Especially with larger sites, the expanded view makes it much easier to check that everything is present and correct, and to generally manage the files and folders.

Assuming that everything seems to have been uploaded properly, it is then a matter of using the "acid test". Exit Dreamweaver and use an Internet browser to access your new site. Figure 14.9 shows the page of the dummy site used for this demonstration. Unfortunately, the browser used to view the page has been set for large text, which has caused the caption to word-wrap. This does illustrate the point that things can easily go wrong with web page layouts, even with the most simple of pages.

Fig.14.9 The dummy page did not look right when viewed in a browser

Fig.14.10 A minor adjustment and the page displays correctly

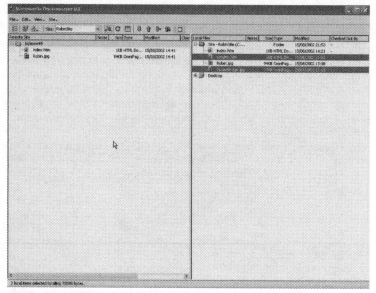

Fig.14.11 The two highlighted files on the right need updating

With the text setting of the browser set at Medium the page is displayed properly (Figure 14.10).

Note that the homepage in your site must be called index.htm or index.html if you wish to have it available using the basic address of your site without any extensions to the address being needed. For example, if your site address is at www.mymegasite.co.uk, this is all that users will need to type as the address in their browsers in order to reach the index page. It is also worth noting that there is often a delay between an FTP upload and the site actually being available at the HTTP address. If everything seems to be all right but you can not contact your site, wait an hour or two and try again.

Synchronising

It is likely that before too long it will be necessary to update your web site. If new pages are added but no changes are made to any of the other files, there is no problem. Just go through the standard upload process and the new file or files will be added to the site. In most cases some existing pages will have been changed, if for no other reason that some new links will be required for the new pages. Dreamweaver will not automatically overwrite any old files with new ones.

With Dreamweaver connected to the remote site a check can be made to determine which files have newer versions on the local site than on the remote site. In other words, Dreamweaver can detect the files that need to be updated. To do this, go to the Edit menu of the Site window and choose the Select Newer Local option. The files that need updating will then appear highlighted in the right-hand section of the window. In the example of Figure 14.11 there are just two files that need to be uploaded.

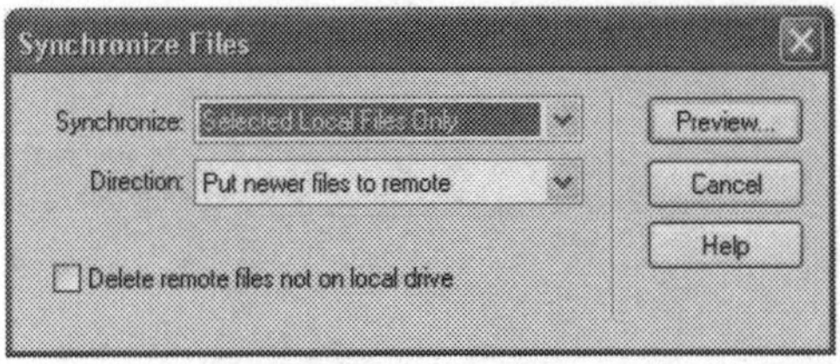

The safest way to update files is through the synchronising

Fig.14.12 The Synchronise Files dialogue box

feature. This is available from the Site menu of the Site window, and when selected a window like the one of Figure 14.12 will appear. In the upper menu you can opt to synchronise only the selected files or the entire site. The default setting in the lower menu is the one we require, and it will result in newer files on the local site overwriting those on the remote site.

If the checkbox is ticked, files that exist on the remote site but not on the local site will be deleted. This will automatically delete any files on the remote site that are not currently in use, but if a file has been accidentally deleted on the local site this will result in its removal from the remote site as well. It is safer not to use this option, and to manually delete unwanted files on the remote site. This is done in the same way as deleting files from the local site. Select them in the Site window and then select the Delete option from the File menu.

To proceed with the synchronisation operate the Preview button. A form showing any files that will be changed is then produced (Figure 14.13), and the proposed action for each file is included in the list. Each action will only be carried out if the corresponding checkbox is ticked, so you have a chance to review things and abort any actions that you do not wish to go ahead with. Left-click the OK button to continue, and the appropriate files will be updated.

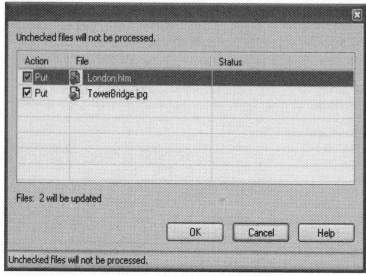

Fig.14.13 *This window lists any files that will be changed*

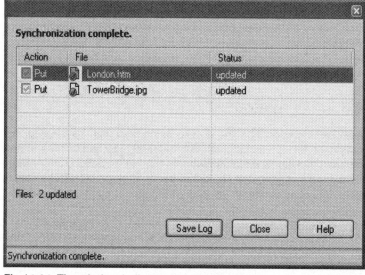

Fig.14.14 *The window indicates the changes that have been made*

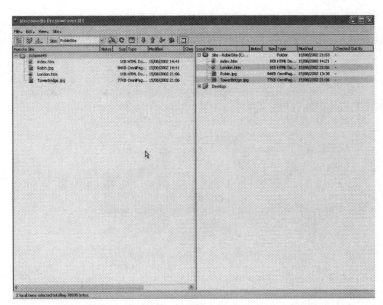

Fig.14.15 The Site window shows the new files on the remote site

A window like the one in Figure 14.14 will then appear, giving a summary of the changes that have been made. Operate the Close button to return to the Site window, and your site should now be fully updated (Figure 14.15). The "proof of the pudding is in the eating" and Figure 4.16 shows the additional page of the dummy site viewed in Internet Explorer.

File manipulation

When Dreamweaver is connected to the remote site it is possible to manipulate the remote files in much the same way as the ones in the local site. However, unless you have some form of broadband connection Internet it might be better to perfect things in the local site and then upload them to the remote site rather than trying to do much work direct on remote files. In order to avoid confusion and mistakes it might be better to do things this way even if you do have a broadband connection. The usual facilities are available from the pop-up menu if you right-click on a file or folder (Figure 4.17). This enables files and folders, to be pasted, deleted, etc.

Fig.14.16 The new dummy page as viewed using a browser

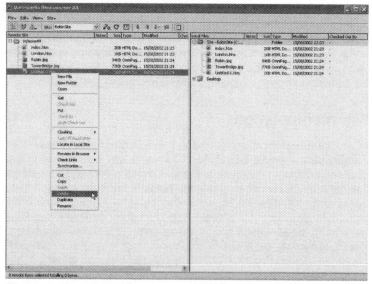

Fig.14.17 The usual facilities are available from the pop-up menu

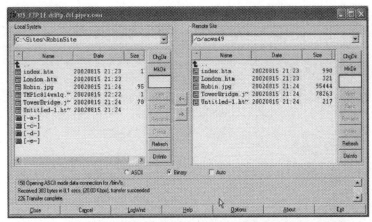

*Fig.14.18 Files can be uploaded using a separate program. In this
case the popular WS_FTP LE program has been used*

As pointed out previously, it is not essential to use Dreamweaver's facilities
to upload and maintain web sites. Any program for uploading to and
downloading from FTP sites should be able to handle the task. It is just
a matter of directing the program to the folder that contains the local
site, and giving it the information needed to access the remote site. This
information is the same as that used to enable Dreamweaver to contact
the remote site. Figure 14.18 shows the popular FTP program WS_FTP
LE in action with the dummy site used for the uploading demonstration.

14 Uploading

Appendix

Useful Web addresses

http://www.macromedia.com

http://www.macromedia.com/support/dreamweaver/

http://www.macromedia.com/exchange/dreamweaver/

This is the web site of Macromedia Inc., the company that produces Dreamweaver. A fully working 30-day demonstration version of Dreamweaver can be downloaded from this site (Windows PC and Macintosh versions), and there are also demonstration versions of other Macromedia products available. The Flash and Fireworks programs are well worth trying. The second web address takes you direct to the Dreamweaver Support Centre. The third address is for the Dreamweaver Exchange, where various Dreamweaver extensions are available. These enable the capabilities of Dreamweaver to be increased, and the extensions provided here are designed to be easy to install.

http://www.dreamweaverfever.com

This site also provides Dreamweaver extensions, but there are also some documents about various aspects of Dreamweaver.

http://www.andrewwooldridge.com/dreamweaver/

This is the Dreamweaver Depot web site. It provides Dreamweaver extensions and general Dreamweaver news.

http://www.macromedia.com/support/coursebuilder/

Various extensions for Dreamweaver are available for download here provided you are a Dreamweaver owner.

http://www.owlnet.net/dwnews/

A Dreamweaver news site, but it actually has a lot more than news. There is a good FAQ section, numerous links to other sites, etc.

http://hotwired.lycos.com/webmonkey/

Not a Dreamweaver site, but one that provides general news and information about the web, such as web standards.

http://www.w3.org

Again, not a Dreamweaver site, but one that covers HTML, XML, Png, and a great deal more. A very useful reference site.

http://www.htmlhelp.com

The name of the site tells you what this one is all about. In addition to the substantial amount of reference material available from the site there are useful links to other sites.

http://www.dhtmlzone.com/

The Dynamic HTML Zone web site. Again, not a site specifically for Dreamweaver, but one devoted to DHTML. There are articles, forums, tutorials, etc.

http://wdj.co.uk/JavaScriptWeenie.html

A general JavaScript site which has tutorials, discussions, articles, and all the usual things.

http://home.netscape.com/browsers/

If you need to try out your web pages with the latest Netscape browsers they are available for download here.

http://www.microsoft.com/windows/ie/

This section of the Microsoft Inc. site has the latest version of Internet Explorer ready for downloading.

http://www.opera.com

You could be forgiven for thinking that Netscape and Microsoft are the only companies that broduce browsers. However, there are others available, and Opera is probably the most popular apart from the big two. It is available for download at this site in various versions, including Windows, Macintosh, and Linux types.

These web addresses have been checked, but note that web sites do sometimes change addresses. There are numerous sites devoted to Dreamweaver and web topics, so any search engine should provide a huge range of additional sites.

Index